C^^ ^^^1386

D0755376

HARRIER

Jonathan Glancey is well known as the former architecture and design correspondent of the *Guardian* and *Independent* newspapers. He is also a pilot and a steam-locomotive enthusiast. A frequent broadcaster, his books include the bestselling *Spitfire: The Biography*; *Giants of Steam*; *Nagaland: A Journey to India's Forgotten Frontier*; *Lost Buildings* and *The Story of Architecture*.

Also by Jonathan Glancey

Giants of Steam

Car: A History of the Automobile

Nagaland: A Journey to India's Forgotten Frontier

Tornado: 21st Century Steam

Lost Buildings

*Modern Architecture: The Structures That
Shaped the Modern World*

Spitfire: The Biography

Architecture (Eyewitness Companion)

London: Bread and Circuses

The Story of Architecture

HARRIER
THE BIOGRAPHY

JONATHAN GLANCEY

Atlantic Books
London

First published in hardback in Great Britain in 2013 by Atlantic Books,
an imprint of Atlantic Books Ltd.

This paperback edition published in 2014 by Atlantic Books.

10 9 8 7 6 5 4

A CIP catalogue record for this book is available from the British Library.

Paperback ISBN: 9781843548928
E-book ISBN: 9781782394433

Printed and bound by CPI Group (UK) Ltd, Croydon, CR0 4YY

Atlantic Books
An Imprint of Atlantic Books Ltd
Ormond House
26–27 Boswell Street
London
WC1N 3JZ

www.atlantic-books.co.uk

CONTENTS

'The airplane won't amount to a damn until they get a machine that will act like a hummingbird, go straight up, go forwards, go backwards, come straight down and alight like a hummingbird.'

Thomas Alva Edison

'All modern aircraft have four dimensions: space, length, height and politics.'

Sir Sydney Camm, Hawker Aircraft

LIST OF ILLUSTRATIONS

PREFACE

The weather was hostile. Blustery. Ice-cold winds. Grey skies barely visible through banks of low cloud. Conditions, in fact, that would have been all too familiar to the pilots of the Royal Navy and Royal Air Force who flew to victory in the Falklands War nearly thirty years earlier. As some two thousand military personnel, their families and friends – and not forgetting the media – stared into the unforgiving sky, sixteen Harrier jump jets, in diamond formation, each of four aircraft, thundered towards RAF Cottesmore to land, vertically, and to shut off their engines simultaneously. But not before one of these GR.9A Harriers – the final development of this legendary military aircraft, painted for the occasion in glossy 'retro' camouflage – stopped in mid-air, turned to the control tower, and, landing light blazing, made a deep and courtly bow to those assembled below and, by extension, to everyone who, one way or another, had been a part of the story of the Harrier over the previous half-century.

That aircraft was ZG506, flown by Group Captain Gary Waterfall, commander of Joint Force Harrier, controlling Harrier squadrons of the Royal Air Force and the Fleet Air Arm (Royal

Navy), and the last station commander of RAF Cottesmore, which itself was closed shortly after this final, highly emotive flight of Britain's jump-jet force. That afternoon – 15 December 2010 – the sixteen jets had flown low in homage, and as a farewell, over the RAF bases of Cranwell, Coningsby, Marham, Scampton, Waddington and Wittering, with their ghosts of Spitfires, Dambusters, Cold War V-bombers, Phantoms and generations of officer cadets earning their 'wings'. They flew, too, above the still-handsome town centres of Stamford and Oakham and over the soaring medieval towers of Lincoln Cathedral before returning to their Rutland base, by now wreathed in eerie and ever-shifting tendrils of low rolling mist.

As the Rolls-Royce engines of the pugnacious jets span on cue to a collective stop, and a haunting silence, those gathered on the ground or clambering from cockpits knew all too well that this was truly the end of an era. The Harrier had been in service with the RAF for forty-one years, and in action, from the Falklands War to the most recent missions in Afghanistan. The Harrier was a development of the Hawker P.1127, the world's first successful vertical take-off and landing (VTOL) aircraft. On the drawing board in 1957, the revolutionary P.1127 made its maiden flight on 19 November 1960; one way or another, the jump jet born and nurtured in Kingston upon Thames, Surrey spanned half a century in the service of the country that invented and manufactured this magnificent flying machine – a fighter aircraft that, perhaps justly, has been dubbed the jet-age Spitfire. It is a machine – the product of an optimistic new Elizabethan age when British design, technology, engineering and aircraft not only matched but led the world, if only for what proved to be an unduly brief time – that has spanned my life, too. As much an emotion as a brilliant invention and a finely resolved and hugely characterful machine, the Harrier ranks in the pantheon of the world's greatest aircraft.

Now, out of the blue, one of the world's most potent and proven combat aircraft was to be taken out of service to save the British government some £900 million. That decision had been announced to Parliament on 12 October 2010, shortly before the fiftieth anniversary of the P.1127's first hover, as a result of the latest Strategic Defence and Security Review. The effect of the cuts was immediate. The following month, the aircraft carrier HMS *Ark Royal*, like her sister ship *Invincible* another victim of the latest round of government spending cuts, made a final voyage with Harriers on board, from Tyneside, where she was built, and launched in 1981, to Hamburg.

On 24 November, four Harriers, led by Lieutenant Commander James Blackmore, blasted off the ship's deck on a flight to RAF Cottesmore. This would be the last time a British military aircraft would operate from a carrier. A replacement carrier, HMS *Queen Elizabeth*, and the supersonic Lockheed Martin short take-off and vertical landing (STOVL) F-35B stealth jets she is meant to take to sea, will not be ready for active service until 2020. Watching the Harriers abandon their floating nest, the *Ark Royal*'s skipper, Captain Jerry Kyd, said it was like 'taking the teeth from a tiger', while General Sir David Richards, Chief of the Defence Staff, noted in a decidedly low-key manner that the decision to decommission the *Ark Royal* had provoked an 'understandable emotional response'.

'Understandable' and 'emotional'? Certainly. And besides, by axing both such a formidable fighting machine as the *Ark Royal* and the seventy-nine-strong Harrier force, Britain had deliberately opened a gaping hole in its defence strategy. The ever-controversial Commander Nigel 'Sharkey' Ward, who had led Sea Harriers to victory from the deck of HMS *Invincible* in spectacular style in 1982, and whom we will meet again in this book, told the British media:

> The connived withdrawal of the Harrier from service is an appalling miscarriage of justice, and of operational wisdom; the reprehensible actions of those who contrived this as 'a logical operational decision' must be condemned as disloyal and against the direct interests of our national defence capability.

To make matters seem much worse than they were, the perfectly serviceable, and saleable, *Ark Royal* was sold, like *Invincible* before her, for scrap to Leyal Ship Recycling, a Turkish company on the Aegean coast, while the Harriers were flogged off, at bargain-basement price, to the US Marine Corps to be broken up for spare parts for the Americans' highly prized AV-8B Harrier II force. In 2013, these Harriers are still active in Afghanistan, and the Marines intend to hang on to them until 2030 if they possibly can.

The GR.9A Harriers that flew for the last time in service that December afternoon at Cottesmore were not machines, or a type of aircraft, due or fit for retirement. In fact, the latest Harrier model had only been delivered to RAF Cottesmore, and so also to the *Ark Royal*, between 2004 and 2009, while in July 2008 a contract had been awarded to QinetiQ, the Farnborough-based aerospace company, to further upgrade and maintain the Harrier fleet until 2018. Imagine buying dozens of Aston Martin DB9s, kitting them out with every latest James Bond-style gizmo and then selling them to an American car dealer for a few thousand quid, each to be broken up into spare parts for DB9s built under licence in the United States. Madness? Well, yes. And yet, as this biography of the Harrier will show, while tracing its genesis, development and action-packed service history, politics have toyed with this magnificent British flying machine from one end of its long, if now truncated, life to the other.

In November 2011, perhaps stung by criticism both within and without the armed services, Peter Luff, a junior defence minister and former PR man, announced that seventy-two of the Harriers bound for the United States would be converted to match the Marine Corps's AV-8B fleet, but as the career of junior ministers rather resembles that of inexperienced pilots flying into fog for the first time, it was hard to know. The following year, Mr Luff was no longer a junior minister of defence and was, in any case, due to leave Parliament at the next general election. As it was, in 2012 the US Naval Air System Command said that at no time had there been plans for upgrading and operating British Harriers for service with the Marine Corps. The aircraft were for spare parts, and that was that.

Intriguingly, the Harrier – in the guise of the prototype Hawker P.1127 – was nurtured into RAF service at a time when a Conservative government was hell-bent on destroying the very idea of fighter aircraft in favour of ground-to-air missiles. Half a century on, meanwhile, a coalition government of Conservatives and Liberal Democrats ditched the Harrier while setting its cost-cutting eyes on pilotless 'drones' that would, if possible, supersede jet fighters and more or less every other fixed-wing military aircraft in the near future. It was, however, a Conservative government that had gained most, politically, from the sheer efficacy of the Harrier in the early 1980s: British victory in the Falklands War in 1982, in which Harriers flown by the Royal Navy and the RAF played a vital and legendary role, had led to a landslide political victory for Margaret Thatcher in Britain's 1983 general election. Indeed, on 17 December 1982, Mrs Thatcher had paid a visit to the Hawker Siddeley factory at Kingston upon Thames. The prime minister had posed, beaming, for press photographers from the cockpit of a Harrier. 'I would have loved to have flown in it,' she had said. No one had doubted her.

Inevitably, the prospects of any British military aircraft are highly susceptible to the Mad Hatter logic of Westminster and Whitehall. The loops, stalls and spins of politicians can either buoy up or bring down the very same machines – from Spitfires to Harriers – that have fought for our hard-won freedoms. And the Harrier was, of course, very much a servant of democracy: it should never be forgotten that, in one of its finest moments, it did its bit in helping to bring down the cruel and puerile military government of the Argentine Republic, a dismal regime that had killed many of its own people – some 20,000 – including students, trade unionists, journalists and the daughter of Livio Dante Porta, one of the country's finest engineers, who had pushed so hard for the development of a clean and efficient steam-railway technology fit for the twenty-first century. Many of the 'disappeared' were pushed from aircraft over the Río de la Plata or the South Atlantic. These 'death flights' were planned by Vice Admiral Luis Maria Mendia (1925–2007), the former head of Argentine naval operations; a document signed by the admiral called for the 'physical elimination by using planes that, in flight, would throw out the prisoners drugged beforehand'.

Back under the cold, grey clouds of Rutland on 15 December 2010, Air Vice Marshal Peter Dodworth, one of the first four RAF pilots to be trained on Harriers, told reporters:

> [The Harrier] was an exciting adventure for us.
> The first time I did a conventional take-off I was
> astonished by the acceleration. My first vertical
> take-off was exhilarating. It is pretty sad to see
> the demise of the aircraft after forty-one years. I
> watched it develop into the formidable and effective
> fighter jet it is today. It has been amazing for me to
> see it fulfil its potential.

Air Vice Marshal Graham Williams, who delivered the first Harrier into service at RAF Wittering in 1969 and who flew the triumphant return leg of that year's Transatlantic Air Race from New York's Empire State Building to London's Post Office Tower, added:

The Harrier means everything to me. It is just one
of those planes that becomes a part of your life. It
was so different from everything else, and it was the
greatest fun, almost better than sex. Today is also a
very sad day for me, because it seems that politics
and finance has got in the way of what still is a very
viable aircraft. The Harrier still has ten to fifteen
years of life left in it. To go and dump it like this is
almost criminal.

Walking away from Harrier ZG506 without stopping to look back, Group Captain Gary Waterfall, one of the 135 RAF Harrier pilots and fifty-three Navy pilots facing an uncertain future, was stoical. 'Without doubt this is an emotional day for all those who have been fortunate to be involved in one of the true icons of aviation, alongside Concorde and Spitfire.' But, he added, 'life goes on, and it's always important to look forward, not back. Right now, though, our thoughts are with everybody involved with Harrier over the years as we bid a fond farewell to a truly remarkable aircraft.'

As he said this, Harriers and Sea Harriers were still reaching for the sky, in their inimitable way, with the Indian, Italian and Spanish navies as well as the US Marine Corps. It is not quite time to say farewell to the instantly recognizable, compact and much-loved British jet that revolutionized flight and could not just fly like a hummingbird but sting like a bee, wasp and hornet rolled into one.

TO TREAD UPON THE AIR

History records, in myth, legend and fact, all too many vertical descents, from hilltops, temples and church towers, which led to the deaths of early would-be aviators. The dream of flight is as old as the hills – and certainly as old as the temples of the ancient Greeks. According to Aulus Gellus, the second-century Roman author, it was the Greek philosopher, mathematician, astronomer and politician Archytas (482–347 BC) who designed and built the world's first self-propelled flying machine. A steam-powered jet called the *Pigeon*, it was said to have flown 650 feet. Did it? Who knows? But Hero of Alexandria, a Greek mathematician and engineer, published notes on a steam turbine, and possibly built and demonstrated it, so perhaps the Greeks were as ahead of their times and the rest of the Western world in this respect as they were in architecture, science, sculpture and philosophy.

For all the intriguing flying machines that may or may not have taken to the air between Archytas' *Pigeon* in Athens of the fifth century BC and the Wright brothers' *Flyer* in 1903, the ability to take off and land vertically was far beyond the capabilities of heavier-than-air machines, whether legendary or not. Interestingly, though, vertical flight by lighter-than-air machines was achieved some two hundred years before the prototype Hawker P.1127 rose into the air, by itself and with no guiding strings attached, on 19 November 1960. While attempts had been made, on paper at least, by Roger Bacon in England in the thirteenth century and Leonardo da Vinci in Italy in the fifteenth century to develop vertical take-off ornithopters, the first successful vertical take-off with humans on board – in fact, the first ever free flight by humans – was made by the Montgolfier brothers, inventors and paper manufacturers, from the grounds of Château de la Muette on the edge of Paris on 21 November 1783.

What a magnificent and thrilling sight this great paper and varnished taffeta hot-air balloon must have made as it rose 3,000 feet above cheering spectators. The blue-and-gold balloon was seventy-five feet high and adorned with images of fleur-de-lis, signs of the zodiac and suns emblazoned with the face of King Louis XVI. The crew, Jean-François Pilâtre de Rozier, a chemistry and physics teacher, and the Marquis d'Arlandes, an Army officer, flew the best part of six miles in twenty-five minutes and brought their craft down to land safely.

The sheer exoticism of its decoration, and the magic nature of its flight, must surely have set Parisian minds racing back through childhood stories of fairies, dragons and flying carpets. Antoine Galland's French translation of *The Arabian Nights*, published between 1704 and 1717, had been a huge success; by the time of Pilâtre de Rozier and d'Arlandes' flight, many Parisians would have been familiar with tales of magic carpets, of how Prince Husain, the eldest son of the sultan of India, bought such a carpet in Bisnagar that could rise in an instant – vertical take-off, of course – and transport him, in 'the twinkle of an eye', to places 'many a day's journey and difficult to reach'. Stories of flying carpets go back even further than these tales, a thousand years old or more. King Solomon was said to have flown on a green-and-gold silk carpet measuring sixty miles square; it could carry 40,000 passengers, or a hundred times more than a Boeing 747 jumbo jet. Even today, Iranians tell wondrous stories of magic carpets used, at least in one case, for warfare. In 1213, or so the story goes, Prince Berhoz of Khorasan in eastern Persia married a young Jewess, Ashirah, whose father wove magic carpets. Berhoz commissioned from his father-in-law two dozen flying carpets supported on bamboo frames. Two soldiers were assigned to each carpet, which was equipped with bows and poison-tipped arrows and fireballs, and when Berhoz's father launched a war against the neighbouring shah of Khwarzem, this mythical thirteenth-century fighter-bomber squadron made a successful attack on the shah's castle, setting it ablaze. It was not so very different from a Harrier operation in Iraq or Afghanistan some eight hundred years later.

In India, meanwhile, many stories are still spun, often with impassioned seriousness by fervent Hindu nationalists, concerning 'vimanas', or highly advanced rocket-powered aircraft that were flown across the subcontinent very many thousands of years ago by the enlightened high priest-kings of the Rama empire. The 'ancient' manuscript relating to flying machines, however, seems to have been dictated by the mystic Pandit Subbaraya Shastry (1866–1940) some time after the end of the First World War. A Hindi translation published in 1959 included diagrams of complex jet engines, although these were the work of T. K. Ellappa, a draughtsman at an engineering college in Bangalore.

Flying chariots are, of course, staples of tales told in India's national epic, the *Mahabharata*, dating from much the same time as the Bible. One such spherical vimana was apparently able to fly up, down, backwards and forwards. In the Sanskrit *Samarangana Sutradhara*, a wide-ranging treatise on classical Indian architecture written in the eleventh century by Paramara, king of Bhoja of Dhar, we learn that a vimana must be:

> Strong and durable… like a great flying bird of
> light material. Inside one must put the mercury
> engine with its iron-heating apparatus underneath.
> By means of the power latent in the mercury,
> which sets the driving whirlwind in action, a man
> sitting inside may travel a great distance in the
> sky. The movements of the Vimana are such that
> it can vertically ascend, vertically descend, move
> slanting forwards and backwards. With the help of
> the machines, human beings can fly in the air and
> heavenly beings come down to earth.

Quite clearly, the design team at Hawker Siddeley, the best part of a thousand years later, had been extraordinarily slow on the uptake.

British observers, meanwhile, appear to have missed the flight of a latter-day vimana, allegedly constructed by Shivkar Bapuji Talpade (1864–1916), a Sanskrit scholar, his wife and an architect friend, and flown successfully to a height of 1,500 feet over Chowpatty Beach, Bombay (now Mumbai), in 1895. It landed automatically. The *Marutsakha*, or 'Friend of the Winds', was powered by a 'mercury ion engine', but sadly, said Talpade, a paucity of personal funds, a lack of sponsorship and imperial animosity ensured that this sensational performance was a one-off. After his death in 1916, his relatives are said to have sold the machine to Rally Brothers, a firm of British exporters based in Bombay. Presumably the brothers Rally assumed that the British government would have no interest in the world's first successful heavier-than-air flying machine, or perhaps they were simply too dull to make sense of its highly advanced Vedic jet technology.

However fanciful, stories like these drawn from across at least two-and-a-half thousand years continued to haunt the imaginations not just of poets, novelists and artists, but of inventors and pioneer aviators, too. Even so, the first reliable VTOL aircraft were the rigid airships – an advanced form of hot-air balloon – that took to the air at the beginning of the twentieth century. The very first was Ferdinand von Zeppelin's *Luftschiff Zeppelin 1*; it made its maiden flight, over Lake Constance, on 2 July 1900. During the First World War, the Zeppelins became the first successful long-range bombers. On

13 October 1915, L.15 bombed central London, damaging the Lyceum Theatre at Charing Cross, killing seventeen people and injuring twenty more.

The aim, post-war, sought by the Germans, the British and the Americans was to nurture enormous dirigibles or rigid airships that could fly across continents and oceans, and take off, land and moor in city centres. Rather fancifully, it was assumed that mighty airships would tie up at the top of the Empire State Building. The idea of using airships as airliners and bombers was abandoned after a number of spectacular accidents – in particular, the loss of the British government-sponsored R101 over France on 5 October 1930, and the fire, caught on newsreel, that destroyed LZ 129 *Hindenburg* as it attempted to dock at Lakehurst Naval Air Station, New Jersey on 6 May 1937. Still, these impressive, if flawed, machines highlighted some of the advantages of what might be achieved by aircraft that could take off and land vertically, and that could hover, whether benignly or menacingly, over 'targets' and city centres – which, as the Zeppelin raids over London proved, had become one and the same thing.

It was the Germans who took the next successful step in the story of vertical flight with the maiden flight of the world's first practical helicopter on 26 June 1936. This was the Focke-Wulf Fw 61, designed by Heinrich Focke and Gerd Achgelis. It was an instant success, and a step forwards from the autogyro, a small aircraft invented by the Spanish engineer Juan de la Cierva and first flown on 9 January 1923. The helicopter blades of the autogyro were not driven by or connected to the aircraft's engine, but, rotating in flight, they allowed the pilot to fly very slowly, something that fixed-wing aircraft were unable to do without stalling. The arrival of the Fw 61 meant that pilots were now able to take off and land vertically, to fly just above the ground if necessary at low speed and, of course, to hover. This ability to stay still a few inches above the ground was, although it sounds odd to say so, a giant leap for aviation.

What neither the airship nor the helicopter could do, though, is what aircraft like the Sopwith Camel and Fokker D.VII had been doing in the late stages of the First World War: flying fast and aerobatically. These, in modern parlance, were 'air superiority' fighters and their latest equivalents, the Supermarine Spitfire and Messerschmitt Bf 109, were both making their maiden flights in the mid-1930s. But despite the undoubted success, and omnipresence, of the piston-engined fighter and bomber in the Second World War, the next challenge for military aircraft design – a step aside from the helicopter, an aircraft that was to succeed brilliantly in its own right, and from the burgeoning dream of supersonic flight – was surely a fighter that could take off, land and hover like the Fw 61, and shoot off at great speed and with great dexterity to engage the enemy. If such an aircraft proved feasible, it would also mean that air forces would be able to fly it from the most basic forward air bases; there would no longer be a need for long grass strips or concrete runways. The potential was enormous. But how to get there?

There were several routes that, one way or another, led to the Hawker P.1127 prototype and so to the Hawker Siddeley Harrier. Equally, the development of pilotless aircraft, or drones

– which might yet altogether replace manned fighter aircraft, however ingenious these can be, in years to come – evolved at much the same time. In 1941, Robert Lusser (1889–1969), a German aircraft engineer, moved from Heinkel, where he had been working on a rival to the Messerschmitt Me 262 jet fighter, to Fieseler. Here he played a key role, with Fritz Gosslau of the engine manufacturer Argus, in the design and development of the Fieseler Fi 103, dubbed the V1 flying bomb (V standing for *Vergeltungswaffe*, or revenge weapon) by the Nazis. Wernher von Braun, meanwhile, was at work on the V2, a vertical take-off rocket and worryingly effective long-range ballistic missile against which there was then no defence. Both V1 and V2 were produced too late in the day to radically affect the outcome of the Second World War. However, Lusser and von Braun teamed up after the war, working at Huntsville, Alabama in the United States on the rocketry projects that would see Neil Armstrong and Buzz Aldrin landing on the Moon less than a quarter of a century after VE-Day.

The importance of these weapons – one leading to the 'drones' employed frequently by the US military in recent years, the other to NASA's successful manned space rockets – had much to do with the urgency that had driven their development. With Germany under aerial assault night and day by British and US bombers, escorted later in the war by powerful and well-armed long-range fighters, scientists and engineers were propelled into thinking quickly and creatively. What was the type of aircraft, or drone or rocket, best able to defend Germany from Allied bombers?

One answer, which led to a cornucopia of imaginative ideas, was for aircraft that could be deployed from makeshift airfields established along the bombers' anticipated flight paths. These machines needed to be cheap and quick to build, easy to transport, and yet capable of climbing rapidly and hitting the enemy's bombers hard. Here truly, as the Allies approached the German border from the west and the Russians from the east, were desperate measures for desperate times. The sheer ingenuity of many of the designs called for by the Luftwaffe's Emergency Fighter Programme of spring 1944 – which featured various forms of high-speed jets, some with swept wings, others with delta wings and vertical take-off aircraft too – was extraordinary. A number of books have been published in recent years on these 'secret' Nazi aircraft designs. While some were little more than sketches on scraps of paper, others were not only promising but were even taken up after the war by the Allies, especially in the United States and the Soviet Union.

One of the most promising was the Bachem Ba 349 Natter (Viper), a small vertical take-off rocket-powered interceptor designed by Erich Bachem, a Fieseler engineer, and produced under the auspices of Heinrich Himmler's SS at a purpose-built workshop at Waldsee in the Black Forest. The idea for such an aircraft had, in fact, been proposed by Wernher von Braun in 1939, and although enthusiastically received by Field Marshal Ernst Milch, the partly Jewish Air Inspector General who had done much to create the new Luftwaffe that went to war that same year, it was rejected by the Reich Air Ministry, which believed it to be both unnecessary and unworkable.

Designed to be constructed using semi-skilled labour, the Natter was essentially a wooden aircraft powered by the Walter 109-509A rocket motor. This produced 3,740 lbs of thrust boosted by a further 4,400 lbs generated by four Schmidding 109-533 solid-fuel rockets bolted in pairs to either side of the fuselage. Launched from a steel guide tower, the Natter should have climbed vertically at the astonishing rate of 37,400 feet a minute, reaching a top speed of 621 mph; as Allied bombers rarely flew much above 20,000 feet, the rocket plane, armed to the teeth with a formidable cluster of Henschel unguided rockets in its nose cone, might well have spelt sudden death for many unsuspecting bomber crews. Once the rockets had been released, the Natter's pilot would escape and parachute back to safety and the next mission, while the expended fuselage would, ideally, strike another enemy bomber and destroy it.

Progress on this secret machine was rapid. On 3 November 1944, a prototype, piloted by Erich Klockner, was carried, it seems, up to 18,000 feet by a Heinkel He 111 bomber, and then released. It flew surprisingly well and landed safely. In late February 1945, a successful vertical rocket launch was made with a dummy pilot. On 1 March, a Natter lifted off with Oberleutnant Lothar Siebert aboard. The launch was radio-controlled; the pilot was to take control as the machine descended towards enemy bomber formations. At about 1,600 feet, however, the aircraft inverted and, flying at fifteen degrees to the vertical, vanished into the clouds; it reappeared and within thirty seconds smashed into the ground, killing Siebert. The war, of course, was all but over at this point, and although the Germans are said to have had ten further Natters ready on launchers at Kirchheim, near Stuttgart, these saw no action – despite Squadron Leader Paddy Payne, Warrior of the Skies, nobly attacking a fully functioning, bright-red Natter with his late-model Spitfire in the pages of the *Lion* comic I pored over as a young boy in the 1960s. One of the surviving Natters was shipped to the United States for inspection; today, it rests, unrestored, in a warehouse belonging to the Smithsonian.

There were several other intriguing designs on the drawing boards of German aircraft manufacturers as late as the end of March 1945, some of which seem even more futuristic, and might have been more successful, given time, than the Bachem Ba 349, of which a total of thirty-six appear to have been built. Focke-Wulf offered the Triebflügeljäger, or Thrust-Wing Fighter, an astonishing wingless VTOL interceptor. Sitting on its tail with its nose cone pointing skywards, the Triebflügel was to have been powered by ramjets located on the tips of the three blades of a giant propeller designed to spin around the centre of the fuselage. The aircraft would have taken off vertically, rather like a helicopter, and then levelled out with the jet-powered blades acting like a giant airscrew and propelling the fighter forwards at what Focke-Wulf engineers calculated would be a top speed of 621 mph. It looked like a machine Dan Dare's mortal enemies, the Treens, might fly on short missions across Venus in the pages of the *Eagle*, the British boy's comic launched in 1950 that celebrated the kind of technological progress that led to the Harrier and men on the Moon. It was not until 1955 that the Americans released information on this top-secret VTOL jet.

Meanwhile, Heinkel proposed the Lerche (Lark), a VTOL fighter and ground-attack aircraft that was also to have stood on its tail at take-off. Eschewing jet or rocket propulsion, the Lerche was to have been powered by a pair of 2,000 hp Daimler-Benz 605D V12s, the ultimate development of the engine produced in tens of thousands and fitted to the Messerschmitt Bf 109 fighter. These were to have driven two large contra-rotating propellers set within an 'annular' wing – a metal ring encompassing the centre of the fuselage – and, theoretically, would have given the Lerche a top speed of 497 mph and a ceiling of 46,910 feet. This remarkable aircraft might well have flown successfully. Its appearance, at the bitter end of the battle for Germany, would certainly have been a shock to Allied aircrew. It would have seemed wingless, an aircraft, or spaceship, from the pages of a science-fiction fantasy, a machine inhabiting a parallel universe to that of Spitfires, Mustangs, Thunderbolts and Flying Fortresses. Even today, the Lerche retains something of the look of a flying machine that might have been dreamed up by NASA scientists and engineers twenty years later – and NASA was, of course, well staffed with brilliant young ex-Nazi engineers and scientists.

Heinkel drew up a further design, very similar to the Lerche, for a turboprop version designated Wespe (Wasp). Although the first turboprop plane to fly was a specially adapted British Gloster Meteor in September 1945, the idea had been proposed and tested, although neither in flight nor with a full-scale aircraft, by György Jendrassik, a Hungarian mechanical engineer, in the late 1920s. German industry had access to this research, and during the Second World War various companies – BMW, Hirth and Daimler-Benz among them – invested in turboprop development. But as the fruits of their experiments were not expected to be seen until sometime late in 1945, and probably later, the Wespe was never going to be built, still less flown in action. While it was fortunate that Hitler's Thousand Year Reich missed its target by 988 years, the pace of research and development in the German aero-industry in the last two or three years of the war was unprecedented and remains unsurpassed.

The memory, and perhaps the blueprints, of such aircraft lived on well into the following decade. In 1959, SNECMA, the French engine company, unveiled its sensational C.450-01 Coléoptère. A test bed for its latest, experimental pulse-jet engine, the Atar 101 E.5V, this tail-sitting jet featured an annular wing and was very much the jet descendant, or younger sibling, of the Lerche and Wespe. Promising great things, it did actually take off, on 6 May 1959, but crashed two months later while attempting the transition from vertical to forward flight; the pilot ejected safely, although the aircraft was written off.

If the Coléoptère was to be a product of prolonged post-war experimentation with new forms of military aircraft, the wartime VTOL machines proposed, or tested, by the Germans were the products of an ever-increasing urgency. For pilots, they were, or would have been, uncomfortable machines to operate. Even if the Lerche and Wespe could have been built in time to take on the aerial armadas of four-engined Allied aircraft carpet-bombing German towns and cities in 1945, pilot error would surely have led to any number of accidents. Lying prone in a cockpit staring up at the sky was never going to be an easy way for a pilot to take off, while having to land an aircraft vertically on its tail after an adrenaline-sapping mission was asking a lot of even the coolest and most competent airman. In any case, such landings would have made these aircraft easy prey for marauding and highly potent Allied fighters, which were by now capable of flying at very nearly 500 mph and diving close to the speed of sound and were armed with batteries of cannons and large-calibre machine guns.

The boundless ingenuity and invention of German engineers, however, was to be redeployed and nurtured once the Axis powers had been defeated and especially during the Cold War, when, as we will see, a VTOL fighter capable of tackling some of the very same missions originally plotted for these Nazi 'science-fiction' aircraft became both desirable and then a reality. That aircraft – the Harrier – was, of course, a jet. One wartime German design that was to use piston engines showed that there was an alternative route to vertical take-off and landing. This was the Focke-Achgelis Fa 269, a tilt-rotor VTOL fighter. In this design, a piston engine – BMW or Daimler-Benz – was to have been mounted in the fuselage behind the pilot. Transverse drive shafts were to set two giant propellers, one fitted in either wing, spinning downwards and so lifting the Fa 269 vertically like a helicopter. These would then pivot behind the wings and push the aircraft forward.

Much test work was carried out, using a wind tunnel, at the Focke-Achgelis works at Hoykenkamp in Lower Saxony, founded in 1937 to manufacture helicopters. The factory, however, was bombed heavily and work on the Fa 269 ended in 1944; Focke-

Achgelis engineers were not exactly relieved, but they knew full well that the aircraft was unlikely to fly before 1947. Forty-two years later, the first US Bell Boeing V-22A Osprey took to the air; it had taken that long to make the Fa 269 concept a reality. Even then, the Osprey was beset by development problems and several machines crashed with fatal results during the 1990s. Although taken into service with the US Marine Corps in 2000, the Pentagon only sanctioned full-scale production as recently as 2005. Today, the Osprey operates with the Marines, the US Navy and the US Air Force. Like the Harrier, it can be based on land or fly from carriers at sea. It has seen action in rescue and combat roles in Iraq, Libya and Afghanistan and has become, after a long, expensive, controversial and even tragic birth, one of the brightest stars in the constellation of current US military aircraft.

While the Osprey proves that the Harrier is not the only solution to vertical and/or short take-off and landing (V/STOL) flight, its role is and always will be quite different from that of the jump jet still flown, and enthusiastically so, by the US Marine Corps. The turboprop Osprey is a successful marriage of helicopter and aeroplane; it can seat twenty-four troops and has a top speed of around 300 mph. A combat US AV-8B Harrier is a single-seat interceptor and ground-attack fighter and flies close to the speed of sound. It nonetheless remains intriguing that this military tilt-motor aircraft, a type that might have made its debut in Germany in 1947, took to the air nearly thirty years after the Hawker P.1127.

Mention has to be made of one other type of Nazi German VTOL aircraft, although this one remains the stuff of apocryphal stories, bar-room tales, internet conspiracies and blurred photographs. Given the German proficiency in photography at the time, technically and artistically and in the most demanding theatres of war, it does seem odd that those involved in such specialist design were unable to take one half-decent snap of a flying saucer. Allegedly, a certain Dr Richard Mehta, 'sometimes known as the "Father of Saucerology"', according to a host of copy-cat websites, was hired by the Luftwaffe, or even by a secret branch of the SS, to build a 'flying saucer' to take out Allied bombers by rockets and, presumably, to take them by goggle-eyed surprise, too. Dr Mehta was, it seems, then recruited by the US after the war to work at Avro Canada, where he worked on classified designs for flying saucers.

In 1953, Avro Canada did, in fact, reveal a mock-up of a flying saucer, the Avrocar designed by John 'Jack' Frost, a British engineer who had arrived in 1947 from de Havilland, where he had been chief designer of the DH 108 Swallow, a small jet based on the Messerschmitt Me 163 Komet. Flown by test pilot John Derry, DFC, a former RAF Typhoon pilot, the Swallow was the first British aircraft to push through the sound barrier. From 1952, Frost worked on the development of a new form of gas turbine, or what he called the 'pancake engine', with jet thrust exiting around the rim of the engine. This configuration led, naturally enough, to a machine with a central engine and exhausts all around its rim that did indeed look very much like a flying saucer.

Visiting US Air Force officials were clearly impressed, agreeing to fund the aircraft along with Avro Canada. Later on, the US

Army came on board, and eventually, despite some terrifying tests with the proposed power plant – engine fires were endemic – the first Avrocar was completed at Avro Canada's Malton plant, Ontario, in May 1959. A first free flight was achieved on 12 November 1959 – although, far from boldly going where no man had gone before, the Avrocar rose just a few feet above ground and wobbled precariously at a top speed of 35 mph. On 9 June 1961, a demonstration flight for USAF and NASA witnessed a second prototype lifting itself over a six-foot-wide ditch and flying at just under 25 mph. The scream of its exhaust was painful to anyone coming anywhere near the Frisbee-shaped aircraft, while the heat generated inside the cockpit was enough to melt instruments. Many Americans claim to have seen flying saucers spinning in the night skies above them in the years 'Jack' Frost toiled away north of their border trying to make this type of machine an earthly, as opposed to an extraterrestrial, reality. Whatever those many Americans saw – especially those abducted and subjected to X-rated probing by inquisitive visitors from other worlds – Avro Canada would have been able to assure them, categorically, that their UFOs were not from Planet Ontario. The project was cancelled by the US military in December 1961. By then, the Hawker P.1127 had been flying successfully for over a year.

Back in 1945, however, with Hitler and the Third Reich dead and disposed of, German ingenuity was being forcibly exported in human form to the Soviet Union and the United States and, to a lesser extent, to Great Britain and France. But if the Second World War was over, leaving sixty million dead in its devastating wake, a Third World War threatened almost immediately. This was not simply the result of a clash between political ideologies, of communism – 'the Red Menace' – versus freedom, democracy and capitalism; rather, it was due to the simple fact that Stalin's Soviet Union had either invaded or controlled Eastern Europe, and from 1949, with its new-found ally, the People's Republic of China, seemed hell-bent on some form of world domination. This is certainly how many ordinary people, as well as politicians and the military, felt in the West, and in fact they continued to do so right up to the fall of the Berlin Wall in 1989 and the collapse of the Soviet Union two years later. While the threat of the Cold War prompted the design and accelerated the development of an enormous variety of fast, powerful jet interceptors and fearsome long-range bombers to carry nuclear weapons, it also led to the genesis of the Hawker P.1127, an aircraft that the military thought of as almost effete in its early years. If there was to be a shooting war with the Soviet Union, the Warsaw Pact and China, then most RAF and USAF officers, not to mention politicians and military strategists, believed this would be fought in the air with Mach 2 fighters and Mach 1 bombers, with guided missiles and stand-off nuclear weapons.

But such an insane contest would have seen the probable destruction of every key military airbase in Europe, East and West, if not the kind of Armageddon that many feared and was so brilliantly satirized in Stanley Kubrick's 1964 film *Dr Strangelove*, in which a crazed, cowboy hat-toting US pilot, Major 'King' Kong, signalled the end of the world by riding an H-bomb like some bucking bronco onto a Russian target from his Boeing B-52

Stratofortress. Any air force units that survived might only be able to take to the contaminated skies again to protect what was left of democratic Europe in aircraft that could be operated from a secret bunker, road or forest clearing. And if they were to do so, discreetly, suddenly and unexpectedly, those aircraft would need V/STOL capability. Which is why, even while the main thrust of military aircraft development in the US, USSR, Britain and France was towards conventional supersonic jets requiring sophisticated and high-maintenance airbases, the dream – fast becoming a necessity – of VTOL and V/STOL flight was harboured in the late 1940s, nurtured throughout the 1950s and became a reality in the 1960s.

Winston Churchill, the British wartime premier who had done so much to help destroy Hitler, the odious Nazi regime and all its 'perverted science', was on the attack again mere months after the defeat of Germany and Japan. On 5 March 1946, now Leader of the Opposition in Britain, he gave a speech at Westminster College, Fulton, Missouri:

> From Stettin in the Baltic to Trieste in the Adriatic,
> an 'iron curtain' has descended across the continent.
> Behind that line lie all the capitals of the ancient
> states of Central and Eastern Europe. Warsaw,
> Berlin, Prague, Vienna, Budapest, Belgrade,
> Bucharest and Sofia; all these famous cities and the
> populations around them lie in what I must call
> the Soviet sphere, and all are subject, in one form
> or another, not only to Soviet influence but to a

very high and in some cases increasing measure of
control from Moscow.

The term 'iron curtain' was not new. Writing in *Das Reich* in spring 1945, Joseph Goebbels, Hitler's minister of propaganda, expressed concern at agreements made by Stalin, Roosevelt and Churchill at the Yalta Conference that February to carve up Europe after the imminent German defeat, and made the point that 'an iron curtain would fall over this enormous territory controlled by the Soviet Union, behind which nations would be slaughtered'. If this was rather rich coming from a man who himself condoned the savage and senseless slaughter of millions of hapless people, Goebbels was not altogether wrong. As the war drew towards its appropriately *Gotterdammerung*-style finale in Europe, senior Nazis outdid one another in seeking last-ditch alliances with the Allies, who they believed were, at heart, as fiercely anti-communist and anti-Stalin as they were. While there was more than a grain of truth in this, the Allies were determined to force Nazi Germany into an unconditional surrender and, as this required the full force of the Red Army and a huge sacrifice from the Soviet Union in terms of human life, no one in Britain or the United States in their right political mind in 1945 was going to turn against Stalin at that point. Indeed, such was the support for good old 'Uncle Joe' that Churchill's iron curtain speech was widely condemned. Churchill despised Stalin and communism as much as he loathed Hitler and Nazism. And yet, he was one of the very politicians who, even if he had little choice in the matter, had allowed the iron curtain to descend in the first place.

The reality of this new political divide in Europe was soon evident. In June 1948, Stalin blockaded Berlin in a blatant attempt to isolate the city, cutting its transport links to West Germany and so to supplies from the Allied powers – Britain, France and the United States. These, along with the Soviet Union, had been the occupying nations in Berlin, a city geographically stranded since the Nazi surrender in the new Democratic Republic of Germany. An iron curtain had indeed descended around Berlin, and the one way in was by air. In a spirited and defiant rescue operation that lasted the best part of a year, Allied aircraft flew 200,000 missions bringing food and supplies to Berlin, for the loss, through accidents, of seventeen US and eight British aircraft and the death of 101 military personnel and civilians.

NATO, the North Atlantic Treaty Organization, was founded the following year: its mission, according to Lord Ismay, its first secretary-general, 'to keep the Russians out, the Americans in and the Germans down'. The Russians retaliated with the establishment of the Warsaw Pact in 1955. In between, the United Nations went into battle, with South Korea against North Korea and its backer, China, in the Korean War of 1950–53. The United States was to be militarily engaged, in one part of the world or another, from then on and up until the present day.

It was the US Navy that made the first demand, in 1948, for VTOL aircraft and, curiously given the nature and design of aircraft carriers, it asked for tail-sitters. The idea, however, was for these fighters to operate from platforms mounted on the afterdecks of cruisers and destroyers. So where a warship might have been equipped with a helicopter, now it might carry its own high-speed fighter escort on patrol and into battle. On paper, at least, the idea seemed attractive. It led to two dramatic, if profoundly flawed, prototypes that the US Navy was to abandon in the mid-1950s. If nothing else, the Convair XFY Pogo and the Lockheed XFV put paid to the tail-sitter concept. The wonder of it is that these two rival experimental VTOL fighters performed as well as they did. From a practical point of view, however, they would have made precious little sense operating at sea in anything other than the calmest conditions. At the same time, it was always going to be hard for even the most athletic pilot to scramble in anything like a hurry into or out of the cockpit of one of these turboprop-powered machines – not least because he would have had to clamber up some sort of gantry and then shift himself from the vertical plane to the horizontal, like an astronaut manoeuvring himself into a space capsule. And as for coming in to land at sea, this was trying at the very best of times, even for the most experienced test pilots, and would have been fairly hellish for less specialized service pilots, especially in poor weather and low light with the sea – and warship – rolling and pitching.

The Lockheed XFV was the first of the two into the air, on 23 December 1953, flown by Lockheed's chief test pilot, Herman 'Fish' Salmon, although its maiden flight was little more than a tentative 40-foot hop. It was powered by a 5,332 hp Allison YT-40-A-14 turboprop that drove three-bladed contra-rotating propellers. This gave insufficient power to allow the Lockheed to take off vertically, and so all thirty-two test flights were made with the help of a temporary, clip-on and non-retractable undercarriage that enabled the 'Pogo Stick', as Lockheed staff dubbed the aircraft, to take off conventionally from a runway. It landed this way, too. Transitions from horizontal to vertical flight and back were made in the air. No attempts were made to land the aircraft vertically, although it could hover – just – in mid-air. In this configuration – in fact, in nearly all configurations – the dangling XFV would have been a sitting duck for enemy aircraft and ship's gunners. In any case, the XFV was uncomfortable to fly and lacked anything like the performance of contemporary US Air Force and Navy jets. Although there was talk of a 7,100 hp version of the Allison engine that would have boosted performance, there seemed little point in pushing further ahead with a type of aircraft that was clearly wrong-headed.

In contrast, the Convair XFY Pogo achieved some success. A more compact machine than Lockheed's, its 5,500 hp Allison YT-40-A-16 engine gave it sufficient thrust to take off vertically, and on 5 November 1954 Lieutenant Colonel James F. 'Skeets' Coleman made a successful transition from vertical to forward flight and back again to land vertically, and safely. It had been a noteworthy achievement, although it was more of a conjuring act than a performance the US Navy would really have wanted its pilots to enact day to day, at sea and in combat. A colour film of this first twenty-minute flight, made under a deep-blue sky from the Naval Auxiliary Air Station at Brown Field, California, is oddly moving. While watching it, I read a note – it could have been written by a comedian – to the effect that Convair had provided the pilot with twenty-five feet of rope to shin down if he had to make an emergency landing away from base. Something interesting had been achieved with this stubby, delta-winged fighter, but to what purpose in an age of fast and competent jet fighters that could shoot off from the decks of the existing carrier fleet? The Pogo continued to fly until November 1956, by which time the US Navy had lost interest in tail-sitters. Happily, both the Convair and Lockheed prototypes have been preserved, although neither is ever likely to hop, let alone fly, again.

What these tests, and earlier experiments, confirmed was that a practical VTOL design should be as close in general arrangement to a conventional aircraft as possible, and that it should be provided with the same amount of power that by the mid-1950s jets were well able to deliver. The first VTOL jet, however, also took off with the nose pointing skywards, although, unlike the turboprops from Lockheed and Convair, the Ryan X-13 Vertijet was suspended off the ground by a nylon cable hanging from the bright-yellow ramp of the lorry-mounted trailer that carried this compact, delta-wing machine. The ramp was raised from the horizontal to the vertical by hydraulic arms. The pilot, left dangling above the ground, was to fire up the X-13's powerful Rolls-Royce Avon jet and to release the hook holding the nose of the aircraft as he applied power and then made a quick transition to forward flight. Coming in to land, the X-13 was brought back to the vertical and lowered close to the ground, where the pilot would manoeuvre it back to the trailer ramp, hook up and switch off. Mission accomplished.

This was a complex way of going about VTOL flight, and yet the X-13 did exactly what it was asked to do. As did Bell's X-14. There is a delightful promotional film shot by the company on

11 April 1957 to demonstrate the progress it made with this experimental aircraft that year. Resembling a mechanical moth, the silver machine, which had been commissioned by the USAF, performs faultlessly from and over Edwards Air Force Base, California – a performance repeated that summer in front of the Pentagon for an invited crowd of three thousand military officials, politicians and journalists. The precise nature of the flying, and the obvious control the pilot had over the experimental aircraft, were due in part to the vectored thrust of the jet engines and the provision of 'puffers', or jet reaction controls, housed in the wing-tips. It was also down to the great skill of Bell's test pilot, Peter Gerard, a highly experienced glider pilot who, raised on a Californian cattle ranch, studied mechanical engineering at the University of California, Berkeley, and flew B-24 Liberator bombers with the USAF during the Second World War. Gerard lived to the ripe old age of ninety-two, his soul slipping into the blue yonder in 2011. On 24 November 1953, he had been the first man to hover in vertical flight, although this was at the controls of a test rig, rather than an aircraft, that Bell had been working on since 1947.

Bell itself was no stranger to bold experimental aircraft design. The company, based at Niagara Falls Airport, New York, had designed and built the first US jet, the P-59 Airacomet in 1942; the X-1 rocket plane that first broke the sound barrier in 1947 with Chuck Yeager doing the 'right stuff'; and, of course, the thousands of P-39 Airacobra and P-63 Kingcobra fighters with their piston engines mounted, unusually, behind the pilot, many of which were supplied to and flown very successfully by the Soviet Air Force during the Great Patriotic War against Germany of 1941–5.

The pieces of the complex development jigsaw that culminated in the Hawker P.1127 were slowly coming together: engineers, on both sides of the Atlantic, started to see the big picture. At much the same time as Bell built and hovered its jet test-rig, Rolls-Royce produced its Thrust Measuring Rig (TMR), or 'Flying Bedstead', a device designed under the direction of Dr Alan Griffith, the company's chief scientist, and powered by a pair of Rolls-Royce Nene turbojets. The contraption, which looked like some early prototype for a British lunar landing module, was used for research into controlled hovering. It was a dangerous machine to fly, with sluggish throttle control, little in the way of stability, and just ten minutes of fuel. Rolls-Royce test pilot R. T. Shepherd managed a free test flight on 3 August 1954, but when the machine was transferred soon afterwards to the Royal Aircraft Establishment (RAE) at Farnborough, it crashed, killing its pilot; the second TMR crashed in 1957. This risky machine did lead, however, to the development of Griffith's RB.108 engine, a jet designed specifically for VTOL and hovering aircraft. The British government took an interest and, in October 1954, Short Brothers of Belfast was awarded a contract for two experimental VTOL aircraft based around the Rolls-Royce engine. Griffith himself was toying with the idea of a VTOL supersonic airliner powered by dozens of RB.108s that would have flown confidently from London to Sydney.

The tiny, bug-like Short Brothers aircraft, designated SC.1, were packed off to the RAE at Boscombe Down when complete in 1957. With its four RB.108s, mounted in the middle of the fuselage, blasting down and test pilot Tom Brooke-Smith at the controls, the second aircraft achieved the first untethered hover on 25 October 1958, two years ahead of the P.1127, while the all-important transition from vertical to forward flight, aided by a fifth, tail-mounted RB.108, took place on 6 April 1960. The SC.1 was a low-performance aircraft, with a top speed of 246 mph and a ceiling of just 8,000 feet, but the point of the exercise was to see if a jet aircraft could take off and land vertically, hover, and make the transition from vertical to forward flight. These things happen at low speeds. To ensure stability at low speed and when hovering, the engines of the delta-wing aircraft provided thrust to small control jets under the nose and tail and at the wing-tips. Information gathered from the RAE tests was supplied to Hawker, while the aircraft made themselves known to the public at the Farnborough and Paris air shows between 1958 and 1961. Sadly, the second aircraft, XG905, crashed at Belfast on 2 October 1963 when an auto-stabilizer failed, killing its pilot, J. R. Green, who had joined Short Brothers from the RAF, where he had been flight commander of 2 Squadron, based in Germany and flying Supermarine Swifts. Green's death was a reminder of the fact that the SC.1, as indeed the P.1127 was to be, was very much an analogue aircraft from an era largely innocent of computers, although the Belfast-built aircraft were among the very first to employ fly-by-wire technology. The two aircraft, XG900 at the Science Museum, London and XG905 at the Ulster Folk and Transport Museum at Cultra, Northern Ireland, have both been preserved. They led long lives for experimental aircraft, only retiring in 1971.

The 'missing link' between the SC.1, and all the earlier VTOL experiments, and the P.1127 was the work of neither an American nor a German or British engineer. The inventor of the idea of vectored jet thrust – the heart and soul of the Harrier and the Lockheed Martin F-35B or Lightning II scheduled to replace the British jump jet – was a Frenchman, Michel Wibault (1897–1963). Born in Douai, Wibault had established his own aircraft company in 1919. He made early use of all-metal construction and was well known to Vickers in England, a company interested in this aspect of his work. With the Germans closing in on Paris in 1940, Wibault escaped to London where, soon afterwards, General Charles de Gaulle, leader of the Free French, appointed him technical director of France Forever, an organization dedicated to galvanizing support for de Gaulle, in the United States. Wibault made his way to New York, where he took on a job with Republic Aviation and worked on designs for the XF-12 Rainbow, a sleek, four-engined, long-distance reconnaissance aircraft of which just two were built in 1945 before their role was usurped by now-redundant Boeing B-29 Superfortresses, and for the low-cost RC-3 Seabee seaplane, of which 1,060 were built, and some two hundred and fifty still fly today, a number of them in regular commercial service.

In New York, Wibault was introduced to Winthrop Rockefeller, the billionaire politician and philanthropist, who was to fund the French inventor for the rest of his career. While still in the United States in the early 1950s and now having the luxury of time to think, Wibault took out a number of patents related to VTOL flight. In 1955, he came up with the idea of an aircraft driven by a single turbine feeding four centrifugal compressors, which looked like giant 1950s hair-dryers, or snail shells, mounted in tandem on either side of the fuselage around the centre of gravity. These could be turned to any angle from straight down to the ground to facing horizontally rearwards; in other words, Wibault had come up with a convincing patent for a vectored VTOL jet. His design was a little complex in terms of mechanical engineering, but this was something that Hawker would sort out over the next few years.

The connection between Wibault and Hawker, however, had yet to be made. This came about when, after Wibault had failed to interest the French military and industry in his patent, an officer in the USAF, Colonel John Driscoll, introduced the French designer to Stanley Hooker. Hooker was the brilliant aero-engine designer who had formerly worked with Rolls-Royce and is famous today – or should be – as the brains behind supercharged variants of the wartime Rolls-Royce Merlin and the Bristol Olympus turbojet fitted to the Avro Vulcan and Concorde. He was also the engineer who came back from retirement to oversee the transition into production of the then-threatened but ultimately highly successful Rolls-Royce RB.211 jet engine, an achievement for which he was awarded a well-deserved knighthood in 1974.

At the time of this first meeting in Paris in late 1955, Driscoll was senior air officer with the Mutual Weapons Development Programme (MWDP), a NATO organization funded by the Pentagon and based in Paris. Driscoll had passed Wibault's design on to the chairman of NATO's Advisory Group for Aeronautical Research and Development, Dr Theodore von Karman of the

California Institute of Technology, who strongly recommended the proposal. The following March, Wibault sent Hooker a copy of a brochure outlining details of his VTOL design. Hooker forwarded this to Gordon Lewis, his young number two, who was to be jointly responsible for the Olympus turbofan and later, as technical director of Rolls-Royce, led the design of jet engines up to and including the EJ200 that today sends Eurofighter Typhoons rocketing and pirouetting through footless halls of contested air. Lewis simplified and lightened Wibault's engine layout and, following a momentous meeting between Wibault, Hooker and other interested parties, the Frenchman agreed to work with Bristol. A patent for the revised VTOL power plant was filed on 29 January 1957; the names attached were those of Michel Wibault and Gordon Lewis.

Lewis and his colleagues did much work during 1957 on the design of a power plant that would be much lighter and simpler, as well as more powerful and efficient, than the original Wibault proposal based on the Bristol Orion jet. This was the Bristol Orpheus, and although Hooker had expected Shorts in Belfast to take up the bait, it was Hawker in Surrey who became interested. A week before he paid a visit to the 1957 Paris Air Show, Hawker's legendary chief designer Sydney Camm (1893–1966) dropped a note to Stanley Hooker at Bristol:

17th May 1957
Dear Dr Hooker,
I saw recently a film on the Ryan V.T.O aircraft and it started me wondering whether we ought to give

more attention to this possible development. I have also heard that you have given some consideration to it and I should very much like to have your views. My own view is that before we can go very far we would have to have in mind the practical application of the aircraft; in other words it could not be merely a research aircraft.

There are many aspects, of course, of this development. Up to the present I have thought that the arrangement in which engines are carried merely for take-off and landing would be bad for the overall efficiency but Rolls, on the other hand, have suggested that this is probably the best arrangement.

I am sorry I omitted to discuss this with you when I was down at Bristol. Perhaps you can drop me a line about it.

Best wishes,

S. Camm

Camm was to British military aircraft what Hooker was to the engines that sent some of the very best of them soaring skywards. Nurturing his career through the Windsor Model Aeroplane Club, by 1925 Camm was chief designer for the Hawker Aircraft Company. To the genius of Camm, we owe the Fury, Hurricane, Typhoon, Tempest, Sea Fury, Sea Hawk and Hunter fighters. Now he was about to add what was to become the Harrier to this pantheon of inspired, highly effective and quintessentially British military aircraft.

At the Paris Air Show, Camm was taken around by Major Gerard Morel, the French representative of Bristol and Hawker, who asked him if he knew what Hooker and his colleagues were up to. This piqued Camm's interest further. When he returned to Kingston, Hooker had sent him a brochure of the proposed Bristol BE.53 VTOL engine. Camm was not altogether convinced. He doubted Bristol's claim that the engine would develop 11,000 lbs of thrust and, because of this, he thought it would be best fitted to a small STOL aircraft, although he was unsure quite what that aircraft might be. In any event, he sent one of his young senior design engineers, Ralph Hooper, to Bristol to see what was up and what Hawker might do with this undoubtedly interesting proposition.

This correspondence and these trips were made at the very same time as Duncan Sandys, the newly appointed minister of defence in Harold Macmillan's Conservative government, was defending his White Paper on Defence in Parliament. Aiming to cut £100 million from Britain's defence budget, Sandys's *Defence: Outline of Future Policy* took careful aim at the RAF and the aircraft industry.

'We are unquestionably moving toward a time when fighter aircraft will be increasingly replaced by guided missiles and V-bombers by ballistic rockets,' the White Paper stated, adding soothingly, 'but all that will not happen overnight. The introduction of these new weapons will be a gradual process, extending over a good number of years, and even then there will still remain a very wide variety of roles for which manned aircraft will continue to be needed.'

Would they? In fact, the Sandys report led to the cancellation of several key military aircraft projects, including Hawker's supersonic P.1121 fighter, a promising successor to the superb and best-selling Hunter. In the event, only the English Electric P.1, the glorious and long-lived Mach 2 Lightning interceptor, was allowed to go ahead because work on the project was far advanced. The Lightning had made its maiden flight in April 1957, the same month the Defence White Paper was announced to the House of Commons, and it would have been very expensive to cancel it at this late stage. The only other aircraft approved was the TSR-2 (Tactical Strike and Reconnaissance Mach 2), a potentially very fine aircraft indeed developed jointly by English Electric and Vickers Armstrong. This project was to be cancelled in 1965 by Harold Wilson's Labour government, which preferred instead to buy American McDonnell Douglas F-4 Phantom fighter-bombers to the detriment of British industry and its workers – the latter were only rarely a Labour priority – and a few British Blackburn Buccaneer strike aircraft. Furthermore, the decision to buy Phantoms was only made after the Wilson administration had ordered and then cancelled swing-wing General Dynamics F-111 bombers from the United States. Huge sums had to be paid in compensation.

It is possible to see the logic of the Defence White Paper. How could fighters be of any use against nuclear missiles, and what fighters would there be to prosecute any kind of war if a single Soviet bomber got through to West Germany and dropped an H-bomb? At my London primary school in the 1960s, we used to sing these words to the tune of 'Ten Green Bottles':

Ten little H-bombs hanging from a wall,
Ten little H-bombs hanging from a wall,
And if one little H-bomb should accidentally fall,
There'll be no more H-bombs and no blooming wall.

Recalling a well-known post-war Pepsodent toothpaste ad, older children had sung:

You'll wonder where your mouth has gone
When you brush your teeth with Atom bomb.

However, as future Paris air shows at Le Bourget were to prove, such apprehensions did nothing to stop either the Soviet Union or the United States showing off one new advanced supersonic jet after the other. In 1961, the United States stole the limelight with a line-up of fighters and fighter-bombers that included the McDonnell Douglas F-4 Phantom, Republic F-105 Thunderchief, Lockheed F-104 Starfighter and Vought F-8 Crusader. The North American A-5 Vigilante, a carrier-based strike and reconnaissance aircraft, also put in an appearance, while a menacing USAF Convair B-58A Hustler strategic bomber capable of Mach 2 flew to Paris across the Atlantic in just three-and-a-half hours.

If the cancellation of prized British supersonic projects that were also essential for the cash flow of aircraft companies like Hawker wasn't bad enough, the government went a step further and pressurized the industry into mergers. As a direct result of the 1957 White Paper, English Electric, Bristol and Vickers Armstrong became the British Aircraft Corporation in 1960, while Hawker Siddeley subsumed Blackburn, de Havilland and Folland. The aero-engine divisions of Armstrong Siddeley and Bristol had merged the year before to form Bristol Siddeley, only to be taken over by Rolls-Royce in 1966. By this time, more than 70,000 skilled jobs had been lost.

The year 1957, then, was not exactly the best time for a hard-pressed British aircraft company with an illustrious past but an uncertain future to embark on a revolutionary new fighter aircraft. Remarkably, and despite Duncan Sandys and his White Paper, cuts and mergers, Hawker's VTOL jet project was to triumph in adversity, and given what became its fifty-year history, forty-one of these in front-line service with the RAF, the Harrier was to score a great victory over political short-termism.

Appraisal of the Sandys review by those who love aircraft has, perhaps, always been as emotional as rational. Aspects of the report did, though, make a certain sense: Bloodhound missiles might well, for example, have provided a surer and more economical means of shooting down Soviet bombers over Britain than scrambled jet fighters. But, given the technologies of the time, the White Paper was at best over-optimistic, and it is only now, some five-and-a-half decades later, that the world's military is contemplating, with some fervour, future generations of remotely controlled fighters and bombers. The controversial deployment of UAVs (Unmanned Aerial Vehicles) or drones like the General Atomics MQ-1 Predator and MQ-9 Reaper is just the start.

As it was, Sandys was to be disappointed since, rather annoyingly, manned aircraft continued to prove themselves useful instruments of war. And just as his review was discredited, so too, in due course, was he, when Lonrho, a company of which he was chairman, was found to have bribed a number of African companies and also to have broken sanctions against Ian Smith's Rhodesia after the former Hurricane and Spitfire pilot made a Unilateral Declaration of Independence in 1965, breaking away from Britain. Sandys was also implicated in the notorious, and rather hilarious, Headless Man Affair of 1963, which involved a set of Polaroid snaps taken in 1957 with a Ministry of Defence camera, showing Margaret Campbell, the duchess of Argyll, naked save for three strings of pearls, fellating a naked man, his head out of shot, while a second naked man masturbated behind him. Sandys was accused of being the 'headless man'. But all this was not before, in a great blow to British pride, Sandys had given two fingers to the RAF and announced the abolition of Fighter Command itself, although this was delayed until it was merged with Bomber Command in 1968 to form Strike Command.

Aside from furthering his ministerial career by making budgetary cuts, it is hard to see quite what Sandys expected Britain, and indeed NATO, to gain ultimately from the 1957 Defence White Paper. Cancellations of what may well have been excellent aircraft depleted Britain's aircraft industry of money, talent and skills. To his credit, Sandys introduced the Clean Air Act of 1956, established the Green Belts, now threatened by David Cameron's coalition government in the 2010s, and formed the Civic Trust – he was keen on historic architecture and was made an Honorary Fellow of the Royal Institute of British Architects in 1968, although his government had been responsible for the wilful and unforgivable demolition of the Euston Arch. Yet he did more than many other politicians to undermine an aircraft industry bristling with fresh ideas in the 1950s. That the Harrier – a resounding British success – ever got into the air was something of a miracle. There was more than a grain of truth to Sydney Camm's famous dictum, stated at the time of the cancellation of the TSR-2, that 'All modern aircraft have four dimensions: space, length, height and *politics*.'

Camm might have added that he was saddened, although not at all surprised, by the 'politics'. In 2009, history was to repeat itself in comments reminiscent of Sandys's White Paper on Defence made by Quentin Davies, Minister for Defence Equipment and Support, at an Unmanned Air Systems exhibition held that summer at the Ministry of Defence in London. 'My own working assumption,' Davies told his audience, 'is that we certainly need the manned combat aircraft and are investing in some very good ones at the moment... that will take us through to the 2030s, but beyond that I think the name of the game will be UAVs.'

This is not to say that Davies, who had recently abandoned the Conservative party to side with Gordon Brown's New Labour government, was wrong. At the time of his speech at the Ministry of Defence, progress on the Northrop Grumman X-47B UCAV (Unmanned Combat Air Vehicle) was making determined progress. The prototype X-47B had been completed at Air Force Plant 42 in Palmdale, California on 16 December 2008, and the first flight of this carrier-based fighter had been planned just weeks after the Unmanned Air Systems exhibition in London. In the event, this striking jet was to make its maiden flight from

Edwards Air Force Base on 4 February 2011. Sea trials began from the deck of the 103,900-ton aircraft carrier USS *Harry S Truman* on 29 November 2012; according to the US Navy, the aircraft is said to have performed 'outstandingly'.

Capable of flying 2,000 miles without refuelling, and kitted out with every latest byte of computer wizardry, the X-47B is an attractive proposition. Only rising costs might shoot it down, yet as the development of the Lockheed Martin F-35B has proved in recent years, the pockets of the US government can be very deep indeed when it comes to ensuring that the country has a military advantage over what it sees as real or potential enemies. Quentin Davies was up to speed on development of this future long-range and pilotless strike, reconnaissance and interceptor aircraft and, unlike Sandys, he was at least untainted by scandal – even though an MP's expenses claim he had made in 2008 did include £20,000 for the restoration of a bell tower at his 'second home', the much-modified eighteenth-century Frampton Hall, near Boston in Lincolnshire.

Back in the late 1950s, however, the cost of developing machines like the English Electric Lightning and the putative Hawker jump jet made it difficult to sanction ever more money for the development of other new aircraft: Britain's economy was still only just recovering from the devastating financial cost of the Second World War. Yet the politicians who made these decisions had their own, invariably self-interested agendas to pursue, and never mind the poor old British aero industry, which admittedly sometimes didn't help its own cause – while some companies were highly innovative and productive, others remained deeply complacent and inefficient. The politicians might also, of course, have been profiting in other ways: influence and favour can always be bought, for a price. And there were bound to be lost chances and missed opportunities. Britain, for example, certainly possessed the technical expertise to develop a Mach 2 two-seat fighter-bomber like the US F-4 Phantom, which went on to become a great global success story, being purchased by no fewer than eleven air forces around the world. But instead we ordered the American aircraft to replace our own Lightnings and Sea Vixens, then proceeded, albeit with the very best of intentions, to degrade its performance by refitting it with Rolls-Royce Spey engines. Who knows what deals were done, when, and by whom?

Yet war itself, as Carl von Clausewitz, the German-Prussian soldier and military theorist, put it, is always 'the continuation of politics [or policy] by other means'. And war, or the looming threat of it, can have the most unexpected consequences. I once interviewed Lieutenant General Günther Rall at his beautiful house, a seventeenth-century hunting lodge set high over Bad Reichenhall, a spa town in the Bavarian Alps. 'Wars – idiotic things – might be caused by weak or morally cretinous people,' Rall told me, 'but they are fought and endured by very decent ones.'

Rall had been a highly publicized young Luftwaffe fighter ace in the Second World War. Flying for all six years of the conflict, against the British, French, Russians and Americans, he shot down 275 enemy aircraft, all of them through the gun-sights of Messerschmitt Bf 109s, and was decorated, by Hitler personally, with the Knight's Cross, followed by an Oak Leaf Cluster and then Crossed Swords. He had joined the Luftwaffe in 1938. What, I asked him, were his politics? 'I was twenty years old then,' he replied, 'naïve politically, happy to see Hitler bringing the German peoples of Europe together again. We were no longer to be humiliated by the Treaty of Versailles. We were a new Holy Roman Empire.'

Marriage, during the war, to a young Viennese doctor who helped Jewish friends and colleagues escape under the nose of the Nazis brought Rall to understand the vile politics that had led both to the development of his beloved Bf 109s and to a war that cost the lives of sixty million people. Later, in the mid-1950s, Rall was asked to help form the new West German Bundesluftwaffe. He jumped at the chance and was soon training alongside former wartime colleagues, including Erich Hartmann, the greatest fighter ace of all time with 352 kills, over the American deserts from San Antonio, Texas. 'Goering's finest fly again!' shouted the headline of a local paper with undisguised relish.

Rall was duly appointed director of the German F-104 project, through which the brand-new and pencil-thin Mach 2 Lockheed Starfighter – capable of climbing 48,000 feet a minute and reaching 100,000 feet, or the bounds of space – formed the backbone of the Bundesluftwaffe's fighter fleet. With good reason, German pilots came to know this unforgiving machine as the *Witwenmacher* or 'Widow-maker': 110 of them lost their lives flying it. Meanwhile, Rall himself went on to become Chief of Air Staff in 1971 and the Federal Republic's military attaché to NATO. His story is rich in irony. Here was a former enemy who was now, as a West German, an ally in the icy stand-off between

NATO and the Warsaw Pact, and who could usefully oversee his country's acquisition of a new and capable air force – and all this only a decade after the end of a war throughout which the Luftwaffe had been an ever-present threat.

The relationship between the body politic, defence industry and armed forces has, then, been often fraught and always complex. So no designer or producer of military combat aircraft, and no one who flies them, can truly detach themselves from the vagaries and vanities of politics. These machines, no matter how special, will always be shaped in the uncertain crucible of the political, be it domestic or international. Of course, fine and alluring aircraft like the Harrier hold a particular appeal that derives from the ingenuity of their design and engineering excellence – and from their dangerous beauty and charisma, too. But it is Camm's 'fourth dimension' that can both give them life and take it from them.

CHAPTER 1

A LEAP OF IMAGINATION

When I was a schoolboy, one of my friends lived in Kingston upon Thames. The last stage of the long journey to this prosperous Surrey outpost was by the 65 bus from Ealing Broadway. This was operated by London Transport's handsome and beautifully engineered RT double-deckers – buses that, resplendent in their guardsman's outfits of red, black and gold, ran all but faultlessly through London streets and country lanes around the capital for forty years. The route was fascinating for any young person alert to interesting architecture, engineering and history. The RT would gargle steadily past Ealing Library – originally Pitzhanger Manor, a house rebuilt in an imaginative classical style from 1800 by John Soane, architect of the original Bank of England – on the way to the factories at Brentford, where, allegedly, Julius Caesar had forded the Thames in 55 BC, and so along to Kew Bridge and its pumping station built for the Grand Junction Waterworks Company in 1838. Inside, there brooded one of the largest of all Cornish beam engines, a 'monster' according to Charles Dickens, built to pump water to London, which it did for very nearly a century. Luckily it has been preserved, and you can gawp at it, in steam, at Kew today.

From here, the bus picked up speed to Richmond, before threading cautiously through the town's narrow shopping streets and then giving a tantalizing glimpse of the Thames as we skirted Richmond Bridge, a graceful spring of stone arches across the tidal river designed by the architects James Paine and Kenton Couse, Secretary to the Board of Trade, in the 1770s. South of Richmond, and on to Ham and Petersham, the bus entered a stretch of genteel suburbia resembling rolling countryside, picking up and dropping off passengers to the accompaniment of the conductor's bell in an enchanting realm of fine Georgian villas, before making its stately way down a long straight road to Kingston.

And here, all of a sudden, was what I used to think of as one of the most awe-inspiring and special buildings within reach of my beloved St Paul's Cathedral. It was the principal façade and offices of the Hawker factory, Kingston upon Thames, a commanding, part-classical, part-modern design, rather like the 1930s Underground stations designed by Charles Holden, although writ on a much larger scale that spoke eloquently of the confidence and nobility of British manufacturing industry. To make it all the more exciting, I knew that behind that palatial façade, and its great stretch of steel windows, Harrier jump jets were being built for the RAF, the Royal Navy, the US Marine Corps and other armed forces abroad that clearly knew that British was still best. This will sound hopelessly naïve today, yet until the end of the 1960s, it was still possible to feel a part of a Britain that appeared to be able to design and make wonderful things on its own back. Of course, things had changed, although nothing prepared me for my return to that long straight road leading down to Kingston upon Thames when I came this way in 2012 to meet Ralph Hooper at the old Hawker social club set between the factory and the Thames.

The RT buses had long gone, replaced by heavy, noisy, ugly provincial buses with squealing brakes bought off-the-peg from God-only-knows where and appearing to cock a snook at London, its history and design culture at every turn of their loutish wheels. What had also gone on Richmond Road was the Hawker factory itself. This came as a shock, and not least because this great workplace and its grand façade had been replaced by a dismal estate of the most banal and indifferent homes, a development careless of architecture and urban design. Here was a story, all too graphically expressed by these new buildings, of how Britain had turned its back on manufacturing industry and engineering prowess wherever possible over the past forty years. The blame for this has partly, and with justification, been laid at the door of Margaret Thatcher's Tory governments from 1979. And yet, Mrs Thatcher would never have been voted into office a second time by such a sweeping margin without British victory in the Falklands War and without the Harriers, built here in Kingston upon Thames, where the vapid new housing estate now stood in all its gormlessness.

On my journey down to Kingston, I read an article from the *Surrey Comet*, dating from 7 March 1959. 'For almost half a century,' it began, 'Kingston has been closely associated with the aircraft industry and lays proud claim to being the birthplace of machines which bear some of the most famous names in the history of military aircraft. Mention the name of Hawkers and one phrase springs immediately to mind – renowned fighter aircraft. In all the successes and setbacks that have attended it since its early days, the people of Kingston have come to look upon the Company as an organisation in which they can take personal pride. The admiration is not one-sided: it is matched by the regard which the Company has for the town.'

The litany of fighter aircraft built by Hawker at Kingston is indeed a wonder: Hart, Fury, Hurricane, Typhoon, Tempest, Sea Fury, Sea Hawk, Hunter, Hawk and, of course, Harrier, all of these under the design direction of the brilliant Sydney Camm. At times in the 1930s, eight in ten RAF aircraft were one of the powerful fighter biplanes designed by Camm in Kingston. The Hawker legacy, however, stretched back further than these legendary piston-engined and jet fighters. Hawker had been founded by Tommy Sopwith – or, to give him his full name, Sir Thomas Octave Murdoch Sopwith (1888–1989) – in partnership with Harry Hawker (1889–1921), who had been chief engineer and test pilot for the Sopwith Aircraft Company, which had been wound up, after great success in the First World War, by a punitive government tax called the Excess War Profits Duty and by the simple fact that thousands of its new fighters were no longer needed.

Sopwith was a debonair, Kensington-born sportsman who taught himself to fly in 1910 in a Scottish Aeroplane Syndicate Avis, a 40 hp JAP-engined machine that resembled the aircraft Louis Blériot, the French aviator and engineer, had designed, built and flown across the English Channel in 1909, the first pilot to do so. Sopwith founded his first aircraft company in 1912 when he was just twenty-four years old. His biographer, Bruce Robertson, wrote:

> Sopwith had four great assets: a private income
> from his father [a successful civil engineer]; a bevy
> of devoted sisters conveniently placed socially and
> geographically; a mechanical aptitude fostered by an
> education in engineering and certainly not least, an
> abundance of pluck and drive.

His friends included the pioneer British aviator Charles Rolls, who was soon to team up with Henry Royce, A. V. Roe and Hugh 'Boom' Trenchard, the legendary, and famously loud, 'Father of the RAF'. Young Sopwith could hardly have fallen in with a more influential, brilliant and effective crowd.

Sopwith taught Boom to fly. He also taught Harry Hawker, a young Australian and blacksmith's son who had sailed to England in 1910 in search of work in the fledgling aviation industry. After brief stints with the Commer Car Company and the English branches of Mercedes and Austro-Daimler, Hawker was taken up by Sopwith in June 1912. He flew solo after three lessons and became not just the Sopwith Company's first test pilot, but also the first professional British test pilot. Sopwith built two Wright-style aircraft at Brooklands that year before founding his own factory in an old ice-skating rink close to Kingston station. A highly competitive sailor as well as a pilot, Sopwith was also a skilled ice-skater and a member of the British national ice-hockey team. Beginning with the Sopwith Bat flying boat designed with S. E. Saunders in 1913, the new company responded immediately to the demands, and opportunities, of the Great War. Hawker had already designed the Sopwith Tabloid, a small, fast and lively biplane that, in seaplane guise, won the 1914 Schneider Trophy held that year at Monaco; its fastest two laps were timed at 92 mph.

Significantly for the future of the company, single-seat variants of the Tabloid flew with both the Royal Flying Corps and the Royal Naval Air Service (RNAS) during the First World War; significantly, too, they were employed as fighters, scouts and bombers. In fact, two RNAS Tabloids flying from Antwerp on 8 October 1914 made the first British aerial bombing raids over Germany. In August 1915, one of the Schneider seaplane variants of the Tabloid was launched from the carrier HMS *Campania*; it was a close call, with even this lightweight aircraft finding it hard to take off despite the ship steaming hard and fast into the wind. And yet, it was not long before *Campania* was sailing with Sopwith Pups, Babies and 1½ Strutters on board, all of them able to operate successfully from the ship's 245-foot flight deck. In 1917, the Pup became the first aircraft to land on a moving ship.

Sopwith employed a staff of five thousand during the war and, working with a wide network of subcontractors, produced 18,000 aircraft between 1914 and 1918. These included 1,850 Pups, 5,500 1½ Strutters and no fewer than 5,747 Camels. The Camel was a demanding machine but, along with the superb German Fokker DVII, it became one of the most effective and best-known fighters of the Great War. In fact, 60 per cent of British single-seat aircraft produced by the time of the German surrender on 11 November 1918 were Sopwiths. During the conflict these machines also flew with the French, Belgian and American military, by which they were much appreciated and greatly admired. The many other aircraft types produced at Kingston during the Great War included the Buffalo, Bulldog, Cuckoo, Hippo, Salamander and Snipe, their entertaining names prompting those within and without the industry to refer fondly to the 'Sopwith Zoo'.

Sopwith himself was a remarkable fellow. An enthusiastic sportsman, who raced cars and yachts, and who at the age of ten had accidentally shot and killed his father in a hunting accident on a Scottish island, he built his own J-Class yachts in the 1930s, designed in collaboration with Charles Nicholson, to compete in the America's Cup. He was at the helm of one of these beautiful boats, *Endeavour*, in June 1940, sailing to pick up British troops stranded on the beaches at Dunkirk. As its chairman, he oversaw the creation of the Hawker Aircraft Company in 1920 and remained a consultant with Hawker Siddeley and British Aerospace until 1980. Sopwith was always very much up to date with the very latest, and often futuristic, developments. A fifteen-year old when the Wright Brothers took to the air with *The Flyer*, he went on to oversee Sopwith Pups and Camels, Hawker Furies, Hurricanes, Typhoons and Hunters. One of the first men in Britain to hold a pilot's licence, he lived to see Concorde soar across the Atlantic at Mach 2, men land on the Moon and, best of all from his point of view, one of his company's aircraft take off vertically. Interviewed in 1979 by Sir Peter Allen, president of the Transport Trust, Sopwith was asked: 'On looking back, which of your planes were you proudest of? Would it be the Camel, or something later, say one of the later Hawker Siddeley machines?' He shot back: 'I would say, undoubtedly, the Harrier... the Harrier flies forwards, backwards, sideways. Once I'd seen an aeroplane fly backwards under control, I thought I had seen everything.'

Sadly, Harry Hawker, who lent his name to the superb line of fighter aircraft that ended with the jet-powered Hawk and Harrier, was killed in July 1921 when he crashed a Nieuport Goshawk at Hendon while practising for the Aerial Derby – a race of 200 miles over two laps with turning points at Brooklands, Epsom, West Thurrock, Epping and Hertford, and won at 163 mph on a blisteringly hot summer's afternoon by Jimmy James, in jacket and tie, flying a Gloster Mars I. Hawker, who would have given James a run for his money, may well have suffered a haemorrhage while pulling a high-g turn and died while attempting to land.

As it was, the Hawker Aircraft Company bought the Gloster Aircraft Company in 1934, and merged with the automotive concern Armstrong Siddeley and its aircraft subsidiary Armstrong Whitworth the following year. Hawker Siddeley then took over A. V. Roe (as in Avro and Lancaster). Until 1963, however, Hawker aircraft were marketed under their own name, as were the products of other Hawker Siddeley subsidiaries. British aircraft manufactured in the 1960s as diverse as the Blackburn Buccaneer, Gloster Javelin, de Havilland Sea Vixen, Folland Gnat and Avro Vulcan were all Hawker Siddeley products, as were the Blue Streak, Red Top and Sea Dart missiles. Railway locomotives, metro trains and Westinghouse brakes and signals were too. In the late 1970s and early 1980s, a Canadian railway industry Hawker Siddeley subsidiary built new trains for the Massachusetts Bay Transportation Authority; other MBTA trains at the time were built by Messerschmitt-Bölkow-Blohm, a fascinating case of old wartime sparring partners turning swords into ploughshares.

Throughout this long and convoluted history, and even into the era when, in 1977, Hawker Siddeley was made a part of state-owned British Aerospace (BAe, later privatized in 1981), Sopwith remained a consultant to the aviation giant he had spawned in Kingston in that former ice-skating rink two years before the outbreak of the First World War. His centenary was celebrated with an appropriate military fly-past, and he died at the age of 101. Intriguingly, William Manning, the engineer who had built the Avis machine Sopwith learned to fly on in a workshop in Battersea, went on, after a spell working with Fiat on the racing seaplanes of the 1930s, to a research post at the Royal Aircraft Establishment, Farnborough, where he was co-inventor of the probe-mounted valve that allowed the Harrier, among other RAF aircraft, to refuel in mid-air.

The RAF has flown Sopwiths and Hawkers made in Kingston from its inception in 1918 to the present day: the Harrier may have bowed out in 2010, yet the Hawk trainer, developed from 1968 by a design team led by Ralph Hooper and John Fozard, and first flown in 1974, is still in production. It serves with the RAF and many other air forces around the world and has been the choice of the virtuoso RAF Red Arrows display team since 1979. The Hawk, though, is not built in Kingston; the factory closed in 1992, to be replaced as we have seen by that other great British product, horrid housing.

But back to the *Surrey Comet* of 1959:

> A huge new office block housing the Company's administrative section, design and pre-production departments has been built on the Richmond Road frontage... for all its size it does not obtrude but enhances the landscape, hiding as it does the gaunt factory buildings to which it is attached.

And its grandeur notwithstanding, this was not a luxurious building:

> Plainly, almost austerely, panelled in oak, the boardroom, situated centrally on the first floor, is flanked on each side by the offices of the directors and their immediate staff. On the other side of the corridor is a department which is a source of great pride to the Hawker team – the design section under

Sir Sydney Camm. He is able to step across from his offices and see an army of experts at work on many various projects.

The design section is where Ralph Hooper and his colleagues worked. Their open-plan office covered 50,000 square feet under a 400-foot span 'daylight roof'.

The county newspaper was giving me a very good idea of what it might have been like to work here in the heyday of the transformation of the experimental P.1127 into the world's first successful V/STOL fighter jet, the Harrier. 'There is,' the article went on, 'an almost monastic calm in the design office and thus it is a dramatic moment for the visitor when he is conducted through the double doors to a platform overlooking the factory floor. Contrasting the cloistered quiet of the office is the din of the Hunter production floor.' This was 'Aircraft Factory No. 1', built by the government and used by Sopwith throughout the First World War. It was meant to have been a temporary structure, but endured until 1992. The P.1127 is not mentioned in the newspaper article except in reference to work being carried out on 'a vertical take-off machine' in a new 11,000-square-foot Research and Development building facing the Thames behind the factory. Significantly, though, the *Surrey Comet* noted a new 'computing section' next to the design department in which the 'most expensive piece of furniture' was 'a £40,000 electronic computer which works out problems that could not be attempted by mere humans'. In 1959, the average salary of a 'mere human' in Britain was a little under £900.

That new company computer is a reminder of the fact that the design of P.1127 pre-dated the digital age. Most of the design work on the jump jet was done with pencils, paper and slide rules, and on drawing boards. In fact, when later in 2012 I spoke to test pilots of the Lockheed Martin F-35B, they all made the point that, as far as they were concerned, the Harrier – which they all knew and most had flown in combat – was a distinctly analogue aircraft, while the F-35B, its much bigger and hugely more complex successor, is digital.

I met Ralph Hooper at the former Hawker social club. The club, now a local authority sports centre, is where ex-Hawker employees still gather. Hooper, who lives within walking distance of the club, is tall, alert, drily and even sardonically witty, and not a man given to unnecessary reminiscence. Like so many engineers, he seems as if he might have no time for anything like small talk. He wondered what on earth we might talk about given that the story of the Harrier had been told so many times and suggested that, if I had the patience, I could find everything I needed to know in a library. When I explained that I was as interested in the politics that had shaped, driven, buffeted and undermined the Harrier and in the tortured story of twentieth-century British manufacturing, Hooper then sat down and duly proceeded to reminisce until we agreed that mutual exhaustion had set in. Modest British engineers like Hooper, and the many others I have met over the years, seem to be wholly unaware of the fact that meeting them face-to-face is an honour. And, unlike architects, for example, they do not talk about themselves without a good deal of prompting.

Libraries can indeed fill in the gaps. Ralph Spenser Hooper, lead designer of the P.1127 and chief designer of the Harrier until 1965, was born in Hornchurch, Essex in 1926. In 1933, the family moved to Kingston upon Hull, Yorkshire. Hooper's father was a civil servant with the Board of Trade, and his mother, a nurse in the First World War, was a descendant of Edmund Spenser, the author of the epic Elizabethan poem, *The Fairie Queene*. The young Ralph Hooper, however, was more interested in Meccano construction sets – he connected his alarm clock to the bedroom light-switch – and his Hornby trains; his grandfather was a rolling-stock draughtsman with the London and North-Eastern Railway at Stratford Works, London. Ralph made model aeroplanes and was apprenticed, in 1941, to Blackburn Aircraft based at Brough, a few miles west along the Humber from Hull. At the time, the company – later also absorbed into Hawker Siddeley – was working on the Firebrand, a powerful if problematical Fleet Air Arm fighter just too late to see service in the Second World War.

Hooper spent two years in Blackburn's workshops, a further two years studying aeronautics at University College, Hull and a final year in Blackburn's offices. His apprenticeship complete, he went on to the new College of Aeronautics at Cranfield, Bedfordshire – where he learned to fly, going solo in a Tiger Moth after four hours and twenty minutes' instruction – and from there to a job with Hawker's experimental drawing office. He had, he says, been thinking of working for Vickers at Brooklands because the factory was close to the Surrey Gliding Club at Redhill, of which he was now an active member, but, as fate had it, Sydney Camm offered five shillings a week more than Vickers was prepared to pay, and that settled the matter.

At Hawker, the first project Hooper worked on was the P.1052, the forerunner of the graceful, successful and long-lived Sea Hawk, the company's first jet, which served with the Fleet Air Arm and several foreign navies in front-line service until 1983, when India finally replaced its examples with Sea Harriers. After the Sea Hawk, Hooper worked on the P.1067, the future Hawker Hunter, one of the most graceful of all military jets. No fewer than 1,972 were made, and although English Electric Lightnings replaced the RAF's Hunter F.6 interceptors in 1963, four Hunters were still in service with the Lebanese Air Force in 2013. The next project, the P.1121, was a supersonic fighter shot down by the Duncan Sandys White Paper. Hawker's Ron Williams, meanwhile, was hard at work on designs for the highly ambitious P.1129, the company's proposal for a replacement for the RAF's English Electric Canberra long-range nuclear strike and reconnaissance bomber, and rival to the ill-fated TSR-2. In the event, a government contract for that aircraft was awarded to English Electric and Vickers. This proved to be an unexpectedly lucky break, and a turning point for the P.1127. Lucky, because the TSR-2 was, of course, to be cancelled in 1965 – and lucky, too, for the jump jet Hooper was working on, since there was nothing else on the drawing boards at Kingston after the loss of both the P.1121 and the P.1129.

As it was, Hooper's visit to Bristol in 1957 to discuss the B.53 engine, and Stanley Hooker and his assistant Gordon Lewis's mutual visit to Kingston, led him to believe, in tune with Sydney Camm, that it would lack the power needed for a VTOL aircraft. He drew up outlines for the first P.1127, a small, battlefield liaison or Army-support STOL jet, which – being only a very expensive type of air taxi for generals – no one really believed in. Luckily, neither Hooper nor his colleague John Fozard gave up on the B.53 or the idea of a convincing VTOL jet. What they needed, though, was more power from the Bristol engine. The answer lay under their nose at Kingston. The exhaust of the single-engine Sea Hawk was bifurcated – divided into two branches – emitting thrust from either side of the jet fighter. This unusual arrangement reduced the loss of thrust that would have occurred if the Sea Hawk had been fitted with a long single exhaust stretching from its Rolls-Royce Nene engine to its tail. Hooper and Fozard hit on the idea of bifurcating the exhaust of the B.53, and thus allowing it to feed two pairs of exhaust nozzles rather than the single pair proposed by Bristol. Fozard added the idea of counter-rotating the two sections of the engine, the bypass fan and the high-pressure compressor; along with their associated turbine stages, these were to rotate in opposite directions to counterbalance the gyroscopic effect that could otherwise send an aircraft trying to take off vertically into an inelegant and probably dangerous tizzy. The front two nozzles were fed with air from the low-pressure compressor, and the rear two with hot jet exhaust; to move together, front and rear nozzles were connected by motorcycle chains. Now, a dream fusion of power plant and airframe was about to become a reality: the Bristol Siddeley Pegasus and the Hawker P.1127 jump jet.

Two key problems, however, created a dark cloud through which it would take great skill in the coming months to pilot the P.1127 from drawing board to production. The first was the simple fact that there was no demand for Hooper's aircraft; the second that there was very little money to pay for research and development. Camm and Hooper paid a visit to NATO's Mutual Weapon Development Project (MWDP) in the course of 1958, and as the design became ever more convincing – with further improvements to the engine to increase its power, and with reaction control vents, or 'puffer jets', to give thrust to nose, tail and wing-tips to allow the aircraft to manoeuvre in the hover and at very low speeds – USAF Colonel Bill Chapman, the new head of MWDP, offered to stump up 75 per cent of the engine's development costs, leaving Bristol to pay the other 25 per cent.

The Americans were actively looking for a replacement for the Fiat G.91. This was the lightweight Italian machine that had won a competition in 1953 for a fighter that could take off from grass strips and European city streets and would go on to equip a number of NATO air forces, including the Italian and German. The Fiat G.91 would be a hard act to follow. It was a great success, stayed in production until 1977, and was finally retired, from the Portuguese Air Force, in 1993. MWDP was considering the idea of a VTOL successor to the G.91 and the Italian fighter was powered by a Bristol Siddeley Orpheus turbojet with 5,000 lbs of thrust, so it was only natural that it should keep a weather eye on what Camm and his talented young colleagues were up to at Kingston. It was, though, as John Fozard told the BBC years later, a curious and complex set-up:

We had an aeroplane, paid for and funded on UK money, with an engine that was going to fly the aeroplane which was three-quarters owned by some Americans based in Paris, and the rest of it owned by Bristol. And the paperwork for that took some sorting out, I can tell you.

After continuous discussions between Hawker and Bristol, the new BE.52/2 Pegasus 1 first ran, or span, at Bristol's Patchway factory in September 1959. It produced 9,000 lbs of thrust. More would be needed, but the new engine was a success, and five months later the Pegasus 2 offered 10,000 lbs of thrust. A further six months of intensive work by programme manager John Dale and his team squeezed another 1,000 lbs from the compact engine. This was just enough, Hooper, Fozard and Camm believed, to achieve VTOL flight with the P.1127. Indeed, throughout its long life the Harrier and its predecessors were always in need of extra power.

By now Camm, although still not entirely convinced about the project, had committed Hawker to building two prototypes. This was brave, for despite valuable help with wind-tunnel testing from NASA – its German scientists were keen to see proof of a production VTOL jet – and from the Aircraft Research Association at Bedford and discussions with the Structural Research and Transonic Wind Tunnel departments of the RAE, there was no guarantee of a production contract from either the RAF or NATO. Although there had been talks between the various interested parties throughout 1957 and 1958, if anything, the Americans seemed far more interested than the British. Ralph Hooper and Robert Marsh, Hawker's Head of Projects, visited NASA and Bell Aircraft on a trip to the US, as did Hawker's chief test pilot, Bill Bedford, and his number two, Hugh Merewether. Both were able to fly the Bell X-14, which was a less sophisticated VTOL machine than Hawker's, but it had flown successfully from February 1957, and after its Armstrong Siddeley Viper turbojets were replaced by General Electric engines in 1959, it served as a test aircraft with NASA until 1981. As the upgraded X-14A, its flight-control systems were similar to those fitted to NASA's lunar landing module. Neil Armstrong, the first man on the Moon, was another of the twenty-five test pilots who flew the open-cockpit Bell VTOL machine without serious mishap.

Although the US was to play a very important role in the development of the Harrier – notably through the work of NASA's John Stack, who proved with a free-flight model that transition from vertical to forward flight was perfectly feasible with the P.1127 – perhaps it was this early eagerness from across the Atlantic that prompted the new British Ministry of Aviation to offer Hawker £75,000 for work on the two experimental P.1127s in October 1959. The following June a contract was issued asking for these two aircraft and a further four prototypes.

The first of the two experimental VTOL machines, XP831, was unveiled at Hawker's test airfield at Dunsfold, Surrey on 31 August 1960, after arriving from Kingston the previous month. It was compact, rounded and more sparrow than bird of prey. Its small wings – a single unit, in fact, doubling up as a fuel tank – were carried high on its shoulders to protect the fuselage from the hot blast of the exhausts. This arrangement gave the aluminium-clad machine its characteristic hunched look, exaggerated by the two 'elephant ear' air intakes on either side of the cockpit and by the downward-inclining curves of the wings. These were designed, in part, to reduce the incidence of Dutch Roll – tail-wagging and rocking from side to side – endemic to aircraft at a high angle of attack, when there is a difference between where the wing is pointed and the direction of the air flowing over it.

Because the wing was so high, conventional landing gear was out of the question – struts that could stretch far enough down to the ground would be far too long to fold into the wings, and they would also considerably reduce the fuel capacity of the aircraft. So the P.1127 sat on a narrow bicycle undercarriage with the high wings supported by tall and spindly outriggers. In flight, these retracted into the wing-tips. 'They're going to snap off like carrots,' a sceptical Camm told Hooper. This unusual, delicate-looking yet necessary arrangement made XP831 look as if it were just touching the surface, like a long-legged mayfly dancing upon a stream. It also looked impatient to be off.

Its bug or garden-bird aesthetic was certainly very different from Camm's sleek Hunter or indeed from any mainstream jet, either sub- or supersonic, flying from airbases in the United States or the Soviet Union. With a big engine squeezed into a small airframe, the P.1127 did not look like a fighter jet should – certainly not in the eyes of RAF pilots yearning for Mach 2 – nor was it armed; it was a purely experimental aircraft to prove what might be possible in the future. Weight had to be kept to an absolute minimum and, even then, there was still no guarantee that the Pegasus engine would be sufficiently powerful to allow the aircraft to perform the tricks Hawker's sorcerers believed it should. Bristol had increased the thrust of the Pegasus to 11,300 lbs, but stressed that the engine fitted to XP831 would have a brief working life. The extra thrust was vital given that the engine had to raise the aircraft off the ground, maintain a hover, and feed high-pressure air to the reaction control vents at the nose, tail and wing-tips to ensure that the pilot was able to keep the aircraft stable while standing still on nothing more than a column of hot air above the runway. It was these jets of air, passing over ailerons, tailplane and rudder and regulated by movements of the stick (control column) and rudder pedals, that were to allow Group Captain Gary Waterfall to make a final bow with his GR.9A to the assembled crowd at RAF Cottesmore half a century later.

The canopy of this curious-looking aircraft was set low with little in the way of all-round vision, and in this respect the P.1127 would not have made an ideal fighter. Its cockpit, however, would have been familiar to any RAF or Fleet Air Arm pilot, save for the nozzle-control lever positioned immediately alongside the throttle. Although the controls were fundamentally simple, it still took great skill and a steady nerve to fly the new VTOL jets and to get the best out of them. And the best, as we will see, was extraordinarily good by any standards, although given that this aircraft could stop in mid-air and even fly backwards, it was always going to have been an exciting challenge, even for pilots able to take it by the horns and put it through its truly unique paces.

The first to do so was Bill Bedford. Born in Loughborough, Leicestershire, in 1920, Alfred William Bedford had been training as a steeplejack when the Second World War broke out. He was taken on as a sergeant pilot with the RAF's 605 City of Warwick Squadron in 1941, flying Hawker Hurricanes. In the later stages of the war, he was based in Burma, India and Ceylon, and flew North American P-51 Mustangs and Republic P-47 Thunderbolts. A flying instructor with the Empire Test Pilots School at the end of the war, he had a brief spell as a test pilot with the RAE at Farnborough and the National Gas Turbine Establishment, before joining Hawker Siddeley in 1951, where he became the company's chief test pilot five years later, a position he held until 1967, when he went into sales and marketing, retiring in 1983 as British Aerospace's regional representative in South-East Asia. A record-breaking long-distance glider pilot, Bedford was renowned for his ability to send jets into the most dramatic and prolonged spins and to demonstrate, with what appeared to be consummate ease, how best to guide them back into level flight – although he did once come perilously close to the ground in a Hunter at the end of a dive that had seen the aircraft spin eighteen times.

Bedford, whose one serious wartime injury was caused when a lorry in which he was a passenger crashed, liked to say that the only truly dangerous situations he had been in were those involving his being driven in a car – or lorry – by someone else. Almost comically, he turned up for the maiden flight of the P.1127 on 21 October 1960 with one of his legs in plaster. Someone had driven him into a tree. Roy Orbison reached the Number One spot in the charts that week with

'Only the Lonely'; but Bedford was not the type to go through heartbreaks over such a trifle as a broken leg when he was about to take the Number One spot in aviation history. His apparent insouciance and evident stoicism call to mind the story of Lord Uxbridge's leg. Henry Paget, 2nd Earl of Uxbridge, was a cavalry and artillery commander at the Battle of Waterloo. After the eighth or ninth horse was shot from under him, his right leg was hit by a French cannon-ball. He was sitting, on horseback, next to the Duke of Wellington. 'By God, Sir, I've lost my leg,' said Uxbridge. 'By God, Sir, so you have,' replied the duke as the battle raged around them. Uxbridge would have fought on, but had to retire for his leg to be amputated without anaesthetic or antiseptic. The only comment he is said to have made during the surgical procedure was: 'The knife appears to be somewhat blunt.' Recovered, he announced: 'Who would not lose a leg for such a victory?' Uxbridge remained a serving soldier and rose to the rank of field marshal.

It was, then, a very British moment when Bill Bedford arrived at Dunsfold. He was declared fit, although restricted to 'tethered hovering only'. This, though, is all that was needed on that momentous autumn day in the heart of England's Home Counties. Bedford recalls looking at a 'rather ugly aeroplane' perched on the steel grid of a hover pit dug to disperse the downwards thrust of the exhausts, which, if directed just inches below the P.1127, might easily upset its balance. Then, after settling into the cockpit and with the engine spooled up, Bedford opened the throttle progressively, and 'with a certain amount of uncertainty, the aircraft erratically got itself *just* into the air'.

Safely tethered, the experimental aircraft was doing what Camm, Hooper and Fozard had promised themselves it would. It was hovering, although just inches from the ground and tied like a restless dog to a kennel in a back yard. And, like an unruly hound, the VTOL jet needed taming. Hooper and Fozard watched as the bobbing P.1127 did its best during those early tests to topple over and to turn its tail into the wind, among other tricks. There was much to sort out, especially with the air intakes, and improvements were now designed and applied continuously as the P.1127 progressed towards the key moment when it would break free of its tethers and rise high enough to perform the all-important transition from vertical to forward flight. Of these early days, Bedford's number two, Hugh Merewether, remarked that it was rather like 'being a child trying to master learning to ride a bicycle in a corridor': in other words, all rather wobbly, so Hawker assigned the engineer Robin Balmer to look after 'stability and control'.

Even then, that first flight had been a very marginal affair; as John Farley, a test pilot with the RAE in the early days of the P.1127, revealed in a lecture given in 2000 to the Munich branch of the Royal Aeronautical Society, 'about 700 lbs of electrical equipment, cabin conditioning, instruments and undercarriage components' had to be stripped from the airframe before the aircraft would lift itself into the hover. Furthermore, the P.1127 and its first tentative hops were severely compromised by the thirty-five-minute hover life imposed on the engine. After that, the engine required a £60,000 rebuild; there were no flight simulators in 1960, so every hover was a costly adventure.

The more cerebral of the two P.1127 test pilots, Hugh Merewether had been born to British parents in Cape Town in 1924. He studied engineering at the University of Cape Town before joining the South African Navy. He transferred to the Royal Navy and for five years from 1948 worked under Barnes Wallis, the inventor of the Dambusters' 'bouncing bomb' along with the massive Tall Boy and Grand Slam free-fall weapons dropped on Germany by Lancasters in the late stages of the Second World War, and later the pioneer of swing-wing aircraft. Wallis was head of research and development at Vickers Armstrong and had also developed the amazingly robust geodesic structures of the Wellesley and Wellington bombers; he and his fellow boffins shared offices in the Edwardian clubhouse of the defunct Brooklands Racing Circuit, Surrey, where in its interwar heyday many an aero-engined racing car had roared around at reckless speeds.

While working for Wallis, Merewether joined the RAF Volunteer Reserve, flying Gloster Meteors from Biggin Hill with 615 County of Surrey Squadron. His squadron commander was none less than the celebrated Neville Duke, the Tonbridge-born Spitfire ace with twenty-seven 'kills' to his credit. From 1951, Duke was Hawker's chief test pilot; in 1953, the year of the queen's coronation, he broke the world air speed record – achieving 727.68 mph past Littlehampton on England's south coast – at the controls of a bright-red Hawker Hunter. By then, he was also president of the Eagle Club, founded by the *Eagle* comic, and was very possibly the model for the equally legendary, if fictional, Colonel Dan Dare, Space Fleet's unflappable Pilot of the Future. It seems right; after all, Duke and his successors at Hawker really were testing the aircraft that future generations were to fly for several decades to come and with the P.1127 they were taking a leap – or hop, skip and jump – into entirely new territory.

The first conventional flight was made, successfully, from RAE Bedford on 13 March 1961, although on these early flights the aircraft, balanced on their tentative undercarriages, tended to skid around the runway. Transition from vertical to forward flight was made on 8 September 1961, just weeks after the Berlin Wall was rushed up around that city by the East German government. It had certainly been a momentous Cold War year, and one that had seen major advances in new technology. On 27 April, the twenty-seven-year-old Soviet cosmonaut Yuri Gagarin had become the first man to travel into space. On 25 May, President John F. Kennedy had declared that the United States would land a man on the Moon by the end of the decade. And on 30 October, a Soviet Tupolev Tu-95V 'Bear' long-range bomber, flown by Major Andrei Durnovtsev from a base in the Kola Peninsula in the far north-west of Russia, had released a 100-megaton H-bomb nicknamed the 'Tsar Bomb' over Mityushikha Bay on the Arctic Sea. It was the biggest explosive device ever activated.

The Harrier was truly the product of disturbing and even apocalyptic times. Earlier in 1961, an invasion of Cuba planned by Cuban counter-revolutionaries, funded and organized by the CIA and approved some while before by President Eisenhower, was stopped at the Bay of Pigs on the island's south coast by loyalist forces led personally by Fidel Castro. His rather limited arsenal included Hawker Sea Furies, two of which performed well against enemy shipping and ground forces. Today, one is on display at the Playa Giron Museum, Matanzas, the other at Havana's Museum of the Revolution. The upshot of the Bay of Pigs episode was the establishment of Soviet nuclear-missile bases in Cuba. In October 1962, this prompted the Cuban Missile Crisis when President Kennedy, demanding the removal of the missiles, squared up to the Soviet leader, Nikita Khrushchev. For more than a moment it really did look as if Armageddon were about to be unleashed on the world and that Mutual Assured Destruction (MAD) would be the order of the day. Wisely, Khrushchev backed down. The Americans might well have unleashed the nuclear dogs of war and seen the developed world turned into heaps of radioactive ash.

Meanwhile, in December 1961 the second P.1127 prototype had broken the sound barrier, recording Mach 1.2 in a dive. Bill Bedford lost the aircraft a few days later, on its thirty-fifth flight, after a problem with an air intake caused him to lose control. He ejected safely; the aircraft was destroyed. But Bedford's most spectacular accident, caught in full glare of the cameras and in front of 110,000 spectators, came later, with XP831 at the 1963 Paris Air Show. The nozzles refused to vector and Bedford came down with an almighty thump. 'As I was completing my turn to straighten out,' he recalled years later, 'suddenly I found the aeroplane plummeting earthwards, completely out of control, and I arrived ignominiously with a major crash on the concrete platform that had been prepared for our competitor. [There was] dust, dirt, wheels, everything, flying all over the place, and I recall that the ground was much closer than it normally was when I got out of the aeroplane because the undercarriage had been amputated.' Rather like Lord Uxbridge's leg. The P.1127 was restored, but did not fly again; today XP831 is on display, suspended from the roof of a top floor in the Science Museum, London.

Other serious accidents were caused by engine failure. On 30 October 1962, Merewether crash-landed at RAF Tangmere with no power and the aircraft on fire. He could have ejected, but was keen to get the P.1127 down safely to find out what had gone wrong. On 19 March 1965, he was diving through 28,000 feet when the engine of his P.1127 failed. Just able to glimpse the RAF airfield on Thorney Island, a peninsula jutting into the sea at Chichester, West Sussex, he glided the aircraft down to a safe emergency landing.

Four more P.1127s were ordered. These were modified progressively, with the last of them, XP976, equipped with the latest Pegasus 5, boasting 15,000 lbs of thrust and the swept-back wings that would be carried through to the Harrier. Just, though, as it was proving its potential, gaining a good press and wooing crowds at air shows at home and abroad, the P.1127 project was nearly brought to a halt. The rival aircraft that Bill Bedford had referred to after making his heavy landing at Le Bourget in 1963 was the prototype of the Dassault Mirage IIIV, a sleek and beautiful supersonic machine designed in response to a NATO specification issued in August 1961 for a Mach 2 VTOL fighter. Working with Rolls-Royce, Dassault transformed the first of its Mirage prototypes into the Balzac V (the V standing for vertical), a test bed for the NATO fighter. Unlike the P.1127, the Dassault's eight RB.108 engines were fixed; they would lift the aircraft off the ground, but forward flight was to be made with a Bristol Orpheus. The Balzac V first hovered in October 1962 and made its first transition flight the following March. The production prototype, the Mirage IIIV, was a much larger aircraft equipped with eight Rolls-Royce RB.162-1 VTOL engines and a Pratt & Whitney JTF10 turbofan, modified in France by SNECMA. The first IIIV made the transition from hover to forward flight in March 1966; the second prototype, equipped with a more powerful main engine, reached Mach 2.04 in level flight, only to be lost in an accident in November 1966. This loss, along with the two fatalities that had occurred during the testing of the Balzac V, prompted the cancellation of the project. Even if the Dassault aircraft had proved more successful than it did, its sheer complexity and nine engines would have made it unpopular and costly in service.

Other attempts at supersonic V/STOL fighters were made in Germany in the 1960s and 1970s, although both projects were cancelled after tests that proved to be at best inconclusive, at worst disappointing. The first of the two was the EWR VJ-101C, designed and built by EWR, a consortium comprising Heinkel, Messerschmitt and Bölkow. The sleek aircraft was intended to be a replacement for the F-104G Starfighter. It boasted four Rolls-Royce RB.145 turbojets, each with 2,750 lbs of thrust, housed in a pair of tilting nacelles on each wing-tip, backed up by a further pair of RB.145s in the fuselage. Although complex compared with the P.1127, the VJ-101C was certainly fast; first flown on 10 April 1963, the first of the two aircraft built, X-1, became the first VTOL aircraft to break the sound barrier, even if this was achieved in a shallow dive. In September 1964, X-1 rolled uncontrollably as it attempted a vertical take-off. The pilot ejected with the aircraft just ten feet off the ground; although injured, he survived. The second prototype, X-2, was fitted with afterburners increasing the thrust of the wing-tip engines to 3,650 lbs. Although these promised high performance, they also generated a considerable degree of heat during vertical take-off and in the hover; ingesting its own hot gases, X-2 crashed while attempting to land on a raised platform. Back at the drawing board, EWR designers proposed a revised version of the aircraft – the VJ-101D – this time without the tilting nacelles, but its engine arrangement with five RB.162 lift engines and two RB.153 lift-cruise engines was complex, and by then the Federal government was unwilling to foot further development costs. The project was cancelled in 1968.

A further attempt was made by VFW (Vereinigte Flugtechnische Werke) which, from 1962, developed the VFW-Fokker VAK-191B. This was to have been a replacement for the Fiat G.91. First flown on 20 September 1971, the subsonic aircraft was lifted by a pair of Rolls-Royce RB-162-81s, each with 5,587 lbs of thrust, and propelled forwards by a single Rolls-Royce/MAN RB-193-12 with 10,150 lbs. Three VAK-191Bs were built, making ninety-one flights between 1971 and 1975, but although they incorporated new developments including fly-by-wire capability, they, too, were complex machines and, in any case, their performance was underwhelming.

It was their over-complicated engine arrangements that dogged the P.1127's international rivals. The Balzac V, for example, employed much the same engine and nozzle arrangement as the Short SC.1. In 1964, Flight Lieutenant John Farley, who was later to become Hawker's chief test pilot, was given the opportunity to fly both the SC.1 and the P.1127. Farley was with the Aerodynamics Research Flight at the Royal Aircraft Establishment, Bedford at the time; the RAE was keen to compare the performance of the SC.1 and its multiple lift engines with the single-engine and vectored thrust set-up of the P.1127. 'At the simplest level,' Farley recalled in a paper he wrote in 2010, 'both aeroplanes were similar because both were single-seat fixed-wing jet aircraft that could take off and land vertically. Both could fly on their wings, both could hover, both could transition to and from the hover and both used pure jet thrust to achieve this.'

The fundamental difference between the two, according to Farley, was that the SC.1 was very much a research project, while the P.1127 was the product of a company with a long line of highly successful fighter aircraft to its credit; Hawker was always thinking of an aircraft that could be placed into service even though there was no specific military requirement for it. What Farley found in practice was that the SC.1, with so many engines to look after and so much clever technology on board, was 'demanding to operate and easy to handle, while the P.1127 was easy to operate but had demanding handling'. It took him, Farley wrote, 'very many flights in the P.1127 before I could climb down the ladder without offering up thanks that I had not bent the thing. Yet after shutting down the SC.1, I always felt relief that it had not suffered one of several nasty failures.' It was a five-engine aircraft operated by a single pilot, and this certainly felt like four engines too many.

While the SC.1 was like something Dan Dare might fly around Space Fleet headquarters in the then far-distant year 1999 on his way from briefing to spaceship, the P.1127 could be seen, said Farley, as a Hawker Hunter with an extra lever and one or two additional instruments in the cockpit. But if the pilot should pull the right lever at the wrong time, or the wrong lever at any time, the P.1127 might easily drop to the ground while attempting to fly forwards. Moreover, if while hovering the P.1127 was pointing away from the direction of airflow, the aircraft would turn on its tail as intake drag increased. To solve the problem of P.1127s moving around in circles, Hawker fitted them, and all following Harriers, with a simple wind vane in front of the windscreen to show the pilot where the airflow was coming from. So the P.1127 was, at heart, a simple machine, which made it a far more attractive proposition than the multi-engined Dassault.

The loss of French interest in a Mach 2 VTOL fighter would prove very significant indeed for the development of the Harrier, even if the Mirage IIIV had initially appeared to spell the end of the P.1127. The Dassault had been one of the four shortlisted entries in that 1961 NATO competition to find a fast VTOL fighter that would combine the roles of interception, ground attack and reconnaissance. The other entries were the Fokker-Republic D.24 Alliance, BAC 584 and Hawker P.1154, none of which ever flew, although the P.1154 came close. At Hawker, however, Ralph Hooper had already begun work on a design for a supersonic VTOL fighter, the P.1150. Larger than the P.1127, it would have generated its speed by burning fuel in the plenum chambers between the Pegasus engine and the forward nozzles

– a process achieving much the same effect as afterburning in a conventional jet. With the promise of 33,000 lbs of thrust from the new Bristol Siddeley BS.100, the world's most powerful jet engine, Hooper could look forward to a maximum speed of Mach 1.7 or about 1,300 mph.

Picking up on the NATO specification, the P.1150 duly became the P.1154 and won the competition. In doing so, it also put the nose of French manufacturers and politicians out of joint. They refused to support the perfidious *anglais* and, without international co-operation, the NATO project fell apart. At home, the situation, which might have been rescued through domestic orders for the very promising P.1154, had only worsened when the RAF and the Royal Navy disagreed over its specification. The RAF wanted a fighter as per the NATO specification, one that would replace the single-seat Hawker Hunter, while the Royal Navy was adamant that what it needed was a carrier-based high-altitude two-seat fighter to replace the Sea Vixen. This disagreement led, ultimately, to the Navy pressing successfully for the McDonnell Douglas F-4 Phantom, while the RAF continued to root for the P.1154, which had been worked up in detail by chief designer John Fozard and chief engineer Barry Laight with the new Blackburn division of Hawker Siddeley.

The RAF named it the Harrier. It was immensely sophisticated, with advanced digital avionic, navigation and attack systems; and indeed, it was one of the first military aircraft that was as much a 'system' as a jet-powered flying machine with guns attached. It was designed to be easy to service – the powerful BS.100 engine could be unplugged and removed from beneath the fuselage –

while its structure made use of lightweight titanium and bonded honeycomb panelling and other components. The engine's main functions were controlled electronically, while the aircraft was equipped with both auto-stabilization and autopilot, two of the measures aimed at reducing the workload of pilots, who would now be more able to concentrate on missions and combat rather than on the well-being of their aerial mount. Tests, meanwhile, proved that the BS.100 was reliable and able to generate a considerable maximum thrust of 35,900 lbs.

Understandably excited by the prospect, the RAF envisaged eight operational squadrons of Mach 2 P.1154 Harriers based in Britain, Germany, the Middle East and the Far East. Flying as V/STOL aircraft from conventional bases, and capable of carrying an impressive payload of weapons, the supersonic Harrier would also have been flown from roads, forest clearings and other forward bases. With a folding nose, it would also have been able to operate from carriers – if, that is, the Royal Navy were ever to change its mind about the aircraft. The P.1154 was, in effect, the Lockheed Martin F-35B of its day, a supersonic V/STOL fighter designed to do more or less exactly what its twenty-first-century successor will be able to do when, and if, it goes into service with the RAF from 2018 and the Royal Navy from 2020. With the P.1154, Hawker and Britain were well ahead of the international game. Wing assemblies and fuselage jigs were fabricated at Kingston. Hawker expected to supply the RAF with 157 single-seat P.1154s and twenty-five two-seat trainers.

In one of its last gasps, the Conservative government of Sir Alec Douglas-Home announced that orders would be placed for the new aircraft. A few months later, the Tories were out and Harold Wilson's incoming Labour government cancelled the P.1154 in February 1965. Thousands of jobs were lost, as was Britain's lead in supersonic V/STOL military design. It was not a great moment for British aviation, but that's politics, and economics. Labour had no particular animus against Hawker; it was a matter of cost, although a case of short-sightedness, too. Britain's loss was to be America's gain. It had been a truly fascinating few years, with Britain pioneering, developing and realizing a technology that could have been a world-beater, and doing so well ahead of the Americans, French and Russians. Indeed, confidence in VTOL and V/STOL design was riding so high in those years that, at much the same time as Hooper, Fozard and Laigh were developing the P.1154, Armstrong Whitworth was busy at work on its AW.681, a long-range four-engine V/STOL military transport aircraft to replace the piston-engined Blackburn Beverley and Handley Page Hastings. In later stages of the design, the AW.681 was shown with four Pegasus turbofans, each rated at 18,000 lbs of thrust, and with vectored nozzles, mounted on pylons under the high wings. It would have been the most advanced aircraft of its type, with a range of over 4,000 miles and capable of carrying an impressive payload and flying as fast as a Boeing 747. To see an AW.681 take off vertically would have been a thrilling, not to say startling, experience. A prototype was scheduled to fly in 1966, and Armstrong Whitworth was confident of orders for fifty aircraft. In the event, the Wilson government cancelled this remarkable aeroplane on the same day as the P.1154. The decision led to the closure of the Armstrong Whitworth factory in Coventry and the loss of five thousand skilled jobs.

The RAF, though, was not going to throw in the towel and, undaunted by the loss of the P.1154, it now suggested that the P.1127 should be developed into a combat aircraft. The P.1127 was about to turn into the Kestrel.

CHAPTER 2

KESTREL BREEDS HARRIER

'Drei hundert und zwei!' ('Three hundred and two!') It was 1965 and these words were uttered by the dry-humoured Colonel Gerhard Barkhorn as he walked away from XS689, the Kestrel jump jet he had dropped too soon from the hover and badly damaged at RAF West Raynham, Norfolk.

Barkhorn was the Luftwaffe's second-highest-scoring ace of the Second World War, with 301 'kills', and along with fellow top guns and Jagdgeschwader 52 (JG52) veterans Günther Rall, Johannes Steinhoff and Erich Hartmann, he had been asked in the mid-1950s to assist in the formation of a new West German Bundesluftwaffe. Now Barkhorn was one of several German, American and British pilots who formed the Tripartite Evaluation Squadron (TES), and he could mischievously claim the Kestrel as the 302nd Allied aircraft he had brought down.

The TES had emerged from talks held at first between the British and German governments and then with the MDWP and Americans. The idea was to test the P.1127 in the role of a NATO fighter since it was well ahead of US VTOL aircraft, and its potential was being recognized, even if slowly. For once, one of the heroes of the hour was a politician, Peter Thorneycroft (1909–84), a former Royal Artillery officer educated at Eton and the Royal Military Academy, Greenwich, and Minister for Aviation in Harold Macmillan's Conservative government of 1957–63. It was Thorneycroft who took on the tricky negotiations between the German and British governments and armed services and, as a result, helped the P.1127 turn into the Kestrel and so prepared the nest for the Harrier in years to come. Meanwhile, the new civilian head of MWDP, Larry Levy, was soon lobbying vigorously for a NATO squadron of combat-capable P.1127s.

The formation of the TES, funded equally by the three participating nations, achieved two important things. It changed the role of the P.1127 from that of an experimental aircraft to a potential front-line fighter, and it put the Hawker jump jet into the hands of American pilots who were to assure the future of the Harrier for decades to come. In June 1962, nine modified P.1127s had been ordered for the planned international squadron. Equipped with a more powerful Pegasus 5, producing 15,500 lbs of thrust, the new aircraft were different in so many ways from the original P.1127s that they deserved a designation of their own: Kestrel FGA.1 (Fighter Ground Attack Mk 1). Aside from the more potent engine, the Kestrel was readily distinguishable from the P.1127 by its larger, swept-back wing, longer fuselage and higher tail.

Speaking to the BBC years later, John Fozard said that the brief from the Hawker management was to make a much better aircraft than the P.1127 while making as few changes as possible to the specification and keeping the budget to a minimum:

> Well, we changed about 93.5 per cent of the drawings, and I don't regret one drawing change because with the experience we had with the 'Eleven Twenty-Seven' [and] the Kestrel... we got a really proven, been-through-the-fire, operational aircraft that went into service exactly on schedule in 1969.

That aircraft, of course, was the Harrier.

The TES was created on paper in 1963 and formed in the autumn of the following year. It made its first flight on 1 April 1965, while the Kestrel itself had first flown in March 1964. The squadron was led by Wing Commander David Scrimgeour and had a real kestrel as a mascot. Born in 1927 and joining the RAF two months too late to serve in the Second World War, Scrimgeour had experience with the Hawker Tempest and Hunter, de Havilland Vampire and Venom, and the Gloster Meteor. He flew ninety-eight TES test flights and in 1970 was appointed commander of RAF Wildenrath, where he oversaw the introduction of Harriers in West Germany.

In 1956, Scrimgeour had been posted to the US Air Force Base at Nellis, Nevada, as part of a military exchange programme, where he flew F-86 Sabre and F-100 Super Sabre jets. British and American pilots had worked in close collaboration since the entry of the US into the Second World War in 1941, and they would continue to do so in the decades ahead, flying Harriers in combat in Afghanistan until 2010, when the RAF jets were axed, leaving the US Marines to fight on with their McDonnell Douglas AV-8B Harriers. The US Marines, however, had not been asked to join the TES, even though it was they who were to make the Harrier very much their particular weapon of choice.

By November 1965, TES pilots had made 930 flights with the Kestrel. The squadron went quiet after that, although it was not formally disbanded until April 1966. Its Kestrels had flown to and from RAF Bircham Newton, Norfolk – closed the following year – and had landed and taken off from the abandoned airfield at North Pickenham and a field called Rabey's Wood. They were also seen emerging from trees and launching simulated ground attacks in the surreal landscape of the Stanford Battle Area, the immense Army training base near Thetford. This had been created in 1942, as the British and American armies prepared for D-Day, and had involved the evacuation of six villages. A Second World War 'Nazi' village was duly constructed on the site and much later, in 2009, an 'Afghan' village complete with a mosque and marketplace inhabited by Afghan nationals and former Gurkhas. Largely out of bounds to the public, this is where several memorable scenes in *Dad's Army*, the evergreen BBC TV comedy, were filmed between 1968 and 1977; it can be visited just before Christmas each year when a carol service, with music provided by the Royal Anglian Regiment, is held at

St Mary's Tofts, a medieval church which is now surrounded by barbed-wire fencing but had been extended and restored with glorious aplomb by the Victorian Gothic Revival architect Augustus Welby Pugin.

The Kestrel was unarmed, although the TES did fit practice bombs to wing pylons designed to carry long-range fuel tanks. Nose cameras were fitted to record and evaluate the extensive range of tests made, from vertical take-offs and landings in demanding locations to simulated ground attacks. With the tests complete, six TES Kestrels were sold to the US military at a knockdown price – a portent of what was to follow when the RAF's Harriers were withdrawn forty-five years later. Designated XV-6A, they proved immediately popular with the US Marine Corps. In April 1966, a Kestrel was operated successfully from the deck of the 13,600-ton commando assault ship USS *Raleigh*. Commissioned in 1962, the *Raleigh* was named after Sir Walter Raleigh, who had attempted, unsuccessfully, to colonize North America in the 1580s, and decommissioned in 1991 after serving in the First Gulf War, in which Marine Corps AV-8Bs were to see extensive action. Flights on and off the USS *Independence*, a 60,000-ton aircraft carrier commissioned in 1958 and decommissioned forty years later in 1998, followed in May.

So keen, in fact, were US Marine officers to fly the jump jet that in September 1968 a pair of them turned up unannounced at the Hawker pavilion at the Farnborough Air Show to watch the new Harrier perform its party tricks to the usual adoring crowd. They asked if they could have a go. As Lieutenant General Tom Miller recalled years later:

We had not had any experience of asking foreign countries to fly their airplanes before, and when we mentioned it, there was a number of questions as to how much flight experience we'd had of all kinds of airplanes and whether we felt that we were capable of flying it. We felt that certainly there was not any problem for us flying it; it was just convincing the British that we were capable of flying it.

We had hoped we could, and fortunately on a Saturday next to the last day of Farnborough, Mr Bill Bedford came up to us and informed us that we had been approved to fly the airplanes, and we had originally thought if we could get two or three flights each, that would be really all we could ask for. Well, Mr Bedford apologized to some extent that they could only give us ten flights each. So we kind of swallowed and said thank you very much and accepted.

The US Marines have never stopped loving the Harrier. And yet, when the Kestrels, or XV-6As, arrived in America, they were pitted against two hopeful homespun VTOL aircraft, the Lockheed XV-4 Hummingbird and the Ryan XV-5 Vertifan. Two Vertifans were built, one for the military and one for NASA. The two-seat delta-wing aircraft was powered by a pair of General Electric J85 turbojets, each providing 3,000 lbs of thrust; these were used in both vertical and forward flight. In VTOL mode, the engines drove three large fans concealed by what looked like giant garbage-can lids, in the wings and nose of the aircraft. Generating a combined 16,000 lbs of thrust, the fans had no difficulty in lifting the Ryan XV-5 off the ground and maintaining the aircraft in a hover. The problem, though, lay in the fact that, together, fans, ducting and turbines were space-consuming and, if this was to be the basis for a small VTOL fighter, then the resulting aircraft would have little room for fuel, weapons and stores. The fan, however, was a perfectly good idea and was to reappear in the Lockheed Martin F-35B sixty years on. Both XV-5s were responsible for the death of test pilots – Lou Everett in 1965 and Bob Tittle the following year – although tests continued until 1971.

The Hummingbird was a failure. Both prototype aircraft crashed, the first on 10 June 1964, killing its pilot. Theoretically, the downward thrust of this twin-jet aircraft was to have been increased by augmentor ejectors activated by opening large vents in the top and bottom of the fuselage. Although the first aircraft achieved transitional flight, it had been a touch-and-go affair. Its downward thrust of just 7,500 lbs was far less than half that of the Kestrel or, indeed, of the Ryan Vertifan. The project was dropped after the second crash in 1969.

Problematic, and even downright dangerous, neither of these US VTOL prototypes had the obvious competence, nor anything like the performance, of the Kestrel. And as films, photographs and the surviving XV-5 on display at the Fort Rucker Aviation Museum, Alabama demonstrate, they were awkward machines: the Kestrel was much more a case of what looks right *is* right. During their spell with TES, Kestrel pilots had discovered what was to be the Harrier's trump card in aerial combat. This was 'vectored manoeuvring', or what pilots call 'viffing': by rotating the nozzles in forward flight, the aircraft can be made to perform stunts denied to its rivals and enemies. It can jump, and even brake to what feels like a halt, in the air, allowing faster interceptor jets to pass by and turning the Harrier from pursued to pursuer.

Upon completion of testing and evaluation, conducted at Edwards Air Force Base, California, Fort Campbell, Kentucky and NASA's Langley Research Center in Hampton, Virginia, two XV-6As were handed over to NASA for further research. In 1974, one of these aircraft, XS689, was presented to the Smithsonian Air and Space Museum, Washington DC. American interest in the Hawker jump jet had, in fact, preceded the formation of TES, and it had been this early interest that had encouraged British officials to support the international squadron that brought Colonel Gerhard Barkhorn to Norfolk twenty years after the fall of the Third Reich.

When, in early 1961, Peter Thorneycroft had been encouraging the Germans, Hawker was already in discussion with the US military. A senior American military official journeyed to Kingston upon Thames in May 1962 to discuss a proposal whereby, if the P.1127 proved to be a better bet than the Lockheed and Ryan VTOL jets, the US could well be interested in working with Hawker, but on the strict understanding that the P.1127s in service with the US armed forces – as many as a thousand – would be built in the United States. This was exciting stuff, and Hawker was soon holding talks with Northrop, who sent a team to Kingston in July 1963 that, significantly, went on to Germany to view US military operations there. The United States had acquired very few foreign aircraft since the First World War, when American airmen had flown machines like Avro's 504K along with French Nieuport 28s, SPAD VIIs and XIIIs, and later Fokker D.VIIs requisitioned from the defeated Germans. In the jet age, the English Electric Canberra had been built under licence by Martin in Maryland; as the B-57, it was to fly extensively in action, notably in Vietnam, while two survivors owned by NASA continue to fly research missions over Afghanistan. The Americans had become used to selling *their* aircraft around the world. The P.1127, though, appeared to be about to change what had become almost a US military creed, if not exactly an official policy.

The RAF, meanwhile, had viewed the Kestrel as a stop-gap on the way to the supersonic P.1154. When the latter was cancelled in February 1965, it was time for the Kestrel to evolve into the Harrier. A part of that evolution was a further upgrade of the Pegasus engine. One of the Kestrels – XS693 – was selected as the test bed for the Pegasus 6. With the promise of 19,000 lbs of thrust, the latest version of the Bristol Siddeley engine offered the level of performance deemed necessary by the RAF.

On 21 September 1967, Squadron Leader Hugh Rigg was flying the uprated Kestrel from Bristol to the Aeroplane and Armament Experimental Establishment (A&AEE) at RAF Boscombe Down, Wiltshire. A top-secret testing and research centre, Boscombe Down is close to the Army's Salisbury Plain Training Area and to that far older secret, Stonehenge. As Rigg closed in on

Salisbury Plain, and with Stonehenge clearly in sight, the new engine decided to pack up. Once he had decided, correctly, that there was nothing else he could do to save the aircraft, Rigg – an experienced display pilot – ejected at 200 feet.

A few days later, millions of Britons switched on their television sets to watch the latest episode of *The Avengers*, ATV's witty, inventive and hugely popular 'spy-fi' series, starring Patrick McNee as John Steed and Diana Rigg as Emma Peel. Rigg, who went on to become one of Britain's great actors, was Hugh Rigg's sister. Curiously, that particular episode, 'The Return of the Cybernauts', ends with a cameo of Steed mending an electric toaster for Mrs Peel. 'Will it work?' she asks. 'As it has never before,' replies Steed, extolling the world of twentieth-century invention including 'thermostats, computers, transistors...' as they wait for the bread to brown. With a sudden bang, the toaster ejects not just the toast, but itself. 'That's the first thing Great Britain's ever got into orbit,' says Steed as he and Mrs Peel, eyebrows arched, peer up through a hole in the ceiling.

Pure coincidence? Perhaps, yet *The Avengers* was a playful, and often surprisingly pertinent, commentary of sorts on Great Britain at a time when the nation was poised between an old world, represented by Steed, of appropriate dress, impeccable manners, vintage Bentleys and an iron-fist-in-velvet-glove approach to necessary violence, and a new world, embodied in the coolly elegant and intelligently fashionable Mrs Peel, of pop art, Lotus Elans and emancipated women. The sharply scripted *Avengers* was set in a slightly fairy-tale Britain, forever pinstriped, exclusively white and Home Counties, where rich invention, top-secret weapons and ministry testing grounds, very much along the lines of Boscombe Down, were par for the course. Here was a hugely enjoyable cartoon-like take on a nation that, while a fertile ground for novel ideas, was losing the plot not just in terms of its role and status on the world stage, but in manufacturing and industry, too. Within little more than a decade, Britain would have been reinvented as a consumer society that placed all too little faith in machines like the Harrier, and was to find it hard to make pop-up toasters, let alone VTOL fighter jets.

Mrs Peel's husband, Peter Peel, by the way, was a test pilot who had disappeared 'somewhere in the Amazonian jungle'. He popped up on screen, just the once; this was at the end of the last episode Diana Rigg appeared in, 'The Forget-Me-Knot', when we learn of his sudden return. We never see his face, but, as he drives Mrs Peel away – from a Mayfair mews, and from the show – in a silver Mulliner Park Ward Rolls-Royce Silver Shadow convertible, we know that he is the spitting image of John Steed. In the public imagination, test pilots were the twentieth-century equivalent of gallant, chivalrous knights on horseback. Steed would have fitted the frame; as would Hugh Rigg, too, of course.

In its fourth issue, published on 7 February 1962, the satirical magazine *Private Eye* ran a cover depicting the Albert Memorial in London's Kensington Gardens. 'Britain's First Man in Space: Albert Gristle awaits blast-off,' the caption teases. 'Ho ho, very satirical,' says a cartoon Queen Victoria shuffling past. This was amusing, partly because the ornate Gothic monument designed by George Gilbert Scott in memory of Queen Victoria's husband, Prince Albert of Saxe-Coburg and Gotha, does look rather like a nineteenth-century British space rocket might have. But the cover was also a poke at Harold Macmillan's Conservative government, which was seen – not least by satirists – as a club of Victorian fogies trying desperately hard to appear up to date with the latest NASA, computer and jump-jet technology.

For a moment during the transformation of the P.1127 into the Kestrel, it had seemed as if Harold Wilson's Labour government, elected into office in October 1964, were about to take innovative British engineering, technology and military hardware seriously. In a much-misquoted speech he gave at the Labour party conference at Scarborough in 1963, Harold Wilson spoke of a 'revolution' that would change the face of Britain once the Tories were ousted from Westminster. What he actually said was: 'The Britain that is going to be forged in the white heat of this revolution will be no place for restrictive practices or for outdated methods on either side of industry.' Whatever the Labour leader meant, and this remains far from clear, a 'white hot' technological revolution became a potentially vote-catching idea in the minds of politicians and the media. Here was a revolution in which the roles of Marx, Lenin and Trotsky would be played by John Steed's thermostats, computers and transistors, or even VTOL fighters and supersonic airliners.

In July 1966, Tony Benn, formerly Anthony Wedgwood Benn, 2nd Viscount Stansgate, was appointed minister of technology, an entirely new appointment, in Wilson's second administration. As Postmaster General earlier that year, Benn had opened, to an evidently excited public, the 620-foot-high Post Office Tower (today the BT Tower), a beacon of new microwave communications technology and a daring addition to the London skyline. Queues formed around the block for months on end as families, eager to join in the white hot revolution, or simply keen on an exciting day out in town, whizzed up to the viewing galleries of Britain's tallest building. Those with the cash to spare stopped off at the Top of the Tower, a revolving restaurant on the thirty-fourth floor run by Billy Butlin of seaside holiday-camp fame. The restaurant offered an ambitious à la carte French menu. Having dispatched a typical meal of L'Avocado aux Fruits de Mer, La Tortue en Tasse, La Sole Meunière Colbert, followed by Les Noisettes d'Agneau Périgourdine, Les Poires Belle Hélène, a Scotch Woodcock and a Café Hag, accompanied by various cocktails, wines, digestifs and perhaps a Havana cigar or Sobranie cigarette, diners were awarded a Certificate of Orbit before descending, at the rate of 1,000 feet a minute, to the streets of Fitzrovia far below.

The young minister of technology went on to champion the magnificent Anglo-French Concorde, the Mach 2 airliner that seemed to prove that white hot Britain was truly on the right flight path into the future. And perhaps Britain's military aircraft industry would now be in safe hands. After all, Benn himself had joined the RAF at the age of eighteen in 1943. He won his wings in Africa and was just too late to see active service in Europe, transferring as a pilot officer to the Fleet Air Arm in July 1945. His elder brother, Flight Lieutenant Michael Benn DFC, had been killed in June 1944 at the age of twenty-two after the air-speed indicator of his Mosquito had failed, causing him to crash-land near Chichester. Tony and Michael's father,

Air Commodore William Wedgwood Benn, DSO, DFC, Croix de Guerre, Croce al Merito di Guerra, the first Lord Stansgate, had flown as an observer-navigator and then as a pilot in the Great War. He had flown in action with the RAF, despite being in his sixties, in the early stages of the Second World War, becoming Secretary of State for Air in Churchill's wartime coalition government in 1944.

But for all its promise of thrilling all-British things to come, the 'white hot' revolution, if it had ever really existed, soon burned out. Concorde made it, partly because it was a joint project with the French, and the Kestrel flew through the political barrier, too. In fact, it was the Ministry of Technology that placed an order for six pre-production Harriers. The tripartite tests with the Kestrel had finally convinced the Germans and Americans as well as the British – there were many in the various Whitehall ministries, as well as some in the RAF, who had been P.1127 sceptics – that this small subsonic jet really was the Cold War warrior NATO was missing.

The minister of defence, Dennis Healey, had taken against the VTOL aircraft on the grounds of cost and because he believed that investment in American Phantoms and Anglo-French Jaguars offered better value. But 'MinTech', as Benn's fiefdom was known, prevailed, and once built, the six aircraft were dispatched for testing and training at Dunsfold, Filton, the RAE, the A&AEE and the Blind Landing Experimental Unit (BLEU) at RAF Woodbridge and RAF Martlesham Heath, Suffolk. Trials in hot and cold weather were carried out in Sicily and Canada, while, at sea, one of the aircraft was flown successfully from a helicopter platform at the stern of the new 6,500-ton Italian cruiser *Andrea Doria*.

In September 1969, another pre-production Harrier was demonstrated on board the 19,900-ton Argentine carrier *Veinticinco de Mayo* ('25 May'). To say the least, this proved to be a strange meeting. The *Veinticinco de Mayo* had just entered service with the Argentine Navy, but she had been launched on 27 November 1944 as HMS *Venerable*, a Royal Navy carrier. Sold to the Netherlands in 1948, she had operated as the *Karel Doorman* until bought by Argentina in 1968. And fourteen years later, in 1982, she was to find herself in action against the British in the Falklands War. Although the *Veinticinco de Mayo* attempted to engage the Task Force on 2 May with her Douglas A-4 Skyhawk jets, heavy seas made this impossible, and after the sinking of the Argentine light cruiser *General Belgrano* – launched as the USS *Phoenix* in 1938, she had been sold to Argentina in 1945 – by the British Churchill-class nuclear submarine HMS *Conqueror*, the carrier returned to port and stayed there for the rest of the conflict. And yet, if the right deal had been made in 1969 between the British and Argentine governments when the Harrier was wooing the brass hats of the Argentine Navy, the *Veinticinco de Mayo* might well have had a complement of Harriers during the Falklands War, and the outcome of that fight might have been very different. As it was, it would take a further four years before the Harrier entered service with the RAF, yet it had now emerged, almost fully fledged and attracting international attention, welcome or otherwise, from beneath the wings of the P.1127 and Kestrel.

CHAPTER 3

COLD WAR WARRIOR

The race was on. Cheered on by those in the know and curious passers-by, Squadron Leader Tom Lecky-Thompson sprinted from the entrance of the Post Office Tower to a nearby building site where a Westland Wessex helicopter of 72 Squadron whirled him the short distance to RAF St Pancras. This was a coal-yard in Somers Town situated close to St Pancras station, the Gormenghast-like London railway terminus designed by George Gilbert Scott, architect of the Albert Memorial. The RAF test pilot leaped from the helicopter, raced to a specially constructed metal platform, scrambled into the cockpit of XV741, a brand-new Harrier GR.1, and, blowing clouds of coal dust over thrilled spectators, roared straight up into the cool May morning sky. It had taken Thompson just six minutes and fifty seconds to get from the top of the Post Office Tower and into the air on his way to New York.

The occasion was the 1969 *Daily Mail* Transatlantic Air Race, which was held to commemorate the fiftieth anniversary of the first non-stop flight across the ocean separating Britain from America, made by Flight Lieutenant John Alcock (pilot) and Second Lieutenant Arthur Brown (navigator) in a modified First World War Vickers Vimy bomber. (They had won a £10,000 prize sponsored by, of course, the *Daily Mail*.) For those with little imagination, the May 1969 event was considered to be a waste of time, money and fuel. And yet here was a golden opportunity to show an American audience what the new Harrier could do. The 3,500-mile race was from the top of the Post Office Tower to the top of the Empire State Building, and the new British VTOL fighter had the great advantage over every other aeroplane in the race that it could take off and land in both cities. The Fleet Air Arm entered an F-4K Phantom and, although it flew far faster over the Atlantic itself, it had to land at conventional airfields; this meant a long sprint from the cockpit of the Mach 2 Navy jet to and from the Empire State Building and the Post Office Tower. The race was held in both directions across the Atlantic.

Within ten minutes of take-off, and at 36,000 feet, Thompson was taking on fuel from a Handley Page Victor, a former V-bomber that had found a new lease of life as an aerial tanker to British military jets. The Harrier pilot duly landed by the East River at the end of New York's 23rd Street and, riding pillion on a motorbike, was at the top of the Empire State Building in six hours, eleven minutes and fifty-seven seconds, after a flight of five hours and fifty-seven minutes that had included four air-to-air refuellings. Thompson won the £6,000 first prize for the East to West Atlantic crossing, while Sir Billy Butlin, the proprietor of the Top of the Tower revolving restaurant, won a £500 prize for the fastest journey by chartered business jet – eleven hours and thirty minutes – flying in the cocktail comfort of a Hawker Siddeley HS.125. Significantly, the Manhattan landing site for Thompson's Harrier had been chosen and prepared by the US Marine Corps. For within six months, the Marines had ordered the first of the several hundred Harriers that were to be built under licence in the United States and continue to fly on front-line duties today.

The race had been a terrific publicity coup for Hawker, the RAF and the men from the various British ministries involved in the Harrier's development and, now, promotion overseas. For the Americans, the very idea of a foreign military aircraft flying into US air space and over New York came as something of a shock. Yet the gymnastic Harrier was not just a superb aircraft, but an endearing one, too. With a length of under forty-six feet and a wing-span of little more than twenty-five, the Harrier, painted dark sea grey and green and light grey, was positively tiny compared with a McDonnell Douglas Phantom. It was also a magical machine, as any London schoolboy who happened to play truant from school that morning can verify.

When I walked back, grimy from coal dust, to look around St Pancras station after the Harrier had thundered its way west, the 'Peak'-class 45 diesel-electrics thrumming from its platforms in clouds of carbon monoxide on their way to all points Midland seemed as tame as cockney sparrows. This was the first time I had actually seen a Harrier. I had gawped at photographs and devoured newspaper articles. I had made sure I watched every second of the BBC's coverage of Farnborough air shows and noted every word of their knowledgeable and crystal-clear commentaries from Raymond Baxter, a former Spitfire pilot who had flown in raids against Wernher von Braun's V2 rocket sites. I had pored over cut-away drawings in boys' magazines and, of course, saved my pocket money for the plastic-bagged Airfix kits at two shillings each I saw hanging from their racks in model shops and newsagents. There had, I knew even then, always been that dream of vertical and hovering flight. There had been fantastical magic carpets, hot-air balloons and airships, and hummingbirds and kestrels too, but the Harrier was more than just a fulfilment of a long-held aspiration. It was somehow thrillingly modern too.

Observing those same cockney sparrows take wing from London gardens and, most memorably, from the thin blue balustrade of the slender concrete bridge across the lake in St James's Park was always a source of immense delight and mystery. Even when you held out your young hands and the sparrows landed so very lightly on them to pick up breadcrumbs, it was impossible to see how they took off in VTOL – or was it STOL? – mode. An aircraft, even a compact one with a powerful Pegasus engine filling its slightly rotund fuselage, could never move so quickly, or so alertly, even when packed as the new RAF Harriers were with the latest in navigation systems. The power-to-weight ratio of the sparrow is very much greater than that of a Harrier, and this despite the 19,000 lbs of thrust from the GR.1's turbine. But to witness Thompson's Harrier take off in that cloud of coal dust – and this in an era that spelt domestic central heating (coal-powered, of course) as much as it did The Byrds, Led Zeppelin, Jefferson Airplane, Joni Mitchell's *Clouds* and the Moody Blues' *On the Threshold of a Dream* – was to believe in the sorcery of aerospace technology and in Britain's ability to lead the world.

This, too, was the time of what had been the populist 'I'm Backing Britain' campaign, nurtured from New Year 1968 by five hard-working and patriotic secretaries from Surbiton, a south London suburb seen, at the time, as the archetypal English red-brick, lower-middle-class enclave. Harold Wilson's government endorsed the campaign eagerly. The government and the economy had been hard pressed by events, at home and abroad, of the previous year. The Six-Day War between Israel and a coalition of the United Arab Republic (Egypt), Jordan, Syria and Iraq had forced the closure of the Suez Canal for some while afterwards, badly affecting British exports. A major dock strike that had started late in the summer of 1967 and gone on into the autumn had damaged exports further; and there had been a continuing sense of shame and a loss of national pride in the country at large since the government had devalued the pound in November 1966. Although, theoretically, the weakening of the pound against other currencies should have been good for exports – of military aircraft as well as fashion items, music and cars – the general feeling at home was that Britain was on the wane.

Furthermore, it had been the French aircraft industry that received a boost from the Israeli victory in the Six-Day War. Equipped with the latest Dassault Mirage III supersonic interceptors and the older yet highly effective Super Mystère and Mystère III jet fighter-bombers, the Israeli Air Force (IAF) took on what, on paper, was an overwhelmingly superior, Soviet-equipped Egyptian air arm. Israeli crews destroyed thirty Tupolev Tu-16 bombers, twenty-seven Ilyushin Il-28 bombers, twelve Sukhoi Su-7 fighter-bombers, ninety Mikoyan-Gurevich MiG-21, twenty MiG-19 and twenty-five MiG-15 fighters, along with thirty-two assorted helicopters and transport aircraft; in return, nineteen front-line IAF jets were lost. War might be hell, but these spectacular results would have been a heaven of sorts to the management of Société des Avions Marcel Dassault. Nevertheless, Israel had expressed an interest in buying sixty Harriers and Finland – with its extensive forest landscapes and fear of Soviet invasion – considered buying ten. In neither case did the deals come off, yet international interest in the Harrier was growing.

As it was, the 'I'm Backing Britain' campaign got off to a very English start. Campaign T-shirts ordered from the London wholesaler Scott Lester turned out to have been made in Portugal. In defence, Scott Lester's marketing director explained: 'We just cannot find a British T-shirt which will give us the same quality at a price which will compare.' How little has changed.

A tie-in single, written by Tony Hatch and Jackie Trent and sung by the all-round entertainer Bruce Forsyth was issued by Pye Records on 8 January. Despite selling for just five shillings instead of the normal seven shilling and fourpence halfpenny, 'I'm Backing Britain' didn't do well. It sold a grand total of 7,319 copies. Still, as the irrepressibly chirpy Forsyth reminded us, 'The country has always done its best when it is hard up against the wall.'

Even the newly appointed poet laureate joined in, although Cecil Day-Lewis's words were no better than those of Hatch and Trent. The *Daily Mail* commissioned Day-Lewis's poem 'Now and Then'; it appeared on the front page of the paper on 5 January 1968. Comparing Britain's economic plight in 1968 to the Blitz, the poem concluded:

> To work then, islanders, as men and women
> Members one of another, looking beyond
> Mean rules and rivalries towards the dream you could
> Make real, of glory, common wealth, and home.

This was hardly the same Day-Lewis who had written the lyrical 'You That Love England' in the dire economic days of the early 1930s:

> You that love England, who have an ear for her
>   music,
> The slow movement of clouds in benediction,
> Clear arias of light thrilling over her uplands,
> Over the chords of summer sustained peacefully;
> Ceaseless the leaves' counterpoint in a west
>   wind lively,

Blossom and river rippling loveliest allegro,
And the storms of wood strings brass at year's
  finale:
Listen. Can you not hear the entrance of a new
  theme?

The new theme entering my consciousness that May morning in 1969 was the sight of that terse Hawker Siddeley fighter from Kingston upon Thames springing into a cool blue morning sky, and the Jovian sound of its Pegasus jet, made in Bristol. Here, I remember thinking, was a sort of jet-age Spitfire, an aircraft that one could fall for; not as beautiful, perhaps, yet there was definitely something in the way she sounded, looked and moved. And that same morning, the Beatles were at Olympic Sound Studios in Barnes, south-west London, working on George Harrison's sublime song *Something*.

The Harrier, though, was not some catwalk beauty but a dog of war, a bird of prey. Her namesakes are hunting thoroughbreds. There is the lithe, sturdy and cheerful hound bred to hunt foxes and hares and to run all day as part of a spirited pack. And there is the low-flying ground-attack hawk that sights and launches attacks on other birds, reptiles and rodents with a swiftness at once alarming, praiseworthy and admirable. The Hawker Harrier was to be their mechanical counterpart, a war-bird not just for the jet age but for the space age, too. She had been developed, after all, in part, by NASA. That same day I bunked off school to watch Squadron Leader Thompson raise the coal dust with XV741 at 'RAF St Pancras', the US Postal Service issued a handsome six-cent stamp I coveted, commemorating the first circumnavigation of the Moon by Apollo 8. Of the three-man crew, Frank Borman and Bill Anders had been USAF fighter pilots and Jim Lovell a US Navy test pilot. And it had been Apollo 8 that had brought back those famous – and numinous – photographs of the Earth inscrutably afloat in space: images that had shown us all just how special and beautiful our world was, and had reminded us anew that peace on Earth was truly something worth fighting for.

The contract for the first sixty production RAF Harriers had been signed in early 1967, and the first aircraft, XV738, flew on 28 December that year with Duncan Simpson in the cockpit. Simpson, on his way to becoming Hawker's chief test pilot, had been apprenticed to de Havilland in 1945. He worked on designs of late-model Mosquitoes and on that famous aircraft's supremely beautiful, if short-lived, piston-engined successor, the Hornet, before joining the RAF and flying Meteor jets with 222 Squadron. He was enticed to Hawker, his name becoming closely associated with the Hunter. He flew the P.1127 and trained the pilots of the international Kestrel squadron. In January 1969, Simpson was asked to work with a new Harrier Conversion Team at Dunsfold under the command of Squadron Leader Richard LeBrocq AFC. Technically, this proved to be a complex affair as the first two-seat Harriers had yet to be delivered, and so the test pilots had to guide their students through training flights on Hunters and Whirlwind helicopters. The flying circus moved on to Boscombe Down, and finally to RAF Wittering, Cambridgeshire, where the first Harrier was delivered to No. 1 Squadron (motto: *In omnibus princeps*, 'In all things first') on 18 April 1969. A fortnight later, 1 Squadron provided two of the Harriers for the *Daily Mail* Transatlantic Race.

The first Harrier GR.1 flown to RAF Wittering was, however, a different machine in many respects from the P.1127 and the Kestrel. Where these had been experimental and development aircraft, the GR.1 was fully combat-capable. The structure and undercarriage were stronger, the Pegasus 6 engine was more powerful and the systems incorporated into the aircraft were more sophisticated than those of the earlier types. The engine only needed an overhaul every 300 hours, a big improvement over the fifty hours of the Pegasus 5, and it could be self-started. The GR.1 had a maximum speed of 736 mph and was fitted with four underwing pylons to carry flares, up to 4,000 lbs of bombs, or unguided rocket packs, a pair of 100-gallon drop tanks or two 330-gallon long-distance ferry tanks. A central fitting under the fuselage accepted either a 1,000 lb bomb or a pair of 30 mm Mk 4 Aden cannons, each armed with 100 shells fired at a rate of 1,200 per minute. A five-camera reconnaissance pod could be fitted in place of bomb or cannons. The maximum range of a GR.1 was about 430 miles, but a probe allowed refuelling in mid-air. When fully loaded, the aircraft was unable to take off vertically, although it could still get into the air very quickly. And when lightly loaded, it could pull off stunts no other winged military aircraft could.

For pilots, the biggest difference was the cockpit. Although rather cramped, as those of most fighter aircraft tend to be – they need to be as wind-cheating as possible – this was now neatly arranged but dominated by a comprehensive head-up display, or HUD, the first fitted to a British military aircraft in service. Designed by the Spectro division of Smiths Industries, a company best known to the general public for its dials on car dashboards and the alarm clocks that woke us up for school, the HUD projected such essential readings as speed, height and altitude onto the windscreen; these could be read with the pilot looking far into the distance without the need to refocus his eyes. *His* eyes, of course, as there were, as yet, no women fighter pilots in the RAF. Although the GR.1 lacked radar, the aircraft was equipped with a Ferranti navigation-attack system that drove a moving map display in the cockpit covering a distance of up to 900 miles around the aircraft.

Rear vision was still limited and notably hampered by the 'elephant ear' air intakes. This was thought not to be a problem with what was still classed as a ground-support and reconnaissance aircraft. The low canopy helped keep air resistance to a minimum, although with that big engine directly behind them, pilots found the GR.1 a noisy aircraft; it was probably just as well that combat sorties flown on the German border were expected to last only twenty minutes. Some of these problems, or inconveniences, were to change with the arrival of the Sea Harrier (*see* Chapter Four) and with experience, as both the RAF and Royal Navy learned that the Harrier was a natural dogfighter and a truly multi-role warplane. As with the P.1127 and Kestrel, the Harrier's ejection set-up was unlike other aircraft's. When it was triggered, the canopy would be splintered into shreds by a cord wound through it before the Martin-Baker seat was sent hurtling skywards; this arrangement was essential, since if the canopy was shot away upwards in vertical flight, the pilot would smash into it when rocketed from the cockpit.

Orders for the RAF were now up to seventy-seven aircraft, including eight two-seat trainers. No. 1 Squadron received its full complement of eighteen Harriers by July 1970. A second squadron, IV (4), based at RAF Wildenrath on the German–Dutch border, followed. This was to have been it – just the two front-line Harrier squadrons – yet as the RAF took enthusiastically to this spirited and clever subsonic fighter, two more squadrons, 3 and 20, both based at Wildenrath, were equipped with the Harrier GR.1 and GR.1A – this with the uprated Pegasus 10 providing 20,500 lbs of thrust – during 1970. By 1973, all Harriers had been upgraded to GR.1A spec. The German squadrons were moved to RAF Gütersloh, seventy-five miles from the East German border, in 1977, although they were often dispersed into the surrounding countryside, hidden under trees and camouflage netting, and taking off and landing in all weathers from and onto aluminium planking. After the fall of the Berlin Wall and the end of the Cold War, 3 and IV Squadrons moved to RAF Laarbruch back on the Dutch border in 1992, while 20 Squadron was temporarily disbanded; it re-emerged the same year as 20 (R) Squadron, the renumbered Harrier training unit at RAF Wittering.

Built originally for RAF Typhoons and Spitfires soon after D-Day in 1944, Laarbruch has since become Weeze Airport, a haven for the low-budget airlines that have done a great deal, and not necessarily to anyone's advantage, to change the face of European towns and cities over the past quarter of a century. 'The problem with aviation,' said Michael O'Leary, chief executive of Ryanair, in 2012 while seeking to get permission from the aviation authorities for super-cheap standing-only flights, 'is that for fifty years it's been populated by people who think it's this wondrous sexual experience; that it's like James Bond and wonderful... when really it's just a bloody bus with wings.' So much for the sorcery of flight and all the designers, engineers, test pilots and service men and women who have helped make commercial flight a safe form of transport; so much, too, for Concorde and the Harrier and the history of an airbase from where, had war ever come, brave young pilots would have flown on terrifying ground-attack missions to keep Europe a safe and free haven for you, me and low-budget Irish businessmen.

The role of the German Harrier squadrons was to liaise and work closely with British and NATO forces on the ground. The fear of a Warsaw Pact invasion loomed in most West European minds until the glorious sight of the breaching, and then breaking, of the Berlin Wall in 1989. Very few people had predicted the sudden collapse of Stalin's totalitarian empire so soon. In fact, most, if pressed on the subject, had imagined that the communist hegemony, so longed for by C. Day-Lewis and other fellow travellers in the 1930s, would endure for grim decades. Germany would remain the front line, as it had since 1945, and RAF fighters, whether the Harriers or their successors, would be ready to scramble at a moment's notice well into the twenty-first century.

If the Warsaw Pact had launched an attack, the RAF's Harrier fleet – normally thirty-six strong – would have been dispersed to those hidden sites. They would have operated from secondary roads, leaving the autobahnen free for conventional NATO jets. Equipped with chaff – strips of metal strewn from the aircraft to confuse enemy radar – and flares to fox heat-seeking enemy missiles, they would have supported troops on the ground while remaining ready to intercept supersonic Soviet fighters. Even such nimble machines as the MiG-21 'Fishbed', which WarPac air forces deployed in large numbers, would have been unable to outperform, or outwit, the Harrier at close quarters.

One of the Harriers' roles, carried out principally by 1 Squadron, based at Wittering, but joined on occasion by IV Squadron, was to conduct cold-weather operations within the Arctic Circle. The aircraft operated from the Royal Norwegian Air Force base at Bardufloss in northern Norway and continued to do so for many years. In the spring of 1940, before the Allies withdrew from Norway and the Germans marched in, Hawker Hurricanes had flown from Bardufloss alongside Gloster Gladiators in defence of the Narvik Front. In 1982, Harriers from 1 Squadron appear to have been caught up in a disturbing story that has refused to go away. On 11 March that year, a de Havilland Twin-Otter making a routine Wideroe Airline flight from Berlevag to Mehamn on the coast of Finnmark in northern Norway crashed on approach, killing all fifteen people on board. Although the official cause of the accident was air turbulence, witnesses believe the aircraft was in collision with a Harrier, and that the offending aircraft was hidden away very quickly as, despite being a member of NATO, Norway had forbidden military flights over Finnmark for fear of provoking the Russian bear. If nothing else, the story is a reminder of the dangers and costs involved in practising to defend Western Europe against a war that for many years had seemed inevitable.

The new Harrier force, meanwhile, carried out exercises in Cyprus and Sardinia, and demonstrated the RAF's new-found potential to support Royal Navy operations at sea. Significantly, Harriers paid a call on HMS *Hermes* in 1971. This 23,000-ton aircraft carrier had been laid down in 1944 and was to have been launched as HMS *Elephant*. She was finally commissioned in 1959 and, twenty-three years later with ten RAF GR.3 Harriers and sixteen Royal Navy FRS.1 Sea Harriers, she sailed to the Falkland Islands as flagship of the British Task Force. (Today, in the guise of INS *Viraat*, the carrier sails on with the Indian Navy.) Then, in the summer of 1972, a new and specially equipped two-seat T.2 Harrier demonstrator flew twenty-one sorties from the deck of INS *Vikrant*, the 15,700-ton carrier launched as HMS *Hercules* in 1945. Never commissioned into the Royal Navy, the ship was sold to India in 1957 and sailed for many years with a squadron of Hawker Sea Hawks on board until these were replaced by Sea Harriers in 1983. The aircraft carrier is now a floating museum moored at Mumbai (formerly Bombay).

The pilot of the two-seat Harrier was John Farley, Hawker's deputy chief test pilot at the time. Farley flew from Dunsfold, stopping off on his way to Bombay at Naples, Akrotiri (Cyprus), Teheran, Kuwait and Masirah (Oman). This was seven years before the Iranian Revolution that led to the overthrow of the secular Muslim rule of Shah Mohammed Reza Pahlavi in favour of a fundamentalist Islamic regime led by the fiery cleric Ayatollah Ruhollah Khomeini. Farley would have had to fly a different route to India today.

Potential overseas sales, however, could be threatened by politics rooted in old grudges. Clearly impressed by the British aircraft, the Spanish Naval Air Arm was keen to buy Harriers. However, a venerable dispute over ownership of the Rock of Gibraltar meant that the Spanish government refused to buy military aircraft from the British government. Luckily, for both Hawker and the Spanish Naval Air Arm, there was a solution to hand: Spain could buy Harriers, built in Kingston, from the United States. The US Department of Defense added an extra number to the final batch of US Marine Corps Harriers it had ordered from Britain. Designated AV-8A, these were shipped in 1976 to the USA, where Spanish Navy pilots joined their American counterparts for training. Named Matadors by the Spanish, the British-American-Iberian Harriers were finally flown back to Spain where, based at Rota near Cadiz, they flew with Escuadrilla 008 and, at sea, from the timber deck of the carrier SNS *Dedalo,* the former 11,000-ton USS *Cabot*, launched in 1943 and sold to the Armada Espanola in 1972. Such was the antagonism Spain felt towards Britain at the time that John Farley was unable to fly over Spain to meet SNS *Dedalo* soon after the Spanish Navy first expressed interest in the Harrier; the carrier instead sailed to a point off the Portuguese coast, and Farley's GR.3 was obliged to skirt the Iberian peninsula on its non-stop flight from Dunsfold. Relations between Spain and Britain improved after the death, in 1975, of the country's fascist leader, Generalissimo Francisco Franco; British money, settlers and tourists invaded, and did their best to destroy the once beautiful Costa del Sol. In 1977, Spain bought four new VA-1 Matadors direct from Hawker, and, after re-equipping its navy with Mk 2 Harriers, sold its original jump jets to the small but ambitious Thai Navy in 1997.

By this time, the GR.3 Harrier had joined the RAF team, with most of the earlier production Harriers being updated to the latest specification. The GR.3, powered by the Pegasus 11 providing 21,500 lbs of thrust, certainly looked different with its dolphin-like nose. The 'Snoopy Nose', as the RAF knew it, housed Ferranti's new laser rangefinder that allowed pilots, working with forward air controllers on the ground, to seek out and destroy targets with impressive accuracy. A Marconi radar-warning receiver mounted in the tail of the GR.3 meant that pilots could now tell if they were being tracked by enemy radar. These key changes, together with an auto-stabilizer to assist with VTOL manoeuvring and pedals that shook to indicate which one to press as side-force limits were reached when the aircraft took off and landed, made the Harrier a competent and formidable ground-support fighter-bomber.

The number of accidents involving loss of aircraft and pilots' lives, however, was high. Flame-outs, engine fires, loss of control when hovering, sticking nozzles, failure to make the transition from vertical to forward flight and bird strikes all contrived to cause the loss of thirty-two Harriers in British service in the 1960s and 1970s. This led, as we will see, to American commentators damning the Harrier as dangerous. This is not true, although the aircraft has always demanded careful and precise handling, especially at low speed and around airfields.

It was, in fact, a bird strike that took out a GR.3 on 1 December 1975, not in Britain, Germany or the United States, but in Belize, a small, self-governing British colony on the north-eastern littoral of Central America and bordered by Mexico, Guatemala and the Caribbean Sea. Known as British Honduras until 1973, this was Britain's one and only mainland colony in the Americas. Long ago, it had been home to the Mayans. Centuries later, conquistadors declared the area a Spanish colony, although as they could find no gold, they left it to others – English and Scots, and Caribbean pirates – to settle and trade there. The land was rich in mahogany; its motto even today is *Sub umbra floreo* ('I flourish in the shade' – by implication, that of the mahogany tree). The Spanish tried to reclaim this fertile land, with its exquisite stretches of coral reef, at various times but were finally repelled when an armada was taken to task in a brief engagement with the Royal Navy in September 1798. Central America as a whole was emancipated from Spanish rule in the 1830s and what was then named British Honduras became a Crown colony in 1862.

When, though, in the 1950s Honduras began to move towards independence, finally winning it in 1981, neighbouring Guatemala began invoking antique Spanish treaties to prove that it belonged lock, stock and mahogany tree to... Guatemala. This led to increasing fears of an invasion and to British troops remaining in Belize until 1994, two years after Guatemala finally backed down and gave up its claim. The fears were real enough.

Since Washington and the CIA had engineered the overthrow of the populist left-wing government of Jacopo Arbenz, a former Army officer, in 1954, Guatemala had been thrown into turmoil. Military regimes, subservient to Washington, ran the country like some subtropical prison camp. Unrest and civil war became all but synonymous with what, by any standards, was by the mid-1960s one of the most brutal and brutalized countries in the world. Little was to change over the following three decades, during which tens of thousands of civilians were 'disappeared' by government and military, just as they were, of course, in Argentina under the rule of the military junta finally ousted in the aftermath of the Falklands War.

In November 1975, Britain sent a detachment of six GR.3 Harriers from 1 Squadron to Belize. The Guatemalan Air Force had been making threatening noises since 1970, when the whining turbojet of one of its Lockheed T-33 Shooting Stars could be heard as it flew over Belize City on an intimidating reconnaissance mission. At the same time, Guatemalan World War Two-vintage F-51D Mustangs were moved up to a base at Tikal close to the Honduran border. With an attack presumed imminent, in January 1972 two Royal Navy Blackburn Buccaneers of 892 Squadron were launched from the deck of HMS *Ark Royal*, the 38,000-ton British carrier that had sailed, hurriedly and in turbulent seas, from the North Atlantic to Bermuda to meet the challenge. The Buccaneers made a six-hour round trip to make their very determined presence felt over Belize and Guatemala. The Guatemalan Air Force decided not to take up the challenge, although it remains anyone's guess quite what would have happened if Guatemalan Mustang pilots had taken on the Buccaneers at close quarters. One modern jet that could dogfight, though, was the Harrier, and when Guatemala began its next round of sabre-rattling three years later, the RAF's jump jets were in Belize to take up the challenge. Wisely, as events in the South Atlantic were to prove within just a few years, the Guatemalans decided not to mix their Shooting Stars and Mustangs with the RAF's Harriers.

The Harriers were to stay in Belize until 1993. Although they were never called into combat, the exercises they conducted were invaluable and most of those posted to Central America enjoyed their spell in the tropical sun. The pilots made impressive showings at the 1990 and 1991 air shows held at La Aurora International Airport, Guatemala City, by which time relations with Guatemala were somewhat improved. Indeed, watching Harriers, close-up, may well have helped to encourage the Guatemalan government to give up its historic claim on Belize. As for the Harrier, XV788, hit by a vulture, it was repaired and later went to war in the Falklands in 1982. The Belize mission also assured the Harrier's place in the RAF of the future. Even in the mid-1970s, a number of influential senior RAF officers wanted a conventional replacement for the Harrier; the sheer versatility of the GR.3s in Belize proved just what an irreplaceable machine the jump jet was. More GR.3s were ordered, and these were the aircraft the RAF was to fly over the Falklands. Alongside them would be a new, naval version of the Harrier, a machine that would make its mark – and history – suddenly and very dramatically indeed.

CHAPTER 4

BAPTISM AT SEA

What an unlikely pair of antagonists! The British have always fought, to be sure. No nation on Earth can be taken seriously in historical circles unless it has had at least one war with the British; it's like not having an American Express card. And yet the very idea of Britain in a contemporary war is a shock. Britain, one feels, fights in history books and not on TV.

Gene Wolfe, 'A Few Points about Knife Throwing', 1983 (from *Fantasy Newsletter*)

Brian Hanrahan should have been counting in the last of the Joint Force Harriers as they landed at RAF Cottesmore just before Christmas in 2010. Instead he was dying of cancer in a hospital ward. The Harrier crews sent him a get-well card, but this was one mission they lost: the veteran BBC reporter they greatly respected, and whose name will forever be associated with the Falklands War and the Harrier, died as the aircraft were retired prematurely from service, a victim of government cuts. It seemed somehow sadly poetic that Hanrahan, who bowed out prematurely too – he was sixty-one – did so with the remarkable aircraft that had made him a household name.

On 1 May 1982, Hanrahan had been on the bridge of HMS *Hermes*, flagship of the British Task Force assigned to recapture the Falkland Islands from the Argentinians, who had invaded this remote South Atlantic outpost the previous month. Under looming skies the colour of dull pewter, Hanrahan watched nine Sea Harriers roar off from the decks of *Hermes* and HMS *Invincible* on missions to attack the airfield at Port Stanley, the Falkland's capital, and Argentine jets at Goose Green. Hanrahan saved his best shot for the moment the Sea Harriers returned: 'I'm not allowed to say how many planes joined the raid, but I counted them all out and I counted them all back.'

It was a clever and memorable phrase that, while getting around understandable wartime reporting restrictions on sensitive military operations, also gave television viewers in Britain a sense that all was well at the beginning of a campaign that proved to be, in the words of Vice Admiral 'Sandy' Woodward, commander of the British Naval Force, a 'close run thing'. Woodward borrowed the words from the Duke of Wellington, who had said the same thing of the Battle of Waterloo; but the Falklands War had been a remarkable affair. It was the first war – although this was never declared formally – between two Western powers since 1945, and, at 8,000 miles, the supply line Britain needed to rescue the Falklands was the longest in the history of warfare.

To those at home in Britain, it had all seemed surreal and remote until reporters like Brian Hanrahan brought words and images back under the tightest of security blankets. Looking for all the world like a kind and knowledgeable geography teacher on a wet and windy field trip, Hanrahan worked tirelessly, under fire and without body armour, with cameraman Bernard Hesketh and sound recordist John Jockell, to tell us what on earth was happening in this largely unexpected and sudden war on the other side of the world.

Official news from the MoD was channelled through press conferences filmed for television. These introduced us to an unfamiliar litany of 'exclusion zones', Exocets, Super Étendards and, of course, Harriers, the British aircraft that were to steal the show. These press conferences were fronted by the extraordinary figure of Ian MacDonald, the MoD's deputy head of press relations. Sitting rigid behind a big desk, and behind an enormous pair of thick-framed black glasses, MacDonald intoned the news the government wanted the press to hear like some sepulchral Dalek. At each session he would say, 'I will not answer any questions afterwards.' MacDonald's delivery was so strange that this reticent son of a Glasgow fish merchant became a celebrity of sorts. When it was suggested that he should be replaced by a more genial spokesperson, the nation rallied around him. If not as soothing, or as poetic, as the BBC's Shipping Forecast, MacDonald's press conferences were a national fixture, their matter-of-fact calmness a riposte perhaps to the rantings of the loathsome military regime in Buenos Aires that had started this unnecessary fight, and that would lie about its progress as if it had graduated from a journalism course taught by Lord Haw-Haw or Joseph Goebbels himself.

The facts of the Falklands War are fairly well known. In brief, an Argentine military junta fronted by General Leopoldo Galtieri and faced, in 1981, with an inflation rate of 600 per cent, 22.9 per cent unemployment, an 11.4 per cent drop in GDP and general unrest, aimed to divert public attention and appease the masses with a promising little war. Whenever an Argentine government appeared to be in trouble at home, many of us believed at the time, and not necessarily wrongly, the shout went up, 'Malvinas!' This is the Latin American name for the Falklands, a remote, craggy and wind-blasted home, in 1982, to about 400,000 sheep, five species of penguin, the black-browed albatross and some 1,800 people of long-established British stock. This raw if wildly beautiful archipelago lies several hundred miles off the Argentine coast. Essentially self-governing today, it came under regular British rule from 1833.

From a historical point of view, all claims to the islands are spurious. From the sixteenth century, they had been visited by European mariners seeking refuge from fierce South Atlantic storms. There was no indigenous human population, although then as now there were very many penguins. The French were first to settle on the islands, arriving on East Falkland in 1764 and declaring it a colony but ceding their claim to Spain three years later. The British, meanwhile, arrived in 1765, creating a settlement in West Falkland and claiming the archipelago for King

George III. The British left in 1774, although they maintained their claim, and the Spanish left in 1806, also maintaining theirs.

When what is now Argentina declared independence from Spain in 1816, the new republic also declared its ownership of former Spanish territories, including the Malvinas. The British recognized the Republic of Argentina in 1825, and an Argentine settlement was established on the islands three years later with British approval. This proved to be a squally affair. In November 1832, Buenos Aires sent a Commander Mestivier to the islands with orders to create a penal colony. A mutiny ensued, Mestivier was killed within four days of his arrival, and in January 1833 the British returned with two warships, the twenty-eight-gun HMS *Tyne* and the eighteen-gun HMS *Clio*, under the command of Captain James Onslow. This time, the British stayed. Within two months, the ten-gun brig-sloop HMS *Beagle* arrived, charged with conducting a South American Survey and on its way to Tierra del Fuego and the Galápagos Islands. On board the *Beagle* was a young gentleman planning his future life as a clergyman. He wrote:

> The first news we received was to our astonishment,
> that England had taken possession of the Falklands
> islands & that the Flag was now flying. These islands
> have been for some time uninhabited, until the
> Buenos Ayres Government a few years since claimed
> them & sent some colonists. Our government
> remonstrated against this, & last month the Clio
> arrived here with orders to take possession of the
> place. A Buenos Ayrean man of war was here, at

> the time, with some fresh colonists. Both they &
> the vessel returned to the Rio Plata. The present
> inhabitants consist of one Englishman, who has
> resided here for some years, & has now the charge
> of the British flag, 20 Spaniards & three women,
> two of whom are negresses. The island is abundantly
> stocked with animals: there are about 5,000 wild
> oxen, many horses, & pigs. Wild fowl, rabbits, &
> fish in the greatest plenty. European vegetables will
> grow. And as there is an abundance of water & good
> anchorage, it is most surprising that it has not been
> long ago colonized, in order to afford provisions for
> Ships going round the Horn. At present it is only
> frequented by Whalers, one of which is here now.

That young gentleman was Charles Darwin. One hundred and fifty years later, the population of the Falkland Islands remained tiny. Indeed, few people in Britain had even heard of the Falklands Islands, much less Las Malvinas, when news arrived that Port Stanley had been taken by Argentine marines and that the governor, Rex Hunt, a former RAF officer who had flown Spitfires in India with 5 Squadron, had surrendered to the Argentine commander, Vice Admiral Carlos Busser. In his No. 1 (Fighter) Squadron Operation Corporate Diary for Friday 2 April 1982, Wing Commander Peter Squire records:

> The Squadron is... committed to play in a five-
> a-side football competition that afternoon at

1415hrs. Needless to say, however, the crew
room conversation is dominated by news of the
Argentinian invasion of the Falkland Islands. The
GLO [Ground Liaison Officer], Major John Moseley,
is asked to look out a map in order to confirm the
exact whereabouts of the islands.

With just sixty-eight Royal Marines under Major Mike Norman to protect the islands, Hunt had little choice in the matter, although holed up in Government House, governor and soldiers staged a three-hour fire-fight, shooting off 6,450 small-arms rounds and twelve rockets. When, finally, Hunt went to meet Busser, he did so in full dress uniform, complete with feathered hat, telling the admiral, 'You have landed unlawfully on British territory and I order you to remove yourself and your troops forthwith.'

Twenty-seven years after the war ended, Vice Admiral Busser was arrested. He was alleged to have taken part in the torture and disappearance of three men at the Argentine naval base Puerto Belgrano. Although he was not convicted, Busser was placed under house arrest until his death in 2012. Busser, however, was just one of the many members of the Argentine armed forces who led what was an undeclared and savage war against their own people between 1976 and 1983. In those years, up to thirty thousand Argentinians viewed as subversives of one kind or another were 'disappeared', many hurled, drugged and naked, to their deaths in the Atlantic Ocean and Río de la Plata from 'death flights' organized by Admiral Luis Maria Mendia, later sentenced to 640 years in prison in Spain. Before they were herded into the aircraft, prisoners were told that they were going to be 'released' and made to dance for joy, accompanied by upbeat music.

Apocryphal stories have long been told of Adolf Hitler, among other senior Nazis, escaping to Argentina in 1945 and settling there. How they would have applauded the mendacious Mendia and the other vicious and puerile military popinjays who plunged Argentina into political and economic hell and sported rows of medals on their chests despite never having fought in anything other than 'dirty' wars against unarmed and innocent men, women and children. Although this had not been Margaret Thatcher's intention when she launched Operation Corporate – the retaking of the Falklands – almost immediately after news of the invasion reached London, the ending of military rule in Argentina was one of the finest things for which this most controversial of British prime ministers was responsible. The British lanced a singularly nasty boil.

It seems somehow significant that the Harrier was to be known as the jet-age Spitfire, not least because of the role it played in the Falklands War as the plucky little British fighter flown by dashing young men against apparently overwhelming odds, and winning through. There is, though, another reason why the Harrier deserves to be associated with the Spitfire: R. J. Mitchell's superb piston-engined fighter came to be seen as the very spirit of the fight for freedom put up by the British against the odious Nazi regime. If only by default, as far as British politicians were concerned in 1982, the Harrier became a potent symbol of a fight against a nasty tyranny that had very many connections with Hitler, his technicians and minions, as well as an empathy with the Führer's aberrant views on democracy, freedom of speech and the rule of law.

The charismatic General Juan Perón, three times president of Argentina between 1946 and 1974, had been excited by fascism. At the end of the Second World War, his government is said to have sold ten thousand blank passports to Odessa, the shadowy organization established to protect former members of the SS. What we know for certain, from official records in Buenos Aires, is that five thousand former Nazis, many of them war criminals, escaped or emigrated to Argentina in the five years following the German surrender. They included such prize specimens as Joseph Mengele, Adolf Eichmann and Klaus Barbie. Conspiracy theorists say that Adolf Hitler and Eva Braun came too. But even if Hitler did not arrive in person, his spirit was never far away. German emigrants had, in fact, flocked to Argentina since the 1870s. What Nazis would have found decidedly odd, though, is the fact that they would share their new-found land with an ever-increasing number of Jews. General Perón might have been pro-Hitler in many ways, but he was no anti-Semite and today Argentina has one of the world's largest Jewish populations.

What Perón wanted, above all, was German know-how, technology and military hardware. One of his prized German immigrants shortly after the Second World War was Kurt Tank, the former technical director of Focke-Wulf. A brilliant aircraft designer and seasoned test pilot, Tank had been responsible for the superb Focke-Wulf Fw 190 fighter and its successor, the Ta 152. In the guise of 'Dr Professor Pedro Matthies', he brought sixty-two former Focke-Wulf employees with him to Córdoba, where at what was to become the Fábrica Militar de Aviones he produced the Pulqui (Arrow) II, a jet fighter based on the Ta 183, one of the many advanced designs on drawing boards in German factories in 1945. The unsuccessful Pulqui I, the first jet aircraft built in Latin America, pre-dated Tank's fighter by three years; it had been designed by a team led by the French aircraft engineer Émile Dewoitine, who had slipped off to Argentina via Spain when faced with post-war accusations of collaborating with the enemy. French engineers were to have better luck in years to come when Argentine Dassault Mirage IIIs and Vs, and Dassault Breguet Super Étendards equipped with Exocet anti-ship missiles, took on the Falklands Task Force.

Four prototype Pulqui IIs were built from 1950 and flew, the fourth in anger against Perón during a coup in 1955. But the project proved to be too expensive for an Argentina weakened by unstable military governments; eventually, the Fuerza Aérea Argentina was supplied with North American F-86 Sabres. Tank went on to India to develop the country's first jet aircraft, the HF-24 Marut (Tempest) fighter, based on the design for what was to have been the Pulqui III. The Marut flew with the Indian Air Force until 1990. In the 1970s, Tank moved back to Germany, where, as if turning full circle, he became a valued consultant to MBB, or Messerschmitt-Bölkow-Blohm. Messerschmitt had once, of course, mass-produced the many variants of the Spitfire's duelling partner and the Fw 190's great rival, the Bf 109.

So the Harrier went into action for the first time twenty-one years after Bill Bedford's first tentative hover in XP831 at

Dunsfold, and against an enemy with regrettable connections to Nazi Germany. 'The Empire Strikes Back', announced the cover of *Newsweek* as FRS.1 Sea Harriers of the 'Dark Blues' (Royal Navy) and GR.3 Harriers of the 'Light Blues' (RAF) practised attack techniques from the decks of *Hermes* and *Invincible* as these great grey ships ploughed through the Atlantic. Here they were joined by a fleet of British warships that, days earlier, had been taking part in a NATO exercise in the Mediterranean and by surreptitious submarines including the nuclear-powered HMS *Conqueror*.

Towards dusk on 1 May, 801 Squadron's Lieutenant Steve Thomas and Flight Lieutenant Paul Barton shot off on combat patrol from the deck of *Invincible*. Shortly into their flight, they were called from HMS *Glamorgan*, a 6,200-ton County-class destroyer bombarding Argentine positions at Port Stanley: a pair of Mirage III fighters from Río Gallegos, Patagonia, had been detected, heading on course for the patrolling Sea Harriers. Blue Fox radar enabled the British aircraft to sight the enemy, closing at more than three miles a second in a dive from 40,000 feet and a distance of seventeen miles. As the Mirages neared, Barton pulled to the left, under and behind the delta-wing Argentine jets flown by Captain 'Paco' Cuerva and Lieutenant Carlos Perona. A mile behind Perona's Mirage, Barton unleashed one of his two heat-seeking Sidewinder missiles.

'The missile thundered off the rails like an express train,' wrote Commander 'Sharkey' Ward DFC, AFC a decade later in his book *Sea Harrier over the Falklands*, 'and left a brilliant white smoke trail as it curved up towards the heavens, chasing after

the Mirage which was now making for the stars, very nose-high.'
Ward was 801 Squadron's commander.

> Paul was mesmerised as the angry missile closed
> with its target. As the Sidewinder made intercept,
> the Argentine jet exploded in a vivid ball of yellow
> flame. It broke its back as the missile exploded and
> then disintegrated, before its remains twisted their
> way down to the cloud and sea below.

Barton, however, had been uncertain of victory as he released the
missile. He later recalled:

> At first I thought it had failed. It came off the rail
> and ducked down. I had not fired a 'winder' before
> so its behaviour at launch was new to me. I was
> surprised not to see it home straight in. To see it
> duck down was disconcerting. I'd begun to wonder
> if it was a dud. It took about half a mile to get its
> trajectory sorted out, then it picked itself up and
> for the last half mile it just homed straight in.
> The missile flight time was about four seconds, then
> the Mirage exploded in a brilliant blue, orange and
> red fireball.

Perona had no idea the Harrier had been on his tail. Cuerva had
caught sight of the Sidewinder and alerted his wingman, but
he had been too late. Meanwhile, Thomas was in hot pursuit of

John 'Jack' Frost, a former de Havilland supersonic research engineer, developed this jet-powered VTOL 'flying saucer' for Avro Canada in the 1950s. The Frisbee-like VZ-9 Avrocar was no rival for Hawker's P.1127; it looked the part, but was limited by a top speed of 35 mph – above which it became unstable – and never flew more than three feet above the ground.

First flown in 1954, the Convair XFY Pogo was a prototype turboprop VTOL fighter for the US Navy; it was to have been carried on board warships. But it required the skills of test pilots at all times – it was notably hard to land – while its performance, although spirited, was no match for a new generation of Mach 2 jet fighters.

The Ryan X-13 Vertijet pushing away from its launch trailer at Fort Edwards Air Force base, California, before performing a Rolls-Royce Avon-assisted vertical take-off. This delta-wing VTOL fighter was originally designed to operate from US Navy submarines; its slow and complex, if balletic, take-off and landing procedure, and its limited performance, made it redundant even before its maiden flight in December 1955.

The bug-like Short SC.1, of which two were built, was Britain's first fixed-wing VTOL aircraft. Unveiled in 1958, it was used for research into the transition from vertical to forward flight, and vice versa. It was a great help to the Hawker team while developing the Harrier. Never intended for active service, it was a complex machine powered by five Rolls-Royce 108 turbojets. The SC.1 was retired in 1971.

It was the development of light, powerful and reliable Roll-Royce turbojets that made the single-engine P.1127 possible, and the Harrier a success. The wartime team in charge of developing the Rolls-Royce Welland, Britain's first production jet engine, were led by Frank Whittle (centre), the Rover engineer John Herriot (left) and Stanley Hooker (right), who went on to design the Harrier's Pegasus engine.

Bill Bedford (above left), a former Second World War RAF fighter pilot, was Hawker-Siddeley's chief test pilot from 1956 to 1967; he was first to fly the P.1127, the Kestrel and the Harrier. From model aircraft and gliders, Sydney Camm (above right) progressed to take charge of the design of Hawker's magnificent, and beautiful, Fury, Hurricane, Tempest and Hunter fighters as well as the P.1127/Kestrel/Harrier.

Tethered to the ground, XP831, the prototype Hawker P.1127, made its first tentative, hovering flight at Dunsfold Aerodrome, Surrey, on 21 October 1960 with Bill Bedford at the controls. Within a month, the tethers were unloosed and the aircraft flew freely. Despite a crash at the Paris Air Show in 1963, XP831 survived and is on display today at London's Science Museum.

Bill Bedford made the first fixed-wing VTOL flights, with XP831, from the deck of an aircraft carrier – HMS *Ark Royal* – off the English coast at Portland, Dorset, on 8 February 1963. Representatives of foreign navies were on board the carrier to watch the exercise, while the Pathe newsreel team was there to record an event that was quickly publicized around the world.

The nine FGA.1 Kestrels, a more powerful development of the P.1127, equipped the Tripartite Evaluation Squadron formed in 1965 at RAF West Raynham, Norfolk, from a team of British, US and West German fighter pilots including the former Messerschmitt Bf 109 ace, Gerhard Barkhorn. Six of the aircraft were shipped to the US after completion of rigorous trials, two serving with NASA.

Flight Lieutenant Tom Lecky-Thompson brings his brand-new GR.1 Harrier, XV741, down to land, victoriously, from New York at RAF St Pancras – a coal yard in Somers Town alongside the magnificent Victorian Gothic London railway terminus – at the end of the May 1969 *Daily Mail* Transatlantic Air Race. The Harrier had entered service with the RAF the previous month.

Designed under the direction of Ralph Hooper, the Hawker Siddeley P.1154 was to have been a supersonic V/STOL fighter for service with the RAF and the Royal Navy. It would have been a highly able aircraft, but differences in views between the two services combined with financial cutbacks by an incoming Labour government elected in 1964 put an end to the project.

The Soviet Navy's Yakovlev Yak-38 was a VTOL interceptor operating, from 1976, from the decks of new Kiev-class aircraft carriers. Based in part on the P.1154, the Yak was equipped, however, with three engines, two for take-off and landing, and, one – vectorable – for forward flight. The aircraft was badly affected by hot and humid conditions, and its payload was often too little for effective combat.

At heart, the Harrier was an analogue-era aircraft; cockpits of the early marks (above) were little different in layout and instruments from the majority of 1950s combat jets with their seemingly random scattering of switches and controls and simple levers. Throughout its long life, the Harrier has been continually updated, with cockpits (left) adapted to the digital world, and becoming neater in the process. The pilot's view was gradually improved, and notably in the cockpits of Sea Harriers, where the seat was raised to offer a true fighter pilot's field of vision.

Cuerva, who was now spiralling down towards the clouds in a tight escape manoeuvre. Thomas launched a Sidewinder as the Mirage vanished from sight. He missed – just – but this was not the end of the story.

Remarkably, Perona was still very much alive, his aircraft on fire, alarms ringing in the cockpit. The Argentine pilot shut down the damaged engine and ejected low over the shoreline of Pebble Island, a sheep farm established in 1846 and, in 1982, an Argentine naval air station as well as home to thousands of Rockhopper penguins. Wearing a light flying suit, Perona was determined not to ditch in the freezing-cold sea. He broke a foot on landing, touching down on *terra firma* with just fifty feet to spare.

Cuerva was less fortunate. With insufficient fuel to fly back to the mainland, he asked permission to land at Port Stanley, or 'Puerto Argentino'. Under attack from HMS *Glamorgan*, *Arrow* and *Alacrity*, the airbase was on red alert. Three Argentine IAI Daggers, Israeli versions of the Mirage V, were flying low towards the British ships, with two more circling above; Cuerva could only be a danger to them; critical moments were lost as air controllers finally gave in to his urgent request. By now desperate to lose weight, and forward momentum, Cuerva dropped his radar-guided missiles, harmlessly. Inexperienced, or nervous, anti-aircraft gunners opened fire. '*Me están tirando a mi... carajo!*' ['They are shooting at me... fuck!'] were the pilot's last words as, presumably injured and unable to eject, he crashed into the sea south of Port Stanley and his aircraft broke in two.

Soon afterwards, the Daggers attacked the British ships. One was downed with a Sidewinder fired from a Sea Harrier of 800

Squadron, flown from *Invincible*, by Flight Lieutenant 'Bertie' Penfold, one of a number of RAF pilots attached to the Royal Navy during the Falklands War, on his way back from a raid over Goose Green. The pilot, Lieutenant José Ardiles, was killed. At the time, his cousin, Ossie Ardiles, a much-feted footballer, was playing for Tottenham Hotspur. He was booed off the pitch by British supporters and loaned to Paris Saint-Germain for a year to keep him out of their way. Later, in the 1990s, Ardiles was to become Tottenham's manager, both the Falklands War and the provocative headlines of the tabloid newspapers designed to fuel anti-Argentine fervour on the terraces long forgotten. The red tops had certainly had a field day. 'Gotcha!' The *Sun* had yelled when the *Conqueror* sank the Argentine light cruiser *General Belgrano* on 2 May with the loss of three hundred and twenty three lives. And shortly before the war, a proposed peace settlement brokered by Peru had been met by The *Sun*'s 'Stick it up your Junta!' According to Roy Greenslade, The *Sun*'s deputy editor at the time, his boss, Kelvin MacKenzie, was delighted with *Private Eye*'s spoof *Sun* headline: 'Kill an Argie and win a Metro' (a small and then popular British Leyland car). 'Why didn't we think of that?' joked the editor of the 'Currant Bun'.

Killing was certainly no joke for the pilots involved in air-to-air combat. Disturbed by what he had done, Flight Lieutenant Penfold did not fly again, and was sent back to the UK. Speaking about the attack to Peter Archer, a Press Association reporter on board *Hermes*, Penfold said, 'I felt quite sick.' His wife, Susan, was contacted at home in Somerton, Wiltshire. 'I am proud of my husband,' she said, 'but I feel desperately sorry for the family of the other pilot.' Mrs Penfold went on to say that her husband 'had an attack of nerves before he set out with the Task Force, the fear of what you are going to do to other people when you get there'. He had also been apprehensive about the sea passage to the South Atlantic. 'Being in the air force, he is not used to being on board a ship. He has only spent three days at sea, ever.'

A compassionate man, and a fine Harrier pilot, Penfold was not alone in finding the voyage trying. As Sharkey Ward recalled:

> *Invincible* had been built by Vickers, and when they were given the plans for the ship by the naval architects at Bath, they insisted that with the proposed design there would be very high vibration levels in the ship at particular speeds, especially in the aft section where all the officers slept. The naval architects apparently told Vickers to mind their own business and build the ship. After the *Invincible* had been launched on her first high-speed trials, the heavy vibration set in just as the builders had predicted. And, now in a war situation, with the ship regularly having to manoeuvre at high speed, the problem had come home to roost. My cabin was no better than anyone else's. Anything at all left on the desk would be removed by the vibration in less than thirty seconds – it was that bad.

Still, this sounded like luxury compared with conditions on board *Hermes*. As Wing Commander Squire noted in his diary for

Tuesday 18 May, 'I have been allocated a small cabin well aft, but my pilots are sharing cabins (i.e. using the floor) or pitching camp on the wardroom floor. The troops are in the passageways.' Even more challenging than the accommodation on board was the attitude of the carrier's captain. That same evening, Squire noted, 'The ship's commander (John Locke) invites me to his cabin for a drink. There, he tells me in confidence of the captain's aversion to the RAF. He warns me of the difficulties that may lie ahead.' When Squire spotted an opportunity, he commandeered a Sea King helicopter and flew through sea fog to visit Sharkey Ward on *Invincible*: 'What an enormous difference,' he noted, 'in both atmosphere and environment.'

But whatever the inter-service tensions that arose, and whatever their complaints about who was getting the easier missions or better treatment on board their respective ships, the RAF and Royal Navy Harrier pilots held each other in great respect and during the exhausting days that followed, a strong camaraderie grew between them. After an inaccurate 'visual sighting' by pilots of 801 Squadron of what they took to be Super Étendards, prompting a wild goose chase by 1 Squadron Harriers, Squire recorded: '801 Squadron sends across a bottle of malt by way of apology.'

Only after the seventy-four-day war had ended did hard-pressed RN and RAF pilots learn that Margaret Thatcher's government had been prepared, or so it was rumoured, for the deaths of up to ten thousand servicemen and women: this was the estimated value of the Falklands in human life and the maximum number of casualties it was thought the British public would tolerate. Many commentators in the United States and senior members of the US military thought this was a war Britain could not possibly win on its own. In fact, it was the last war Britain fought on its own – albeit with background assistance from the US and Chile – and using largely all-British equipment and weaponry. And as for the Harrier, at the start of the war it was still an unknown quantity in terms of combat, as for that matter were Harrier pilots.

The first of May began with a dramatic attack, at 04.38 hours, on the runway at Port Stanley by a solitary RAF Vulcan bomber, XM607, captained by Flight Lieutenant Martin Withers. The Vulcan had flown 4,000 miles from the Ascension Islands, refuelled by an aerial armada of Victor tankers, to deliver its payload of twenty-one 1,000 lb bombs. At fifteen and three-quarter hours, it had been the longest bomber mission ever flown, and was surpassed only by those of USAF B-52 Stratofortresses flying from the United States to Iraq in 1991. This and six subsequent raids were also the first and last time the RAF's awe-inspiring Avro Vulcan V-bombers, placed in service from 1956 and designed to carry H-bombs at the height of the Cold War, would see combat.

The day ended with Sea Harriers flown by Lieutenant Alan Curtis and Lieutenant Commander Mike Broadwater intercepting three low-flying Argentine bombers heading towards the British ships. 'Tally Ho!' called Curtis as he dived and, turning behind the lead aircraft, let loose a Sidewinder missile. The bomber burst into fragments that rained into a dark sea. Broadwater fired a Sidewinder at a second aircraft, but missed. The two surviving bombers vanished into the cloud and made for home. The odd thing for the British pilots was that the ill-fated bomber had been one of the twelve English Electric Canberras acquired by the Fuerza Aérea Argentina in the early 1970s. A stalwart of the RAF, this first-generation jet bomber made its maiden flight in 1950 and its photo-reconnaissance variant was still in action over Afghanistan as late as 2006. Curtis's kill was akin to a Spitfire taking out a de Havilland Mosquito – the inspiration for the Canberra – during the Second World War. As it was, and by chance, another Canberra became the last Argentine aircraft to be shot down in the conflict, hit not by a Sea Harrier, but by a Sea Dart missile fired from the destroyer HMS *Cardiff*.

In their first day in action, Sea Harriers, or 'Shars', had proved their worth, and to Argentinian pilots these nimble, fierce and inescapable aircraft were soon to be known as *La Muerta Negra*, or 'Black Death'. And the appearance of the Sea Harrier matched its performance: just like the Spitfire, it both looked right and was right. Indeed, I remember the first time I saw Sea Harriers at RNAS Yeovilton in early 1982 on a trip to visit Castle Drogo, the grandiose country house overlooking Dartmoor designed by Sir Edwin Lutyens for Julius Drewe, founder of Home and Colonial stores, at a time when Britain was just entering the age of aerial warfare and the Royal Navy was still in all its imperial pomp. Those FRS.1 Sea Harriers were swans compared to the GR.3, which seemed by comparison an awkward, if not exactly ugly, duckling. Their resplendent pre-Falklands uniform of dark grey, easily mistaken for dark blue, over white, and bold insignia, was very smart indeed. A raised canopy and a finely resolved nose imbued the Sea Harrier with poise, balance and, at last, an elegance lacking in the characteristically hunched-up RAF aircraft.

The Sea Harrier had emerged slowly in the early 1960s from a Royal Navy requirement to replace the de Havilland Sea Vixen and, from the end of the decade, a need to face up to the fact that the Fleet Air Arm's fixed-wing combat aircraft would soon be facing the axe. Harold Wilson's Labour government wanted to rid the Navy of large aircraft carriers like the *Ark Royal* and to replace them with a new type of small carrier – the command cruiser – suitable for helicopters but not for conventional fixed-wing aircraft. This prompted discussions between Hawker and the navy, and between 1972 and 1974 detailed design work on a Royal Navy 'Maritime Support Harrier' was largely completed. Only small numbers would be ordered as it was assumed that each of the three new light carriers would be equipped with just six V/STOL jets apiece. By this time, of course, Britain's sway over the waves had been considerably diminished. The Navy's last battleship, the fast 44,500-ton steam-turbine *Vanguard*, had been decommissioned and scrapped in 1960.

Hawker, meanwhile, had even been working on a proposal for an altogether smaller class of ship than the new small Navy carriers. In discussion with the boat-builders Vosper Thornycroft, the design team at Kingston worked up plans for deckless Harrier carriers. Attached to cranes, the jets were to have been swung out from the sides of the ships. The pilot would start up, hover and then make the transition to forward flight. On return, the aircraft would be picked up from the hover alongside the ship and swung aboard by crane. Demonstrated, without mishap, over land, the experiment was not carried out at sea. It would have been a lot to ask of a pilot returning from combat in challenging weather to perform such a finely calibrated manoeuvre.

The cockpit of this all-purpose interceptor, reconnaissance and strike version of the Harrier was raised by eleven inches to give the pilot a much better all-round view both on the deck and in the air. The extra space beneath the pilot's feet contained new avionics and electronic equipment. The instrument panel included a larger Smith's head-up display, driven by a digital computer. The nose contained the Ferranti Blue Fox radar that was to prove so very valuable in 1982. Revised weapon pylons were designed to carry RAF and US Marine Corps weaponry, including the American AIM-9 Sidewinder air-to-air and Martel and Harpoon air-to-surface missiles, the latter type intended primarily for strikes against ships. As a reminder that the Cold War had yet to go away, the Sea Harrier was also designed to carry a 600 lb WE.177A nuclear bomb; aircraft of this type were withdrawn from service in 1992 after the collapse of the Soviet Union and the subsequent disintegration of the Warsaw Pact. As a further reminder of that undeclared state of conflict, one of the primary tasks envisaged for the Sea Harrier when it was still on the drawing board was to intercept snooping Soviet Tupolev Tu-95 Bears over the North Atlantic and North Sea. Originally designed as a long-range bomber, the swept-wing Tu-95 would later be developed into a very effective missile platform and reconnaissance aircraft. Powered by four mighty Kuznetsov NK-12 turboprop engines designed by a team of Junkers and BMW technicians led by the Austrian SS Standartenführer

Ferdinand Brandhorn and deported from Germany along with their factories, this remarkable machine first flew in 1952, long before the Harrier. It is not due for retirement until around 2040, long after the last US Harrier will have been replaced.

The tail fin of the Sea Harrier was larger than that of the GR.3 and, to deter corrosion by sea winds and salt water, the magnesium-zirconium casings of the Pegasus engine were replaced by aluminium. Larger wing-tip reaction control vents were fitted to assist pilots as they manoeuvred within the tight confines imposed by the superstructure and decks of carriers as they sometimes operated in harsh weather and rough seas. There was an improved autopilot and a faster Martin-Baker ejector seat: the Type 10 'zero-zero' seat fitted to the 'Shar' – it could be launched at zero feet and at zero knots, i.e. with the aircraft stationary on the ground – would see the parachute open within 1.5 seconds of the pilot releasing the seat, compared with the 2.25 seconds of the Type 9 fitted to the GR.3. Three-quarters of a second might not seem a long time if you are sitting at a desk, but it is long enough if you happen to be the pilot of a combat jet that is about to explode or otherwise out of control: the minutest fraction of a second counts.

Since first tested successfully in 1949, Martin-Baker ejector seats have saved the lives of nearly 7,500 pilots. Today, the Middlesex-based company is still family-owned, supplying ejector seats to ninety-three air forces worldwide. Founded by the Irish-born engineer James Martin and the Welsh-born former RFC and RAF pilot Valentine Baker in 1934 to build aircraft, this enduring company changed course in 1942 after a test flight of the prototype MB3 fighter on 12 September 1942 proved fatal for Baker. Deeply affected by his partner's death, Martin switched from aircraft design to ejector seats, although not before his company had created the magnificent MB5, a machine that might well have given the P-51D Mustang more than a run for its money. Since Bill Bedford ejected from XP836, one of the prototype P.1127s, on 14 December 1961 on the approach to RNAS Yeovilton, at least a hundred RAF Harrier pilots alone have rocketed out of their aircraft strapped to Martin-Baker ejector seats; nearly all of them have survived and most have flown again soon afterwards.

All up, the FRS.1 was slightly heavier than the GR.3 – by just 100 lbs – and more expensive, with a unit price of £6.8 million compared to £5.5 million. This was a remarkable achievement by any standards; there was no delay in the project, and perhaps – as events turned out – this was just as well. Roy Mason, a former coal-miner and Secretary of State for Defence in Harold Wilson's Labour administration of 1974–6, announced orders for twenty-four production Sea Harriers in May 1975. Even this small order had been a case of touch and go, as for much of the 1970s Britain was in the throes of a dismal economic recession, peaking, at first, with the infamous Three Day Week of January to March 1974 when electricity was rationed and factories ground along as best they could, and, later on, with the grim Winter of Discontent of 1978–9, when industrial unrest led to serious strikes at a time when Britain was hit by the fiercest blizzards since the Big Freeze of 1962–3. The future of companies like Hawker itself was unsure as both Tory and

Labour governments set about merging and even nationalizing key sectors of British industry.

The first FRS.1 to fly was XZ450 on 20 August 1978. The following month, the new Sea Harrier was thrilling the public at the Farnborough Air Show, taking off in spectacular style from a ski-ramp. Pioneered by Lieutenant Commander Doug Taylor while he researched a doctoral thesis at Southampton University in the early 1970s – although Ralph Hooper at Hawker had been thinking along the same lines – the ski-ramps were incorporated into the curved deck design of the new Royal Navy light carriers. Launching the Harriers on a semi-ballistic trajectory, they enabled the aircraft to take off within a very short distance, and at just 70 mph, with the heaviest permitted payloads. And, just as importantly, they ensured that the aircraft was always pointing skywards when taking off; this was not always the case on conventional flat-deck carriers as the swell of the sea could see pilots lifting off just as a ship's prow end dipped.

The Sea Harrier went into Royal Navy service on 18 June 1979 with the training squadron 700A at the same time as HMS *Invincible* was undergoing sea trials, and after tests and flight training from Yeovilton and RAF Wittering, with three ocean-going squadrons, 800, 801 and 802. No one could have seen the Falklands episode coming, and yet even before these Harriers could be fitted and tested with Sidewinders – this was to be done at sea – they were off south, across the Equator and down to a turbulent South Atlantic. In the event, Sea Harriers shot down twenty Argentine aircraft in air-to-air combat; none were lost in return, although two were destroyed by ground fire and four lost through accidents. Given the suddenness of the mission and the fact that war zone, weaponry and even the aircraft themselves were all new and unfamiliar, it was an exemplary performance.

The Task Force, setting sail under Operation Corporate from Portsmouth and the Mediterranean in April 1982, was certainly a shot in the dark. The cockiness of the Argentine military had been reinforced by their belief that the British would take no action once they had invaded the 'Malvinas', along with South Georgia and the Sandwich Islands. Not only had the junta been in discussion with London during 1981 over potential sales of an aircraft carrier – possibly *Hermes* – and Sea Harriers, and perhaps Vulcans and more Canberras too, but in his defence review of that year, John Nott, Mrs Thatcher's Secretary of State for Defence, had planned the withdrawal of the Royal Navy ice patrol ship HMS *Endurance* on 15 April 1982; there would be no replacement. It was the skipper of the *Endurance*, Captain Nicholas Barker, however, who made the point to Whitehall that the withdrawal of the one and only Royal Navy surface ship for thousands of miles would send the wrong signals to Buenos Aires: Britain would effectively be abandoning its territories in the South Atlantic and ensuring that it would be unable to respond if Argentina decided to invade the islands.

Captain Barker and his ship in fact went on to play a key role in the retaking of South Georgia, with Argentine troops there surrendering eleven days before *Endurance*, launched in 1956 as the *Anita Dan* in Denmark and acquired by the Royal Navy in 1967, had been scheduled for retirement. The 1981 government defence review, however, had gone even further to encourage the Argentine military. The *Invincible*, which was to take Sharkey Ward and his fellow Sea Harrier pilots to war in April 1982, was to have been sold to Australia, while *Intrepid* and *Fearless*, two assault ships that played vital roles in the landing of British troops on the Falkland Islands, were also to have been sold; *Fearless* – the Royal Navy's last steamship and a maritime star in the 1977 James Bond film *The Spy Who Loved Me* – was destined for the scrapheap and *Intrepid* sold to – yes – the Argentine Navy. Both ships carried Royal Marines – a corps Nott had also seriously considered disbanding – to the South Atlantic islands and the formal surrender of the Argentine military was to be signed on board *Intrepid*. Replacements for both ships have since been placed in service.

To his credit, Nott handed in his resignation at the outbreak of what indeed had looked to be the 'Guerras de las Malvinas', but this was refused. In the early 1950s, Nott had served with the 2nd Gurkha Rifles in Malaysia. No one doubted his personal courage, yet he had become blinkered and was thinking only in the short term. 'Expect the unexpected' is a motto all politicians should take to heart. Indeed, when Harold Macmillan, whose own Conservative administration had been rocked by a number of scandals, was asked by Jack Hardiman Scott, the BBC's political editor and part-time writer of thrillers, what was most likely to blow governments off course, he is supposed to have replied with the famous words: 'Events, dear boy, events.'

As it was, Margaret Thatcher's government did react very quickly to the events of 2 April 1982. Military preparations were made, and diplomatic overtures brought the United States and Chile on side. President Ronald Reagan agreed to the Royal Navy borrowing USS *Iwo Jima*, an amphibious assault ship that normally carried a complement of up to twenty-five helicopters, if either of the Harrier-carrying *Hermes* or *Invincible* got into trouble. The US also provided surveillance, as did General Augusto Pinochet's unpleasant military regime in Santiago de Chile, along with missiles and submarine detectors. The French government, under the presidency of François Mitterrand, nominally supported Britain, although an 'intelligence-gathering' team of French technicians remained in Argentina for the duration of the Falklands War to ensure that French-built Super Étendards could launch French-built Exocet missiles at British ships. And Israeli advisers in Argentina looked after the IAI Daggers. It is said that such was the Israeli prime minister Menachem Begin's hatred of the British that he condoned further sales of Israeli military hardware to Argentina during the Falklands War. Such behaviour was surely unforgiveable: here was a Jewish politician supporting an extreme right-wing military regime that had tortured, terrorized and killed thousands of its own people, given shelter to the Nazis, including the nastiest concentration camp commandants, doctors and theoreticians, and which was hell-bent on appropriating territory beyond its borders because it believed such 'living space' was Argentine.

Hernan Dobry, the Argentine journalist who revealed the extent of Israel's aid to Argentina in his 2011 book *Operation Israel: The Arming of Argentina during the Dictatorship, 1967–83*, believes that sales of, among other equipment, anti-tank mines, machine guns, mortars, air-to-air missiles, missile radar alert systems and long-range fuel tanks for Dagger bombers was agreed at this top level as a form of revenge for the hanging of Dov Gruner, a personal friend of Begin who was sentenced to death by the British Mandatory Authorities in 1947 for his part in an attack on a police station. According to Israel Lotersztain, a salesman for the Israeli defence company Isrex Argentina, a meeting was set up between representatives of his company and Prime Minister Begin. 'You've come to talk badly about the British?' asked Begin. 'Is this going to be used to kill the English? Go ahead! Dov up there is going to be perfectly happy with the decision. Obviously, it must all be done perfectly.'

An Aerolineas Argentina Boeing 707 appears to have made five flights from Tel Aviv via Lima, with the collaboration of the Peruvian government, to Buenos Aires, and four further flights to and from Tripoli to collect weapons from Colonel Muammar Gaddafi's ruthless regime in Libya. Even more audacious, claims Dobry, was Argentina's attempt to buy twenty-three Mirage IIIB and C aircraft from Isrex. They were to have been delivered flying in the colours of the Peruvian Air Force, but the war proved short-lived, the junta in Buenos Aires collapsed and there was no longer need for second-hand Mirages.

Could all this be true? After the publication of Dobry's book, an unnamed 'senior official' from the Israeli Defence Ministry told the London *Jewish Chronicle* that it was 'highly unlikely that in the months of the Falklands War, when Israel was preparing the invasion of Lebanon, anyone in the defence establishment, and certainly not the prime minister, would have the time or resources to organize emergency arms supplies for faraway

Argentina'. Herzl Makov, director of the Begin Heritage Centre in Jerusalem, told the paper that the book was 'a distortion of historical reality', and that 'Mr Begin's relations with British prime ministers James Callaghan and Margaret Thatcher were excellent and warm'.

Whatever the truth, this conspiracy-style story reveals the complexities of warfare, and the arms trade, in the decades following the Second World War. While the Falklands conflict might appear straightforward enough to anyone who believes in a people's – in this case, the Falkland Islanders' – right to self-determination and that it is entirely proper to stand up to a vicious military regime that has no respect for its own people, let alone others, it was also a battleground between the old and new worlds and a case of old scores being settled by proxy. In the early 1950s, the United States had fought China and, by implication, the Soviet Union, in Korea. The USA and the USSR clashed again at the time of the Cuban Missile Crisis, while China, the Soviet Union and Cuba backed, and fought, wars in Central and Latin America, Africa and Asia against the United States and the West. The battlegrounds had shifted from central Europe to developing countries and, as has often been said, the Third World War, although never declared, is still being fought in the Third World. Indeed, when Washington learned of Margaret Thatcher's intention to launch a flotilla to retake the South Atlantic islands, the US Secretary of State, General Alexander Haig, tried at first to deter the British; the fear in Washington was that Buenos Aires might ask for, and be given, military and other aid by Moscow. The US had been fearful of 'Reds' in its back yard throughout the

An FRS.1 Sea Harrier blasts off from the 'ski-jump' at the Royal Aircraft Establishment, Bedford. Devised by Lieutenant Commander David Taylor in the 1970s, the ski-jump enabled Harriers to climb quickly and safely from the decks of carriers with heavier payloads than they would in normal STOL operation. Fitted to Royal Navy carriers, they helped the Sea Harrier to success in the Falklands War.

Two generations of Harrier pilots (above left), Commander Nigel 'Sharkey' Ward, who led 801 Naval Air Squadron from HMS *Invincible* during the Falklands War, and his son, Lieutenant Commander Kris Ward. Sharkey took a brand new FRS.1 Sea Harrier to BBC's Pebble Mill Studio in September 1979, landing vertically onto a metal sheet as the pilot of this RAF GR.1 is seen doing on an earlier exercise elsewhere (above right).

An FRS.1 Harrier of 800 Naval Air Squadron coming in to land on the deck of HMS *Hermes* as the British flagship ploughs towards the Falkland Islands through a choppy South Atlantic.

A GR.3 Harrier of RAF No. 1 Squadron, with its distinctive dolphin nose, rests in its hide outside Belize City in March 2008. Six Harriers were on duty at various times in Belize between 1975 and 1993 to protect the Central American state, a former British colony, from threats by neighbouring Guatemala. No shots were fired: the well-armed and supremely agile Harrier was a very credible threat.

A GR.3 in a sylvan hide in West Germany, close to the border with the German Democratic Republic. The Harriers were to have been a last-ditch force designed to undertake the RAF's equivalent of a guerrilla aerial war if the Soviet bloc invaded Western Europe and took out, as it was expected to try to do, easily targeted conventional air bases.

Harriers were designed to take off, all of a sudden, from forest clearings and rural roads – and to surprise the enemy, particularly ground troops and armoured divisions. Here, in November 1978, a GR.3 of No. 4 Squadron practices take-offs and landings from a public road near RAF Gütersloh, a former Second World War Luftwaffe base close to the East German border.

FRS.1 Sea Harriers from HMS *Invincible* soar over the Adriatic as part of the UN Peace Keeping Force in Bosnia. The mission was not all plain sailing; on 16 April 1994, Lieutenant Nick Richardson, flying from HMS *Ark Royal*, was shot down by a hand-held SAM-7 rocket launcher near Goražde while attempting to attack Bosnian Serb tanks; he ejected safely and was rescued.

An AV-8A of the United States Marine Corps lands on the carrier USS *Franklin D Roosevelt*. The USMC had been impressed from early on with the unique performance and combat characteristics of the Harrier; a total of 110 AV-8As were shipped from Britain to the United States between 1971 and 1976; since then the US Marines have remained loyal to the jump jet.

Underside of a USMC AV-8B showing the immense size of its 'elephant ear' air intakes, the four rotating nozzles that allow the Harrier to convert from vertical to forward – and even backward – flight, the air brake and weaponry carried on under-wing pylons. The earlier AV-8A had a relatively poor safety record, but this was due largely to a combination of slack maintenance and pilot error.

RAF GR.5 and GR.7 Harriers were painted in winter camouflage for training exercises over Norway and, in this instance, GR.7s for action in Bosnia. The versatility of the Harrier, as it developed from an experimental aircraft to a multi-role NATO warplane, was one of its chief attractions to various branches of the military and partly why it has lasted so very long in active service.

GR.7 Harriers taxiing in the shimmering heat in Kuwait prior to take off from Ahmed Al Jaber Air Base on mission to maintain the No Fly Zone over southern Iraq in the 1990s. Like the GR.5 and GR.9, the GR.7 was a British version of the McDonnell Douglas AV-8B Harrier II, a larger and much more powerful development of the original GR.1 and GR.3.

A USMC AV-8B Harrier (left). In service since 1985, the Mk 2 Harrier is expected to continue in operation until 2030. Making extensive use of carbon fibre in its construction, the AV-8B is a stronger and more robust aircraft than its predecessors. The aircraft also continues to serve with the Italian and Spanish navies.

A GR.7 of 20(R) Squadron (left), RAF Wittering fires CRV-7 rockets over the sea at Holbeach, Norfolk. Developed as a strike aircraft, supporting ground forces and attacking ground targets, the Harrier has proven to be a highly effective dogfighter too. The aircraft's extraordinary manoeuvrability enables it to pull aerial stunts that allow it to get the better of much faster jets.

An AV-8B Harrier II (right) soaring above desert hills in Afghanistan. USMC Harriers remain on duty in Afghanistan in 2013; their British counterparts were withdrawn in 2010. The latest equipment fitted to these aircraft allows them to undertake precise reconnaissance work and, when called upon, to attack – if properly directed – with pinpoint accuracy.

The shape of fighter and strike aircraft to come? The unmanned Northrop Grumman X-47B (right) first flew from Edwards Air Force Base, California in February 2011. During 2012 and 2013, the subsonic jet performed flawlessly in tests carried out at sea on board the USS *Harry S Truman* and USS *George H W Bush*. The performance of the small aircraft is said to be 'outstanding'.

An alternative, piloted future; this is the Lockheed Martin F-35B (left) , the controversial and expensive STOVL – short take-off and vertical landing – combat jet that may soon enough see service in air forces and navies around the world, beginning with the USMC in December 2015. The Mach 2 F-35 combines supersonic performance, with stealth technology, great agility and formidable weaponry.

Sixteen GR.9 Harriers of Britain's Joint Harrier Force in diamond formation roar over the snow-dusted levels of Lincolnshire on their farewell flight, 15 December 2010.

1950s, toppling left-wing regimes, from that of Colonel Jacobo Arbenz in Guatemala in 1954 to Salvador Allende's Marxist government in Chile in 1973, and ostracizing Fidel Castro's Cuba, a country that sought an ever closer relationship with the Soviet Union as US sanctions hit ever harder after the Missile Crisis.

These nominally local wars, fought almost continuously somewhere in the world from 1945 to the present day, have also been test beds for new weapons designed and manufactured by the superpowers – the United States, the Soviet Union and China – and other leading nations, notably Great Britain and France. And, of course, there have been more minor, yet highly effective, players in these conflicts like Israel, South Africa and Germany, which as both the Federal Republic and a reunified state has been very busy exporting weapons, mainly Leopard tanks, small naval vessels and coastal submarines. Even so, there had been no British intention to fight in the South Atlantic against a Latin American power; London's response to events in the Falkland Islands was more or less spontaneous. This was demonstrated, most graphically, by the composition of the truly extraordinary British Task Force that set sail for the South Atlantic from early April to mid-May. The nuclear submarine *Conqueror* was underway from France on 4 April, followed by the carriers *Hermes* and *Invincible*, and their Sea Harriers, the following day from Portsmouth. The majority of the warships joined the carriers mid-ocean from Gibraltar, while the main body of troops set sail from Southampton on 9 April on board the elegant 45,000-ton P&O ocean liner SS *Canberra*, and on 15 May aboard the last traditional transatlantic liner, Cunard's 70,300-ton RMS *Queen*

Elizabeth 2, better known as the *QE2*. How on earth the *Canberra*, so distinct in her white livery, survived seemed a mystery at the time; after the war, Argentine pilots would explain that they thought she was a hospital ship. It was certainly good to see this superb example of late 1950s design return home some weeks later, although later very sad to learn that she was cut up in Pakistan in 1997. But one way or another, 127 ships sailed south. As did thousands of troops, and a very small number of combat aircraft: a grand total of twenty-eight Sea Harriers, joined, as we will see, by ten RAF GR.3 Harriers from 1(F) Squadron and accompanied by 127 Fleet Air Arm Wessex, Lynx, Wasp and Sea King helicopters.

The British established a Total Exclusion Zone with a radius of 200 nautical miles around the Falklands. Any Argentine ship or aircraft entering this circle of fire would be a 'legitimate' target. The sinking of the Argentine light cruiser *General Belgrano* on 2 May by HMS *Conqueror* outside the exclusion zone proved to be highly controversial. British politicians and commentators keen to score points against Margaret Thatcher denounced the attack as a war crime. With the benefit of hindsight, and newly released Whitehall files, it appears that the *Belgrano* was sailing towards the British exclusion zone, accompanied by the 2,200-ton destroyers *Piedra Buena* (formerly USS *Collett*, launched in 1944) and *Hipolito Bouchard* (formerly USS *Borie*, also launched in 1944) and with orders to attack the British aircraft carriers that day. Whatever the facts, the Argentine fleet returned to port after the *Belgrano*'s loss and remained there for the duration of the conflict. Henceforth, the aircraft carrier *Veinticinco de*

Mayo's Skyhawk attack aircraft would have to fly the hundreds of miles from mainland Argentina to the 'Malvinas' and back. Indeed, all Argentine aircraft had to fly these great distances – a minimum return journey of 700 miles – allowing them little time over targets, and precious little fuel to expend either tackling or evading Sea Harriers.

The wonder of it is that the Fuerza Aérea Argentina and Comando de Aviación Naval Argentina did so well in their fight against the British. On paper, the Argentinians appeared to be far superior in terms of air power. Theoretically, the Argentine Air Force (AAF) could muster some fifty Skyhawks, although the number ready for action at the beginning of May appears to have been thirty-two: fourteen A-4Cs from Grupo 4 de Caza Escuadrón III at San Julián and eighteen A-4Bs from Group V's IV and V Squadrons at Río Gallegos. The same air bases were home to thirty Daggers, but only twenty-four were combat-ready. Eight Mirages out of a total of seventeen flew from Río Gallegos and Comodoro Rivadavia. Six out of eight Canberra B.62 bombers were in service at Terlew, and there were at least twenty-five locally made FMA (Fábrica Militar de Aviones) IA 58 Pucarás, twin-engined turboprop ground-attack and counter-insurgency strike aircraft, dotted about various airfields. Meanwhile, the Argentine Navy listed four Dassault Super Étendards and the eight Skyhawks on board *Veinticinco de Mayo* on 1 May.

The reality was, though, that many of these aircraft were not in the best shape, and although the air force did have two aerial tankers, few Argentine aircraft were able to refuel in the air. In addition, the landing strip at Port Stanley was too short for Skyhawks and Mirages, the Super Étendards had just five Exocet missiles between them, and their pilots had never been in combat. The AAF did have a number of F-86 Sabres at the time, too, but these had neither the range nor, in all probability, the wherewithal to take on modern jets, still less the ability to avoid heat-seeking missiles. They were instead employed along the border with Chile, just in case General Pinochet decided to attack Argentina, or the generals in Buenos Aires decided to attack Chile.

Watching footage of AAF Skyhawks flying low into the attack on British ships and knowing that these jets were equipped with unguided bombs made, as it happens, in Britain and the United States, lacked missiles or any form of electronic self-defence, and were fitted with unreliable ejector seats, it is impossible not to admire the bravery and what proved to be the skill of Argentine pilots. As Admiral Woodward said, 'The Argentine Air Force fought extremely well and we felt great admiration for what they did.' The air force A-4B and A-4C Skyhawks flew 219 sorties, the Daggers 153, Mirage IIIAs fifty-eight, the Canberras forty-six, and the Pucarás a large number of reconnaissance and ground-attack missions.

Skyhawks sank the destroyer HMS *Coventry* and frigate *Antelope* and damaged the destroyer *Glasgow* and the frigates *Argonaut* and *Broadsword* as well as the landing ships RFA (Royal Fleet Auxiliary) *Sir Galahad* and *Sir Tristram* as they brought light tanks, vehicles, fuel and ammunition to shore. The Argentine Navy Skyhawk A4-Qs, flying from Río Grande naval air station in Tierra del Fuego, destroyed the frigate HMS *Ardent*. Nineteen

AAF and three Navy Skyhawks were lost, the majority to surface-to-air missiles and anti-aircraft fire, others to accidents and eight to Sea Harriers. Israel attempted to make up the loss in 1983, but Washington vetoed the sale of these twenty-four Skyhawks that had previously been owned and operated by the US.

Other ships damaged by Skyhawks and Daggers included the frigates HMS *Brilliant*, which shot down three of its attackers with Sea Wolf missiles, *Alacrity*, *Arrow* and *Plymouth*, the destroyer *Antrim* and the landing ships *Sir Bedivere*, *Sir Lancelot* and *Stromness*. Five Daggers attacked HMS *Plymouth*; their 1,000 lb bombs hit the 2,150-ton ship, but failed to explode. On deck, Able Seaman Phil Orr destroyed two of the attackers with Sea Cat missiles. The most famous Royal Navy casualty was HMS *Sheffield*, a guided-missile destroyer sunk by an Exocet launched from a Super Étendard on 4 May.

Eleven Daggers were destroyed, nine by Sea Harriers. The Royal Navy jets also took out a Mirage IIIA, a Canberra, a Pucará and a C-130E Hercules transport plane. Sea Harriers flew a total of 1,435 sorties and Harrier GR.3s 126 ground-attack missions, but not a single one was lost in aerial combat. Altogether, the Argentinians lost 100 aircraft including helicopters, the British twenty-four helicopters, six Sea Harriers and four GR.3s. The Argentine Air Force lost fifty-five men, thirty-six of them pilots. Four Sea Harrier pilots were killed. Lieutenant Nick Taylor of 800 NAS (Naval Air Squadron) was shot down, in XZ450, the first Sea Harrier to fly, over Goose Green by radio-controlled twin 35 mm Swiss Oerlikon anti-aircraft guns. He had transferred to Harriers weeks before the Task Force sailed; his body was recovered by local residents and given a proper military burial, recorded on film by the Argentine military. Investigating an unidentified blip on radar screens, Lieutenant 'Al' Curtis and Lieutenant Commander 'E-J' Eyton-Jones of 801 NAS disappeared into fog, rain and low cloud close to the wreck of HMS *Sheffield*, their deaths a mystery, although it seems likely that they collided in what was truly foul weather. Lieutenant Commander 'Gordy' Batt DSC of 800 NAS died when his aircraft exploded, without explanation, almost as soon as he lifted off from the deck of HMS *Hermes*.

The RAF lost no Harrier pilots, although Flight Lieutenant Grant Hawkins, working with the SAS, was one of many British servicemen killed when their Sea King helicopter flying from *Hermes* crashed into the sea north-east of the Falklands on 19 May. Three days later, Flight Lieutenant Jeff Glover of 1(F) Squadron flew a lone reconnaissance mission from *Hermes* and was shot down by the enemy over Port Howard by what is believed to have been a Blowpipe, a hand-held and British-made surface-to-air missile. Brigadier Julian Thompson, commander of 3 Commando Brigade, compared using the weapon to 'trying to shoot pheasants with a drainpipe'. Some pheasant, some drainpipe: one side of the Harrier's wing was blown clean off. Glover ejected, injuring his shoulder as he disappeared deep under water; picked up by a rowing boat, he was taken to Argentina and held there, starting with a spell in the military hospital at Comodoro Rivadavia, until the end of the conflict.

On his seventh sortie from *Hermes*, Squadron Leader 'Big Bob' Iveson, the handle-bar mustachioed son of the celebrated Second World War Bomber Command pilot, Group Captain

Douglas Iveson DSO DFC & bar who later flew Vulcans from RAF Waddington, was shot down over Goose Green, again most probably by a 35 mm Oerlikon anti-aircraft gun. Ejecting safely – although unconscious for a few seconds – and avoiding an Argentine Army patrol, Iveson holed up in an abandoned house for two days. He switched on his personal locator beacon after a storm, and a gunfight, died down and was winched aboard a British helicopter.

The last of the RAF Harrier pilots to be brought down was Squadron Leader Jerry Pook DFC on Sunday 30 May. On a sortie, with Flight Lieutenant John Rochfort, to take out an Argentine artillery position that was not where it should have been south of Mount Kent, Pook's Harrier was hit by small-arms fire. The Harriers were able to find and attack their target using traditional 'map-and-stopwatch' navigation, but by this time Pook's aircraft was leaking fuel at a rate that meant there was no possibility of his flying back to *Hermes*, 180 miles from Port Stanley. His radio worked only intermittently – a problem with many Harriers during the conflict – and one of his understandable fears was that he would be blasted out of the sky by a guided missile from a British warship. Luckily, Rochfort found him and was able to radio ahead for helicopter assistance. Pook ejected at 10,000 feet: 'My first Harrier ejection was extremely violent, and I clearly remember my head being forced down between my knees by the 3,000 lb thrust of the rocket seat.'

Despite fears that he would be unable to detach himself from his parachute as he hit the sea and struggled into his inflatable dinghy, Pook was picked up quickly by an anti-submarine Sea

King. He arrived on board *Hermes*, bloodied with cuts to his face, very shortly after Bob Iveson. 'We shook hands warmly,' Pook recalled, 'and the conversation went something like this: "Jerry, you're all wet – been for a swim?" "Something like that. I understand you've been taking a few days off in the country – you lazy sod!"' It was an exchange that could have taken place in the summer of 1940, although RAF pilots in the South Atlantic played a very different role from their predecessors in the Battle of Britain. They were flying from an RN carrier 8,000 miles from home, and their missions were ground-attack sorties rather than duels in high skies with enemy fighters. Furthermore, the weather, unlike that forty years before, was generally appalling. It is, perhaps, becoming harder, especially now that GPS, computers and digital technology have transformed the way so many of us communicate today, to envisage the conditions in which combat pilots like Iveson and Pook were flying. Imagine skimming the tussocky hills of the cold, dark, rain-soaked and wind-lashed Falklands in poor visibility, while being targeted and fired at from the ground, with nothing but your eyes, training, intelligence and reactions to guide you. These, and the nimbleness of the Harrier.

As we've seen, the mutual respect between RAF and RN Harrier pilots didn't preclude a degree of animosity. As Pook himself put it when the clouds broke as he returned to *Hermes* one evening and he had a moment to enjoy the view as he listened to controllers 'giving their laconic instructions' to Sea Harriers directed to intercept an incoming raid:

Not for the first time did I feel a twinge of envy
at the Sea Harriers' cushy job, now that they had
given up Ground Attack on the Admiral's orders.
No interminable hassling with an idiotic Air Task
organisation for them, and no sordid grovelling
about in the weeds to attack unseen targets while
their aircraft were shot full of holes by every man
and his dog. No: it would be an air defender's life for
me in the next war – if I survived this one. Plenty
of hanging about admiring the scenery from a safe
height, punctuated by the very occasional burst of
excitement when you were directed on to a 'bogey'
– usually some panicky attack pilot running for his
life after a desperate attempt to hit the target. After
a brief stern chase just a press of the trigger was
enough. No map reading at zero feet, and no return
fire. Just the roaring smoke trail of your American-
built 'Lima' as it sped unerringly on its way to its
speeding target. Finally the animal thrill of elation
as the brief fireball smashed your enemy into the
sea. Shoot down and back home you would be sure
of the medals and adulation of the girls – after all,
only *real* fighter pilots get to shoot down planes,
don't they? Those GR.3 pilots just moved dirt
around – anyone can do that.

The situation was hardly helped when on 28 May a formation of
three GR.3s flying low over Falkland Sound were set upon by a

pair of patrolling Sea Harriers flown by Sharkey Ward and Flight Lieutenant Ian Mortimer. The 'Shars' had dived in behind the GR.3s, their missile switches set, before 'Morts' realized their mistake and, alerting Ward, called off the attack.

The RAF pilots were certainly hard pressed. After just eleven days in action, five of their six Harriers had been lost or severely damaged, and when 1(F) Squadron's CO, Wing Commander Peter Squire DFC, went to see Captain Linley Middleton, the skipper of the *Hermes*, to discuss the possibility of replacement aircraft being shipped to the carrier, he recalled that the reply had been: 'No. I think it's a waste of time: it's just the RAF trying to lay on a publicity stunt.' Middleton, a veteran Fleet Air Arm pilot who had seen action at Suez in 1956 and flown 2,643 hours in Hawker Sea Furies and Sea Hawks as well as Supermarine Scimitars and Blackburn Buccaneers, was overruled by the Admiralty; the replacement Harriers were duly flown the nine gruelling hours from Ascension Island just as the first six had been shortly before.

Wing Commander Squire's experience commanding 1(F) Squadron during the Falklands conflict was to stand him, the Harrier and the RAF in good stead in Iraq and Afghanistan in years to come. Like his fellow pilots, he was forced to learn the hard way, and very quickly indeed. The 'light blue' Harriers had flown from RAF St Mawgan in Cornwall to Ascension Island in the equatorial South Atlantic on 3 May shortly after a transatlantic training flight to Goose Bay, Labrador and back to practise air-to-air refuelling. Together with eight Sea Harriers of 809 NAS, they were then loaded on board the *Atlantic Conveyor*, a

14,950-ton Cunard roll-on, roll-off container ferry requisitioned by the MoD. Shortly after the Harriers arrived safely – the Navy aircraft were split equally between *Hermes* and *Invincible* – the *Atlantic Conveyor* was hit by two Exocets launched from Super Étendards flown by Captain Roberto Curilovic and Lieutenant Julio Barraza. The ship sank, becoming the first British merchant vessel to be lost at sea to enemy fire since the Second World War, and with her went the six Wessex and five Chinook helicopters that had been scheduled to carry men and materiel across to the main island. Now the troops had no alternative but to make their famous, and ankle-wrenching, 'yomp' over sodden heaths and through treacherous bogs to Port Stanley.

In the thick of the action, Squire flew unscathed until late into the conflict before having to eject, after engine failure. Squire's father, Wing Commander Frank Squire DFC, had flown Consolidated Catalinas on maritime patrols with 210 Squadron during the Second World War. Squire himself had flown Hunters from Singapore and Harriers in Germany before the Falklands, and went on to become Air Chief Marshal Sir Peter Squire and Chief of the Air Staff from 2000 to 2003. His input into the development of later-model Harriers was to prove invaluable. Meanwhile, during the Falklands conflict itself, the design team at Kingston had been kept busy working on instant improvements to the jump jets; these included the provision of chaff and flare dispensers, which the Harrier had previously lacked, to fox enemy radar and heat-seeking missiles. The dispensers were rushed into production and dropped from the air to the Task Force by an RAF Hercules transport aircraft.

Squire, Pook and others had voiced concerns at the time about particular faults with the Harrier – that lack of chaff, those intermittently functional radios, faults with the navigation system and, as always, a fundamental lack of power: Harrier pilots always wanted more thrust than the Pegasus was able to deliver. Over and above all this, they felt, quite rightly, that they were being asked to fight a dirty low-level, ground-attack war without the latest weaponry. It was only in the very last days of the conflict that the GR.3s were finally fitted with laser-guided bombs that allowed the aircraft to keep back just far enough away from their targets to avoid being shot down. The RAF pilots had every reason to want to do their duty and get home safely: unlike in the Battle of Britain, most GR.3 pilots were married men with children, and some were approaching forty. They were not flying for old lies – *dulce et decorum est pro patria mori* – much less for hatred of the enemy, or certainly not the enemy they encountered; they were too grown-up, too professional and sometimes simply too cynical to believe in 'sabre-rattling' of any kind. They were certainly not aided in their arduous task by the attitude of some senior Royal Navy officers, and yet the Harriers of the two services still shared a victory fly-past over Port Stanley on 2 July.

The RAF pilots flew from *Hermes* to Port Stanley for the last time soon afterwards on a day when heavy snow was being driven across the carrier's deck by lacerating and freezing winds. Here was a moment to reflect, as Pook did:

> After the long-delayed launch we joined up into a
> loose tactical formation and headed west for the last

time towards the islands that had so nearly claimed our lives. En route we weaved through majestic halls of towering cumulus, which spewed dirty great snow showers into a sea glistening blue-black in the winter sunshine. From the air our erstwhile target, Port Stanley Airfield, looked serene and virginal under a light dusting of the first winter snow, the hand of Nature trying to atone for the violence done to it and its defenders.

The snow might have made take-off difficult for the Hercules that was to take the pilots back to Ascension Island and on home from there in the comfort of an RAF VC-10; here, though, the Harrier came into its own again. One of the newly arrived relief pilots from 3(F) Squadron hovered a Harrier up and down the runway, clearing snow with its powerful downblast. Even then, it was not all over for the exhausted pilots of 1(F) Squadron. They were ordered to return, with their GR.3s, from England to the Falklands for a spell from late August until Port Stanley Airfield was made ready for the fixed-wing jets that would guard the islands from then on.

From the beginning, the Sea Harrier had been designed as an interceptor, just as the RAF's Harriers had been designed primarily as ground-attack aircraft. In combat exercises made in the short period between their being placed in service and sent to the South Atlantic, Sea Harriers took on and won against US Navy Grumman F-14 Tomcats, USAF McDonnell Douglas F-15 Eagles and Northrop F-5E Tiger IIs, as well as RAF GR.3 Harriers.

Meanwhile, in the hands of the energetic, and outspoken, Sharkey Ward, the Sea Harrier had been making a public impact from early on. In September 1979, after the RAF had turned down the offer on safety grounds, Ward had landed a brand-new Sea Harrier – vertically, of course – on the football pitch alongside BBC's *Pebble Mill at One* studio in central Birmingham. *Pebble Mill at One* was a popular daytime television magazine show and the stunt was undoubtedly good PR for the Navy's latest fighter. Ward's landing was accompanied by the band of the Royal Marines, and while still in the cockpit he was given a kiss by the young cockney model Lorraine Chase, something of a latter day forces sweetheart at the time for her part in a television and cinema advert for Campari. 'Were you truly wafted here from Paradise?' asked a well-groomed chap as a dolled-up Chaise sipped a Campari in a 'posh' setting. 'Nah,' she replied, 'Luton Airport.' Ward had wafted in from RNAS Yeovilton, and had done so in just fifteen minutes from take-off as he followed the route of the M5.

As CO of 801 RNAS, Ward was appointed senior Sea Harrier adviser to Naval Command when HMS *Hermes* and *Invincible* set sail from Portsmouth with twenty Sea Harriers between them. Then thirty-eight years old, Ward had begun his naval flying career with Phantoms of 892 RNAS from the deck of HMS *Ark Royal*. He had been an air warfare instructor at RAF Lossiemouth and a NATO nuclear planning and intelligence officer at Kolsas, Ohio, before being asked to fly a desk as Sea Harrier project officer at the MoD in Whitehall. This was, says Ward, 'my first exposure to the "armchair" military and the devious and arguably dysfunctional senior echelons of that organisation'. Such an assessment was typical of Ward, a pilot and commander whose swashbuckling spirit, undoubted skill and courage, and sharp tongue popularized the myth and reality of the heroic, gung-ho fighter pilot into the beginning of the digital age when the very future of fighter pilots was in doubt. He did so, complete with a black Labrador – Jet – at his side, although at the time, as a family man, he drove a Volvo to Yeovilton rather than an MG, or the Lotus Cortina he had rolled in South Wales years before after a heavy drinking session at RNAS Brawdy.

After the sheer power of the Phantom, Ward took immediately to the subsonic Sea Harrier. It might not have been nearly as fast, nor with its high wing could it pull such tight turns as the big American fighter, but Ward was impressed with the aircraft. He liked its ability to fly so well at very low speeds, to get out of stalls and spins with a minimum of fuss, and to brake to a halt in the air; he also appreciated its low fuel consumption. And yet when the *Invincible* slipped anchor at Portsmouth, with Rod Stewart's 'Sailing' lilting from speakers along the quay, Ward was only too aware of the dangers ahead. It was not just that the Sea Harrier was untried in combat, but intelligence was not all it might have been. Performance data for the Mirage IIIA, for example, was gathered at sea from *Jane's All the World's Fighting Aircraft*, as was the number of Exocet missiles supplied to the Argentine navy. Of more concern was the fact that, following the Fairey Gannet's retirement in 1978, there would be no Airborne Early Warning (AEW) aircraft accompanying the fleet, even though later in the conflict missions would be flown by RAF Nimrods from

Ascension Island. As a result, since the Harrier's Blue Fox radar would only detect an enemy aircraft at a distance of fifteen miles – or less than two minutes' flying time if that enemy happened to be a Mirage IIIA or Dagger – pilots would be dependent on information relayed from ships' radar and, at close range, by what Ward and Co. knew as the 'Mk 1 Eyeball'. Furthermore, Blue Fox, although good in certain ways, was unable to look down and search for small targets over land or a rough sea, and the Sea Harrier's Sidewinder missiles could not 'see' over the horizon: they had to be fired in visual range of their targets.

The crews, whatever their fears, took a typically bloody-minded British approach to the situation. In the evening as they drank, they sang, if slightly ungrammatically and to the tune of 'Don't Cry for Me Argentina' from Andrew Lloyd Webber's 1978 hit musical:

On your bike Argentina,
The front line are getting airborne;
You've gone too far now, we've left the bar now
And soon the Falklands will be in our hands.

But not, thought Ward, if the Sea Harriers were in any way prevented from doing their best. And yet in some ways they were. Ward and his 801 Squadron colleagues were convinced that patrols to protect British ships were best flown at low level: this would 'put the frighteners' on incoming aircraft and ensure the Sea Harriers could respond very rapidly. In contrast, 800 Squadron pilots, under the command of Lieutenant Commander Andy Auld, were ordered to patrol at 8,000 feet and above to avoid the approaching enemy and save their Harriers. But this was tempting fate. By the time they had dived into action, a ship might already have been successfully attacked and the aircraft responsible would be racing back to base.

Ward was proved right when, after the conflict, the Argentinians admitted their fear of the Sea Harriers. So if the two RNAS squadrons had co-operated more fully, it is conceivable that fewer British ships would have been damaged or sunk. The fact that their tactics differed, or were allowed to differ, still seems puzzling: the two units had, after all, been formed together in 1933 after a reorganization of the structure of the Fleet Air Arm, with 800 flying Hawker Nimrod fighters and Hawker Ospreys as navigation leaders, or 'pathfinders', from HMS *Courageous*, and 801 flying Nimrods and Fairey Flycatchers from HMS *Hermes*.

Something similar had happened, albeit on a larger scale, in 1940, during the Battle of Britain. Air Vice Marshal Keith Park, the astute commander of No. 11 Group RAF in the south-east of England, was naturally disposed to get his Spitfires and Hurricanes up from their airfields and to altitude as quickly as possible to intercept the Luftwaffe. Others, the famously legless Douglas Bader among them, advocated the Big Wing, an arrangement by which fighters of several squadrons took their time to formate and then attack, theoretically in overwhelming force. There was something to be said for both tactics, although on balance Park's system proved more flexible, and more effective. The dispute caused much undignified acrimony, however, and almost certainly contributed to Park's subsequent removal from his command. Even today, Sharkey Ward believes that he had been fighting two battles in the South Atlantic, one against the enemy and one against the 'Flag', or Naval Command. He was not alone: many Sea Harrier pilots had the feeling that they were somehow only with the fleet on sufferance.

After the war, Ward, now promoted Commander, was appointed to be Air War Adviser to the Naval Staff and the First Sea Lord. 'But,' as he wrote in his thrilling and scathing book *Sea Harrier over the Falklands*, 'the brotherhood of fish-heads [Royal Navy] denied me the opportunity of ever commanding a carrier, and the brotherhood of crabs [RAF] continued to deny the Senior Service adequate organic air resources at sea. I, and many other fighter pilots, became tired of fighting donkeys and soon decided to leave Her Majesty's Service.' In 2001, Commander Ward flew in a Sea Harrier once again, but this time on the cushions of a two-seat trainer piloted by his son, Kris. It was Lieutenant Commander Kris Ward who in October 2010 was to confront David Cameron, the British prime minister, with the words: 'I am a Harrier pilot and I have flown 140-odd missions in Afghanistan, and I am now potentially facing unemployment. How am I supposed to feel about that, please, sir?' Cameron thanked Ward, adding that the decision to retire the Harrier was 'right' at a time of 'difficult decisions'. All too often, politicians simply don't get it, and they simply don't understand military matters. After all, who needs a new generation of Trident submarines when you can still have Harriers?

At it was, the Argentinians had surrendered unconditionally on 15 June 1982, the day before Peter Squire's diary records, 'I have managed to complete a Rubik's Cube', and the Battle of

Britain Association sent a message to 810 Squadron, 'From the Few to the Very Few! Congratulations on a job well done.' The end of the conflict did wonders for Margaret Thatcher at the polls, ousted the military regime, and prompted the return of parliamentary democracy, freedom of speech and the rule of law in Argentina. It also landed the British with a £2 billion bill as a strong military garrison was established on West Falkland to protect the islanders from future attack. Post-war euphoria saw the money voted through Parliament. Intriguingly, this was just the kind of expenditure that Lord North, the eighteenth-century Tory prime minister, had been concerned to avoid after the Falklands Crisis of 1770.

In June 1770, the Spanish governor of Buenos Aires, Francisco de Paula Bucareli y Ursua, dispatched five frigates under General Juan Ignacio de Madariaga with a complement of 1,400 marines to seize the Malvinas. The small British force there under the command of Captain George Farmer RN was forced to capitulate. Westminster reacted angrily, demanding that North act. But, although preparations were made for war with Spain, which by now had allied itself with French ministers spoiling for a fight with the perfidious English, the king of France, Louis XVI, backed off and the Spanish, fearful of fighting the British alone, opened negotiations with North's government. In the event, Spain withdrew and Britain regained its South Atlantic settlement, although the rather vague treaty signed between the two parties acknowledged that the return of the British did not 'affect the question of prior right of sovereignty of the Malouine, otherwise called Falkland's Islands'.

Although the North administration won plaudits for seeing off the French and Spanish, it was concerned not to spend ambitiously on this faraway corner of the world. It commissioned Dr Samuel Johnson, the eminent man of letters, to write a pamphlet – 'Thoughts on the late Transactions Respecting Falkland's Island' – to dissuade too enthusiastic a support for this distant and still tentative British sphere of interest. 'Thrown aside from human use,' wrote Dr Johnson, 'stormy in winter, barren in summer, [this is] an island not even the southern savages have dignified into habitation, where a garrison must be kept in a state that contemplates with envy the exiles of Siberia, of which the expense would be perpetual.'

Britain had other, more important matters at hand and in mind in 1770. In January, British troops clashed with American colonists; in March, they shot dead five Americans in Boston: the US War of Independence was brewing. Elsewhere, British trade and empire stretched to new limits with Captain Cook's discovery of the east coast of Australia. Meanwhile, at home the Industrial Revolution had truly begun: James Hargreaves had that same year taken out a patent for the Spinning Jenny and James Watt was beginning work on his improved steam engine. The modern world was well on its way.

Despite their defeat in 1982, for Argentinians the Falklands were to remain a matter of fervent and even quasi-religious national pride. The unshakeable belief that 'Las Malvinas son argentines' was written into the new constitution of 1994. And, when in 2012 the economy was dipping badly, the Argentine president, Christina Fernandez de Kirchner, began a new bout of sabre-rattling over the sovereignty of the Falklands at the same time as introducing new anti-terrorism laws that many Argentine intellectuals believe may be used against those who disagree with the government. A discussion paper – 'Malvinas: an alternative view' – written by a group of leading intellectuals, academics and 'free thinkers' (doubtless the government knows where they all live) and published on the internet on 2 April 2012, ahead of the thirtieth anniversary of the invasion of the Falklands, stressed that:

> Our worst tragedies have not been caused by the
> loss of territories or the lack of natural resources,
> but rather the absence of respect for life, for human
> rights, for institutions and essential values of
> the Republic such as freedom, equality and self-
> determination... the [Argentine] soldiers fallen in
> Malvinas demand above all that we do not again
> fall to the temptation of 'cheap patriotism' which
> took away their lives, nor use them as an element
> to sacralise positions that in any democratic system
> are debatable.

The Argentine government, however, refused to listen. In February 2013, Hector Marcos Timerman, the country's minister of foreign relations, came to London to tell Westminster how the Falklands would be taken over by his country within twenty years, whatever the people of the islands wanted. As the then twenty-two-year-old managing editor of the short-lived afternoon newspaper *La Tarde* in 1976, Timerman had initially supported the newly installed dictatorship but then changed tack the following year when the regime kidnapped and tortured his father, Jacobo Timerman, the influential editor and publisher of the centrist daily *La Opinión*, which had become increasingly critical of the regime. Jacobo Timerman was released in 1979 and sought exile in Israel. He had believed that he could play ball with 'soft liners' in the junta, yet, as his biographer Graciela Mochkofsky says, 'There were power struggles inside the armed forces, but there were no "soft-liners" when it came to disappearances and torture camps.'

Despite these sorry events, Hector Timerman still evidently believes that the Falkland Islanders have no right to self-determination; they are underdogs and must ultimately pay the price for daring to live in what is apparently Argentine living space, even though it is hundreds of miles across the sea from Buenos Aires. How the Germans who settled in Argentina from 1945 would cheer him on. Even now, at 6 p.m. every day, grenadiers march out of the Casa Rosada, the presidential mansion in Buenos Aires, and goose-step across the road into Plaza de Mayo, where they lower the Argentine flag for the night.

Perhaps some accommodation between Britain and Argentina can be reached in the future, and a way found to share the islands' bountiful fishing rights and, if they prove commercially exploitable, their untapped oil and gas reserves. But it seems unlikely. Some things and some countries never really change, just as some politicians will always appeal to the flag rather than to common sense. That said, the Falklands conflict certainly changed both British fortunes of war and the Sea Harrier. The lessons learned in aerial combat were put to good use in a number of modifications made to the FRS.1 that had been developed rapidly but not in time for deployment in the South Atlantic. In 1985, a contract was issued to British Aerospace – Hawker Siddeley Aviation had been merged into this corporate giant in 1977 – for two updated FRS.1s, the first, ZA195, being flown in September 1988 by Heinz Frick, a Swiss-born former RAF fighter pilot with extensive experience of Hunters, Lightnings, Phantoms, Jaguars and Harriers who had left the service in 1978 and become British Aerospace's chief Harrier test pilot in 1988. A total of forty-seven FRS.2 Sea Harriers were produced between 1993 and 1998, of which twenty-nine were rebuilds of FRS.1s. The aircraft were redesignated FA.2 in 1994; this was because, since the Falklands, the Sea Harrier was seen as first and foremost a fighter attack aircraft rather a than a fighter with reconnaissance and nuclear strike capability.

With a fuselage lengthened by very nearly three feet, a new wing, and greater firepower and load-carrying capability, the FRS.2 was a bigger aircraft than the original Harriers. A new and slightly bulbous nose housed the Blue Vixen all-weather radar system Falklands pilots had longed for; a 'multimode' system, it mapped the ground, detecting and tracking targets. A new surveillance camera was also installed in the nose. A greatly improved GPS air-navigation system, an updated radar-warning receiver and countermeasures were welcome improvements, as was an improved cockpit and head-up display. In terms of weaponry, the FRS.2 was armed with a pair of AIM-

9/L Sidewinders for Falklands-style dogfights and another of Raytheon AIM-120A air-to-air missiles, which now allowed pilots to take out targets fifty miles away, over the horizon and out of sight. The fifth weapon carried was an MBDA Sea Eagle, a radar-homing and sea-skimming missile with a range of over fifty miles. This was a formidable machine that was to see action in both the Balkans and Sierra Leone (*see* Chapter Six). In 2002, however, the Ministry of Defence announced the withdrawal of the Sea Harrier at the behest of Tony Blair's right-wing New Labour government.

The reasons given for the decision were twofold. The Pegasus engine fitted to the FRS.2 was insufficiently powerful when working in hot climates like the Persian Gulf, and a replacement would be too expensive, not least because the future role of the Harrier, whether flown by the Royal Navy or the Royal Air Force, was to be in ground attack. The Sea Harrier was, as we have seen, essentially an interceptor, and this role was presumably considered redundant by the MoD because Britain's future wars would be against countries, or factions within those countries, lacking combat aircraft. This was a point of view, but a typically short-sighted one. As Group Captain Harv Smyth DFC, who flew the GR.9A in action in Afghanistan until the last Harriers were taken out of service in 2010, put it: 'Because we [Joint Fighter Command] are asked to do a lot around the world, and because over the past twenty years every major mission we've undertaken has been a surprise, we really do need to be prepared.'

The last FA.2s, despite having many years of life in them, were retired from Sharkey Ward's old 801 RNAS in March 2006.

This, though, was not quite the end of the story. At least one other navy saw the attraction of the Sea Harrier. In 1979, having considered the Soviet V/STOL Yak-36M and Y-38, the Indian Navy ordered six Sea Harrier FRS.1s, which were delivered in December 1983. These were followed by a further seventeen FRS.1s and six two-seat trainers, although Indian pilots were also trained in Britain. As we have seen, the Indian Sea Harriers replaced veteran Hawker Sea Hawks and, equipped with Sea Eagles for anti-ship missions and French Matra Magic missiles for air-to-air combat, they flew from the decks of the newly modified 15,700-ton light carrier INS *Vikrant*, the former HMS *Hercules*, launched in September 1945 but never commissioned, then laid up and supplied to the Indian Navy in 1957 as part of Britain's war debt to India. Placed in service in 1961, this was India's first aircraft carrier; her Sea Hawks saw action in the war against Pakistan in 1971 and *Vikrant* was only retired in 1997.

Indian Harriers of 300 INAS (Indian Navy Air Squadron) fly today with INS *Viraat*, which is none other than the former HMS *Hermes*, flagship of the Falklands campaign. Launched in 1953, *Viraat* was due to retire in 2012–13, but delays in procuring two large carriers, a new 40,000-ton *Vikrant*, due in 2017, and the 65,000-ton *Vishal*, scheduled for 2023, may yet see *Viraat* celebrate its seventieth year in service. The question of exactly how long the Sea Harriers, which have never been in combat, will remain in Indian service appears moot: by early 2013, just twelve aircraft survived out of the original twenty-nine; the others had all crashed, although the surviving FRS.1s have been upgraded, from 2005 onwards, with new Israeli avionics and Rafael Derby air-to-air missiles made by Hindustan Aeronautics of Bangalore.

To bridge the gap between old and new carriers, the Indian Navy bought the 45,400-ton former Soviet Russian carrier *Admiral Gorshkov*, launched in 1982. Suitably modified, the INS *Vikramaditya* was due to enter service in November 2013. Significantly, this and the new Vikrant-class carriers will be seaborne platforms for Russian MiG 29-K and, possibly, French Dassault Rafale supersonic interceptors. They will mark the Indian Navy's move away from small carriers, V/STOL, the Sea Harrier and British aircraft. The Indian Navy had, in fact, been considering Russian aircraft for its carriers in the 1980s, but the Sea Harrier had won the day. The British aircraft's rival was the Yakovlev Yak-38. For a moment it had looked as if this multi-role Soviet V/STOL aircraft might have been not just a challenge to the Harrier, but a technological leap ahead of it. In some ways it was. The Yak-38 offered pilots an automatic, hands-free landing system, a godsend in bad weather at sea. All the pilot had to do was to fly to a point astern one of the three new Kiev-class carriers for which the Yak-38 was designed. At about 3,300 feet, the ship's electronics took control of the aircraft's computer, guiding it to a precise position on deck, bringing it down to land gently and shutting off its engines.

Unlike the Harrier with its single engine, the Yak-38 had three engines. A pair of Rybinsk RD-38 turbojets with a combined thrust of 15,740 lbs lifted and lowered the aircraft, while forward flight was achieved with a vectorable Tumansky R-28 V-300 turbojet with 15,000 lbs of thrust. This system worked, and the Yak-38, first flown in 1971, began sea trials with the Soviet aviation cruiser *Kiev* in 1975. And yet, although the Yak-38 was faster and notionally more advanced than the Harrier, just 231 examples were built, and all had been retired no later than 1991. In practice, the aircraft suffered so badly from hot weather and humidity on trials in the Black Sea and, critically, in the Indian Ocean that it was unable to carry external stores and take off at the same time. An oxygen-boosting intake system fitted during overhauls from 1979 helped, but the V/STOL Yak was to make a very poor impression when it was deployed in Afghanistan in spring 1980: the aircraft could carry just two 100 kg bombs and were not flown in hot, daylight hours.

The Yak-38, code-named 'Forger' by NATO, was an elegant-looking aircraft and a development of the Yak-36, a prototype developed from 1961 as a Soviet rival to the P.1127. However, because there was nothing like the Pegasus in the pipeline, Yakovlev engineers placed a pair of Tumanksy R-27-300 turbojets alongside one another, each with a thrust of 11,688 lbs, in a rather ungainly fuselage sporting a necessarily massive twin air intake. Each engine provided downward thrust through a single nozzle on each side of the aircraft's centre of gravity. Like the P.1127, the Yak featured a bicycle undercarriage and outrigger on the wing-tips. Two of the initial four Yak-38s were destroyed in crashes. Nevertheless, a first free hover was achieved in June 1963, a successful transition to forward flight six months later. One of the aircraft was given star billing at an air show held at Moscow's Domodedovo airport on 9 July 1967 as part of the official celebrations held that year to mark the fiftieth anniversary of the October Revolution. Yakovlev engineers, however, would have much preferred to develop the first Russian VTOL aircraft around a powerful single engine like Pegasus.

The Yak-38's poor performance encouraged the Indian Navy to look to the Sea Harrier. And, by 2013, the Indian Sea Harriers, although few in number, had outlived both their Russian rivals and their British siblings. Some years earlier, however, a Mk 2 Harrier had been developed, and it was this aircraft that the RAF and Royal Navy pilots flew together, in a Joint Harrier Force formed in 2000, until the end of 2010, and the US Marine Corps remains faithful to it to this day. In fact, it was American involvement in the Harrier story that was to take the Hawker aircraft to new heights even while the Mk 1 aircraft were fighting in the South Atlantic. The second-generation Harrier was, in the very best sense, an Anglo-American hybrid. The final brand-new FA.2s counted in by the Royal Navy from the factory at Kingston upon Thames on 24 December 1998, and photographed alongside a surviving P.1127, were the last all-British Harriers and also the very last all-British fighter aircraft. The future would be international.

CHAPTER 5

FOREIGN LEGIONS

Even after David Cameron's government had axed it in late 2010, the Harrier would always have Paris – and the US Marine Corps. It was in Paris, more than half a century earlier, that USAF Colonel John Driscoll, head of NATO's Washington-funded Mutual Weapon Development Project (MWDP), had met Michel Wibault and introduced him to Stanley Hooker in Bristol; it was in Paris that USAF Colonel Bill Chapman, Driscoll's successor, had agreed to the MWDP funding 75 per cent of the development costs of the Pegasus, the heart of the P.1127 and every last Harrier built. And without the involvement of the US Marines and their enduring enthusiasm for the aircraft, the Harrier would never have flown, nor fought for as long as it has; it was the Marines who had ensured that a second generation of the jump jet from Kingston upon Thames became a reality; and once again, it was the British who were the beneficiaries of

American largesse, as they had been before, especially from the moment when, following the Japanese attack on Pearl Harbor in December 1941, the US government, led by President Franklin D. Roosevelt, was able to lend an enormous helping hand to its old English-speaking cousin on the other side of the Atlantic.

The American love affair with the Harrier was tested from early on. The first US pilot to be killed flying the aircraft was Major 'Chuck' Rosburg at Dunsfold on 27 January 1969. A U-2 pilot posted to Britain to evaluate the GR.1, Rosburg had landed on what was intended to be his last Harrier flight before packing up and going home. For whatever reason, he told Dunsfold Control, 'There's something not quite right. I'm going to take it up again.' He did, vertically; but as Rosburg made the tricky transition with XV743 to forward flight, he lost lateral control and side-slipped at a 90-degree angle towards the ground. He ejected, sideways, and hit the deck.

Neville Duke, Hawker's former chief test pilot, who lived in a house in the grounds of Dunsfold, was among the first on the scene with his wife, Gwen, nursing the stricken pilot as best they could until an ambulance arrived; but Rosburg was dead. Thirty-five years old, he was a father of four children; at home in the States, his wife Shirley was expecting a fifth. Duke, a charming and modest man, was, along with Johnnie Johnson, one of Britain's most successful Second World War fighter pilots; he shot down twenty-seven German aircraft, and probably three more, flying American Curtiss Tomahawks and later Spitfires. Not a man to talk about warfare or 'heroics', Duke told me that Rosburg's death had made him think of how much his generation owed the Americans, and how lucky he was to be alive after his worst accident, when in June 1944, as the commanding officer of 145 Squadron in Italy, the engine of his Spitfire Mk VIII was holed by flak. When he tried to bail out, the harness of his parachute caught in the canopy. Hanging upside down from the stricken aircraft, he broke free at the last possible moment; he, and the Spitfire, plunged into Lake Bracciano, twenty miles north-west of Rome. Unable to release himself from the parachute, he was in real danger, but was rescued by two local village boys who swam out from the shore. The villagers looked after the twenty-two-year-old British pilot until he was picked up by advancing American soldiers and driven back to his squadron.

At Dunsfold, a quarter of a century later, Rosburg had fallen foul of the fact that the Harrier was unstable in the hover and at low speeds; he might have been saved had he booted the rudder and turned the aircraft into the wind to allow the ailerons to do their bit to keep the Harrier steady. Perhaps. As we have seen, Harriers were to be fitted soon afterwards with wind vanes in front of the windscreen, a simple and infallible device that made for much safer hovering. When, however, the Harrier went into service in the US, many of its pilots were to die in accidents, putting a strain on what was to remain a special relationship in spite of these casualties. In the Harrier's first decade of service, twelve US Marine Corps (USMC) pilots were killed, the first on 18 June 1971, when thirty-three-year-old Major Michael J. Ripley, a decorated combat pilot who had flown in Vietnam, crashed into Chesapeake Bay on a test flight from Pax River (US Naval Base Patuxent River, Maryland). The eldest of Ripley's three sons,

Charles, later recalled the excitement of hearing the sound of a Harrier approaching everyday around noon: 'My father would fly over and he'd tip his wings at us.'

Charles Ripley had, in fact, been speaking to two reporters from the *Los Angeles Times*, Alan C. Miller and Kevin Sack, who were to win the 2003 Pulitzer Prize for National Journalism with their long, thoroughly researched and well-written three-part feature on the Harrier that had been published the previous year. Miller and Sack tore into the Harrier with gusto, as if determined to end a relationship that their investigations led them to believe was mad, bad and not so much dangerous as deadly. In their opening salvo they wrote:

> The Harrier is the most dangerous airplane flying in
> the US military today. Over the last three decades,
> it has amassed the highest rate of major accidents
> of any Air Force, Navy, Army or Marine plane now
> in service. Forty-five Marines have died in 143
> non-combat accidents since the corps bought the
> so-called jump jet from the British in 1971. More
> than a third of the fleet has been lost to accidents.

Lesson one seemed to be: never trust the British. 'The Marines have known for years they were flying a plane bedeviled by mechanical problems... just about anything that could go wrong has gone wrong.' There was the 'temperamental engine', a 'persistent source of trouble, playing a role in more than half of all Harrier accidents between 1980 and 2001'. According to retired USMC Major Clinton M. Higginbotham, who had spent much of his career maintaining the Harrier, 'It was just a bad engine from Rolls-Royce.' In any case, it took 550 man-hours to replace this piece of 'cantankerous' British junk compared to the ten man-hours it took to refit an F-16 Fighting Falcon with a proper, all-American General Electric F110. The Harrier's cost per flight hour in 2001 was $5,351 compared to the $3,871 of a USMC F/A-18C Hornet. 'The Class A mishap rate for the first model of the Harrier,' meanwhile, 'was astronomical – 31.77 accidents per 100,000 hours. Notoriously unstable, it had a propensity for rolling over and slamming into the ground. Well over half were lost to accidents. One tragedy-scarred squadron dubbed the plane "the Widow-Maker"' – which, of course, is what Bundesluftwaffe pilots, among others, had nicknamed the Lockheed F-104 Starfighter. To cap it all, the Harrier was apparently useless in combat, and as Michael O'Hanlon, a defence analyst at the Brookings Institution, told reporters: 'You can find missions the Harrier can perform, but I question whether any of them are missions only the Harrier can perform.' As for the very idea of VTOL flight, this was clearly nonsense:

> Named after a low-flying marsh hawk [the polar
> opposite, of course, of a noble, high-flying American
> mountain eagle], the Harrier has a massive Rolls-
> Royce engine that supplies 23,800 pounds of thrust
> through four nozzles that pivot down to produce a
> shimmering blast of hot air. The thrust can propel
> the plane off the ground and into a hover, a process

pilots compare to balancing an elephant on the head of a pencil.

And what could be more absurd than that?

While there was a distinctly and unnecessarily anti-British tone to their prize-winning article, Miller and Sack did, in fact, identify the several key reasons why the USMC Harrier appeared to be so much more dangerous and so much less effective than its British cousins. The first of these related to maintenance:

> [Gunnery Sergeant John Higginbotham,] a senior Harrier mechanic at Cherry Point [North Carolina], said it was not so long ago that, with just three years under his belt, he was the most experienced mechanic in his squadron. In Britain, where maintenance-related mistakes are relatively rare, some Harrier mechanics have worked on the plane for more years than their American counterparts have been alive. Some Marine leaders acknowledge that the Harrier, quite simply, is often too complex for the recent high school graduates who typically maintain it.

Miller and Sack also discovered that all too many USMC pilots flew all too few hours with the Harrier on a regular basis. 'Investigators looking into the 1981 crash of a Harrier flown by 1st Lt. David S. Noble made a disturbing discovery. He had flown just 7.5 hours in the previous 30 days – half of what the Marines say is needed to fly the Harrier safely.' Worse still for the future, perhaps:

> Retired Lt. Col. John W. Capito, a former Harrier squadron commander, interviewed young pilots for the Harrier Review Panel and learned that many were flying just four to five hours a month right out of flight school. 'It's not enough time to fly a Cessna, much less a Harrier,' Capito said. 'These guys were getting a third of the flight time they needed and then people were wondering why they get into accidents.'

Perhaps the most revealing line in Miller and Sack's article was a quote from Susan Page, the widow of Colonel John H. Ditto, the highest-ranking American officer to die in a Harrier, and a pilot with 4,900 hours and two tours of Vietnam in his logbook, for the most part flying A-4 Skyhawks and F-8 Crusaders. In January 1981, with 13.7 flight hours with the Harrier, he lost control in a vertical take-off and ejected into the ground. 'I would love to think that there was something wrong with that airplane,' Page told Miller and Sack, 'love to think that in that heap of metal maybe they missed something wrong with it.' The implication – and certainly the one the *LA Times* journalists wanted their readers to draw – was that it was preferable to believe design flaws in a British aircraft had been responsible for Ditto's death rather than pilot error and, further, that buying British had been a mistake.

At the end of their Harrier-busting mission, Miller and Sack profiled the forty-five USMC pilots who had died flying their 'lawn dart'. Causes of death included flying after too little sleep, a flashlight dropped into the engine during maintenance, becoming disoriented in fog, taking off in heavy wind, flying into a mountain, the sea, or dense low cloud, a control stick jammed by a metal hose-connector left in the cockpit, banking too steeply, parachute failure, colliding in mid-air, being struck by lightning, prematurely exploding bombs, an incorrectly maintained engine, a wrong-sized engine component, being shot down over Kuwait during Operation Desert Storm or hit by an Iraqi ground-to-air missile, a broken fan blade, a fractured canopy and crashing in the hover. Sad and sometimes avoidable, this litany of fatal errors and deadly failures does not tell axiomatically of a poorly designed aircraft. Indian Navy pilots were to have an even worse time with the Harrier than the US Marines. Nevertheless, Miller and Sack's article underlined the fact that too many decent men were dying in training – let alone combat – and enough was enough. Highly trained Harrier pilots, and loving fathers, were surely not meant to be some latter-day equivalent of the Charge of the Light Brigade.

Understandably, the passions of bereaved families were fuelled by speculation – or could it be fact? – prompting concerns that the US Marines had been sold one of the world's very worst aircraft. 'He felt that most of the pilots he knew were very competent,' said Robert Van Sickle of his father, Captain Michael R. Van Sickle, who died when his Harrier crashed in 1992 during simulated bombing runs in Kuwait. 'They were just faced with a machine that was extremely dangerous and hard to control.'

Regardless of whether or not Miller and Sack were suffering from a bout of Anglophobia when they wrote their article, there is no getting away from the fact that the Harrier's US safety record was poor. This, though, does seem to have been the result of a combination of inadequate and even improper maintenance, and pilot error. The Indian Navy's safety record with its Sea Harriers was even worse than that of the US Marines with the AV-8B, while the British, Spanish and Italians fared extremely well in comparison. Perhaps Miller and Sack were also – consciously or not – following in the paths of other aggressive and eagle-eyed journalistic campaigns fought in the States against suspect machinery. One only has to think of Ralph Nader's memorable assault on the Chevrolet Corvair, a rear-engined family sedan that was accused of being 'The One Car Accident' in Nader's 'Unsafe at any Speed: the Designed-in Dangers of the American Automobile', published in 1965. This was the culmination of a campaign Nader had begun from the late 1950s, attacking the US automobile industry's inadequate safety record in both scholarly and mainstream magazines, and his subsequent influence on US journalism was both profound and lasting.

Such anxieties about the jump jet had certainly not been entertained by the USMC's Colonel Tom Miller and Lieutenant Colonel Bud Baker when, packed off to England in 1968 by Major General Keith Barr McCutcheon – himself a highly decorated Marine pilot who had served in the Second World War and the Korean and Vietnam wars, and who had taken a shine to the idea of the British aircraft – they had approached Hawker representatives at that year's Farnborough Air Show, and blagged ten flights apiece at Dunsfold. Their enthusiastic reports did much to encourage the US Navy to order a batch of twelve aircraft from Hawker the following year using money earmarked for F-4J Phantoms, although the hard work of persuading Congress had been down to McCutcheon.

It had been a huge step for the US military: American was biggest and best, but as there was no American answer to the Harrier, the military establishment gave in. Not only did Bud Baker get to command the first dozen Harriers, which were designated AV-8A, with Marine Attack Squadron 513 based at Yuma, Arizona and flying from USS *Guam*, a 19,395-ton Iwo Jima-class amphibious assault ship launched in 1963, but Kingston got to build these machines and, by 1976, another 100 aircraft in four further orders. First delivered in 1970–71, the AV-8As were flown out in kit form from England, by Lockheed C-5 Galaxy and Lockheed C-141 Starlifter jet transports, to the McDonnell Douglas plant at St Louis, Missouri, where they were put back together again. The original plan had been to build the AV-8As under licence at St Louis, with Pratt & Whitney supplying American-built Pegasus engines. The relatively small numbers of aircraft involved meant that the costs would have been too high, although the idea was soon to be revived.

Meanwhile, the Harriers were put through their paces at Pax River and aboard USS *Guadalcanal*, a sister ship to *Guam*, and the newly commissioned 16,405-ton landing ship or amphibious transport dock *Coronado*. Both types of ship had been designed with helicopters in mind, yet the AV-8A proved to be a welcome guest. At Pax River, Major Harry W. Blot, the US Harrier project officer, developed the art of 'viffing', or vectoring in forward flight, using the Harrier's nozzles as extremely powerful air brakes. Significantly, the US Harriers were also fitted with the Sidewinder missiles that were to prove so effective in the Falklands War when fired from Royal Navy Sea Harriers.

The US Marines cherished their Harriers, despite a high accident rate, but were soon asking for more power. A gutsier Harrier would be able to carry more bombs, rockets, missiles, guns and fuel. A proposal for a Pegasus 15 promised 24,500 lbs of thrust, but given the engine had a fan blade 2.75 inches too big to fit into the existing Harrier airframe, clearly a bigger aircraft was the answer. With a larger wing, new avionics and plenum chamber burning, the AV-16, as the project became known, would be supersonic and thus an aircraft with appeal to both the US Navy and the Marine Corps. For a moment, it seemed as if the supersonic jump jet Hawker had wanted to build ten years earlier was a real possibility. Cost and politics soon intervened. The US baulked at the idea of paying the entire cost of the development of the AV-16 with Britain getting the benefits for nothing in strictly financial terms, while the question of jobs – who would get to build the supersonic jet and where – was uppermost in the minds of many US politicians and manufacturers. The tentative 'Joint Advanced Harrier Programme' was dropped in 1975.

It was, however, resurrected soon afterwards, although in a cheaper and more manageable guise, but only after the British agreed to drop their own plans for an improved Harrier. In August 1981, after much wrangling, Britain agreed to buy the proposed new Mk 2 Harrier – the American AV-8B, the British GR.5 – with McDonnell Douglas manufacturing 60 per cent of the aircraft, measured in terms of man-hours, and British Aerospace making the remaining 40 per cent. As for the engine, the latest version of the Pegasus would be built by both Pratt & Whitney and Rolls-Royce which, by now, had taken over Bristol Siddeley: Rolls-Royce would be responsible for 75 per cent of construction and for final assembly. The aircraft would be completed, ready for delivery, at St Louis, with those destined for the RAF being shipped back across the Atlantic. This was not exactly a case of 'coals to Newcastle', but it did mark a fundamental change in the Harrier programme, with the Americans, who had done so much to engender the P.1127 and the AV-8A in the first place, setting the pace and calling the shots from now on, and with the British cast as subcontractors. As it turned out, British personnel involved in the development of the AV-8B found their work much easier in the United States than it had been at home. John Farley, Hawker's test pilot, recalled:

> I didn't always enjoy working on the Harrier/
> Sea Harrier programme in the UK as it was too
> political... we seemed to spend all our time pitching
> the aircraft to politicians to save the project from
> cancellation. With the Marines, the reverse was true;
> there was never any doubt that they would get the
> aircraft they wanted from the project.

The Mk 2 Harrier was not just a bigger aircraft than its predecessor, but a substantially different one. Its new wing, with a 20 per cent greater span and 14.5 per cent increase in area, was made of carbon fibre, 300 lbs lighter than it would have been in metal and four times as strong. To date, this was the largest carbon-fibre component employed in a military aircraft. All told, carbon fibre, also used in the rudder, flaps, nose, forward fuselage and stabilizing surfaces on the tail, added up to 26 per cent of the total weight of the AV-8B, a saving over metal of 480 lbs; and because every extra pound imposes a penalty on small combat aircraft like the Harrier, this was a significant saving. Large slotted flaps allowed greater lift, especially in STOL mode, and more control at slow speed, while the greater strength of the new wing meant the Mk 2 could carry more than the AV-8A and GR.1. The Mk 2 was slower in terms of top speed, but this was not particularly important to the US Marines, for whom the aircraft was to be used first and foremost skimming trees, waves and dunes in support of ground troops.

A larger cockpit, and raised seat, was crowned with a bubble canopy giving the pilot a good all-round view. Instrumentation was quite different. Instead of an array of analogue dials and scatterings of switches, the pilot was faced with a neat display of screens: the Harrier had truly entered the digital age just as, in fact, the mobile phone and desk-top computers were quietly revolutionizing the working lives of manufacturers, politicians and journalists. A new 'hand-on-throttle-and-stick' arrangement allowed pilots to keep their hands on these all-important controls while operating other devices as well as weaponry. Switches and buttons built into the throttle and control stick operated by gloved fingers and thumbs spelt an end to pilots having to fumble, 'hands-off', for the right switch. Such controls would shortly become familiar to Formula One racing drivers and, all too soon, to millions of people around the world as they played the relevant computer games and convinced themselves they could out-fly a Harrier pilot. Yet whatever digitally empowered armchair pilots might like to believe, the virtual experience can only ever approximate to real flight in wind or low visibility, in uncertain and possibly lethal conditions.

A prototype Mk 2, converted from an AV-8A, first took to the air at Lambert-Louis airport on 9 November 1978, three-and-a-half years after the North Vietnamese took Saigon and the tragic twenty-year Vietnam War came to a bruised and bloody halt. It was the sway of public opinion in the United States, along with North Vietnamese military prowess, that had done so much to put an end to a war fought for a dogma – the Domino Principle – which posited that the whole world would go communist if the United States stayed at home and did nothing. In the end, the communist world collapsed pretty much all by itself. If wars had to be fought after the Fall of Saigon on 30 April 1975, they would surely be the kind of small, localized conflicts to which the Harrier would be ideally suited. The Cold War, however, with its threat of Mutual Assured Destruction, still raged, albeit without a single atomic bomb being dropped in Europe or anywhere else, for that matter. No one could predict how warfare would twist and turn in the last quarter of the twentieth century.

Charles A. Plummer, McDonnell Douglas's chief test pilot, had flown the improved Harrier early that morning in November

1978. Among those watching from the ground was Bill Bedford; but where the British test pilot had managed just a perfunctory and distinctly wobbly, if revolutionary, hop on his first flight back in 1960, Plummer held his red, white and blue aircraft in the hover, at 130 feet, for seven minutes. Five years later, Plummer demonstrated the military capability of an early production AV-8B to the Navy and the Marines at Pax River. Making a short take-off, Plummer lifted into the air within 270 yards, carrying seven 570 lb bombs but no external fuel tanks. He flew low and fast 422 miles to his practice target, dropped his bombs accurately and then, soaring up to 42,000 feet, shot back to Pax River to land vertically, the mission having taken two-and-a-half hours; and all this with 800 lbs of fuel remaining in the internal tanks. It had been an impressive performance.

The first production AV-8Bs, replacing A-4 Skyhawks, went to Marine Attack Squadron VMA-331, which was fully operational by September 1986. Eventually, 175 aircraft were delivered to seven front-line squadrons and one training squadron; the number included fifteen two-seat TAV-8Bs. On the other side of the Atlantic, the RAF's No. 1 Squadron went fully operational with its brand-new GR.5 Harriers on 2 November 1989, exactly a week before the East German government announced that its citizens were free to cross the Berlin Wall. The Cold War was over.

The new Harriers were upgraded continually as computer systems and digital technology raced ahead in winking, bleeping leaps and bounds. Digital engine control systems were followed by night-attack radar systems (GR.7; 1990), new weaponry and a final upgrade of the long-lived Pegasus (GR.7A; 2002). Not only could the latest engines produce 23,800 lbs of thrust – more than twice that of the engines installed in the P.1127 – but they now ran at lower temperatures and with far greater reliability than ever before. The last upgraded Harriers (GR.9A, with engines adapted to hot climates) were delivered to the RAF in 2006, just four years before the entire fleet was prematurely retired. The GR.7A and GR.9 variants were all rebuilds of existing airframes, the last of which was manufactured in 1992. Two-seat T. Mk 10 trainers were also built over the next three years; these were converted to T. Mk 12 standard between 2003 and 2006.

The GR.9s went into battle, looking more like birds of prey than ever with their bigger, brooding wings, and armed to the teeth with laser-guided American Paveway IV bombs. Then there was the unfulfilled promise of British Brimstone anti-armour missiles and a host of further improvements, including fly-by-wire, that were scheduled to be made between 2006 and 2015. These last British Harriers were strong enough to have carried a P.1127, in terms of weight, into the skies. They were to prove highly effective war-birds.

The Spanish and Italian navies certainly thought highly of their Harriers too. Both ordered Mk 2s and continue to fly these in 2013. As we have seen, when, in 1996, it had replaced the AV-8As it had ordered during the Franco years, Spain sold seven of its first generation of jump jets to the Royal Thai Navy. These served on board the newly launched flagship HTMS *Chakri Naruebet*, an 11,486-ton carrier built by Bazan (now Navantia) in Spain. Three years later, only one of the Harriers was operational even though the Thai Navy had not been at war. The *Chakri*

Nuruebet had, though, been involved in several humanitarian missions, demonstrating that the military can be a powerful force for good. To date, the Thai flagship has only been to war in virtual fashion, playing the part of USS *Ranger* in Werner Herzog's *Rescue Dawn*, a film set during the Vietnam War and released in 2006. The Thai Navy had been interested in replacing its rapidly diminishing AV-8A, or 'Matador', fleet with AV-8Bs, but the deal fell through during 2003, and the last Thai Harrier was retired three years later.

The US had been in discussion over sales of both versions of the Harrier at various times with Australia, Brazil, Switzerland, Japan and the People's Republic of China, as had the British with the Chinese during the Labour administration of James Callaghan in the late 1970s. However, fears of a Soviet backlash and, then, the Chinese invasion of Vietnam in 1979 in response to the Vietnamese invasion and occupation of Cambodia put paid to any such deal. The Vietnamese action had, though, at least succeeded in ousting the unspeakably vile regime of the mass-murderer Pol Pot, who had killed some two million, or a quarter, of his own people, making the Argentine generals and their stooges look like pale amateurs.

The Spanish, meanwhile, re-equipped with VA-2 Matador IIs, which arrived at the naval air station at Rota, near Cadiz during 1987 and 1988. These replaced the Matador Is, taken out of service by the end of 1996. As a matter of record, the first-generation Harriers flown by the Flotilla de Aeronaves' Octava Escuadrilla (8th Squadron) over twenty years proved to be exceptionally reliable, unlike, it seems, USMC AV-8As in the United States.

Four aircraft were lost in those twenty years, and only one pilot – Lieutenant Cesar Jauregi Garcia, lost off the coast of Cabrera in May 1980 – was killed. The Matador IIs operated from the deck of the Armada's new flagship, the 15,912-ton *Principe de Asturias*, which was launched in 1982 but served a decommissioning notice by the Spanish government in November 2012. At this time, the Spanish economy was performing very poorly indeed, and deep cuts were made in military expenditure. However, the Harrier fleet comprising eleven Matador IIs and five Matador II Plus's – these with engines providing 23,600 lbs of thrust – were still able to fly from the 27,079-ton multi-role warship *Juan Carlos I*, launched in September 2009 but ordered six years earlier, before Europe was hard hit by the deepest recession it had experienced since the 1930s.

The Italian Navy was a fan of the Harrier, too. It had wanted the aircraft since 1967, when the anti-submarine helicopter carrier *Andrea Doria* had hosted a GR.1 Harrier. However, an arcane law dating from 1937 that had survived the Second World War insisted that the Marina Militare was not allowed to fly fixed-wing aircraft. This was rescinded in 1989 and the Navy was able to order eighteen Harriers, sixteen of them single-seat AV-8Bs and all but three of these assembled by Alenia Aeronautica, Turin. Initially, the Harriers flew at sea from the 10,100-ton carrier *Giuseppe Garibaldi*, launched in 1983, but from 2009 they also operated from the new Italian flagship, the 27,100-ton carrier *Cavour*. The Italian Harriers' first mission abroad, with NATO in early 1995, was to protect the withdrawal of UN forces from Somalia, the lawless East African state with an appalling human rights record. They did this successfully, and performed flawlessly.

As the Mk 2 Harrier evolved, so it was to become a more reliable, more accurate and deadlier weapon. It would prove that it could contribute very usefully in serious, set-piece conventional wars like those in Iraq. It would also demonstrate that it could be deployed in a much more 'asymmetric' conflict like the awkwardly named Operation Enduring Freedom in Afghanistan, where its all-round flexibility and reliability would be prized, along with its ability to attack targets with pinpoint accuracy, thereby minimizing collateral casualties. The Harrier's pilots, at least, were never to lose their fondness for an aircraft that, at its zenith, was the brilliant offspring of a sometimes turbulent relationship between Great Britain and the United States of America, and of two very different ways of fighting a war.

CHAPTER 6

NEW WARS FOR OLD

Saddam Hussein was a son of a bitch. This much was known to US, British and other servicemen, including the Harrier pilots involved in fighting in Iraq in 1991 and again in 2003 and, in between, patrolling the skies over what had been the cradle of Western civilization some six thousand years ago. Saddam Hussein was also our son of a bitch – America's, Britain's and Western Europe's – a nasty dictator whose Ba'ath party had been helped into power in 1963 with the connivance of Washington in a country that had been created by Britain after a peevish carve-up of the Middle East by Britain and France after the First World War. A part of the idea had been to keep the Russians at bay and Turkey weakened, and to ensure the safe passage of newly discovered Iraqi oil to Western Europe and the United States.

When Iran became a threat to Western interests after the Shah was toppled in 1979, Saddam, who at the time had been making overtures to the Soviet Union, found himself bombarded by good wishes from the United States. From now on, he would be America's strongman in the Middle East, provided with money, military intelligence, special advisers and armaments of every kind – especially biological weapons and poison gas – and with these he would fight a protracted war against Iran throughout most of the 1980s and against citizens of his own artificial state, the Kurds to the north and Shi'ite Muslims to the south.

The Americans loved the beaming Saddam. In 1980, he was given the keys to the city of Detroit, while in 1983 and again in 1984 Donald Rumsfeld, President Reagan's special envoy to the Middle East, was packed off to Baghdad to reassure and do business with him. The British were clearly fond of him, too. Shortly after Saddam had been appointed deputy president of Iraq in 1969, Glencairn Balfour Paul, the British ambassador to Iraq and a keen Arabist, offered his impressions of this 'presentable young man' with 'an engaging smile' to Whitehall. 'I should judge him, young as he is, to be a formidable, single-minded and hard-headed member of the Ba'athist hierarchy, but one with whom, if only one could see more of him, it would be possible to do business... responsibility may mellow him.' Almost, in fact, the sort of chap Balfour Paul might have played cricket with at Sedburgh and Magdalen College, Oxford. But when the affable British diplomat, who had explored the Ennedi foothills of Tibesti by camel during his years as district commissioner of Sudan, took a somewhat uncritical view of the Ba'athist party,

Saddam went on to gas the Kurds in the mountains of northern Iraq and to drain the marshes in the south of his country where Shi'ite tribesmen had lived in harmony with nature for hundreds of years. It is estimated that over half of Iraq's chemical weapons equipment came from West Germany, but Britain did her bit too, financing a chlorine factory that would manufacture mustard gas. Many other countries, including Austria, Brazil, China, Egypt, Holland, India, Luxembourg, Singapore and Spain, provided Saddam's regime with stockpiles of chemical weapons.

As it was, in December 2003, a deposed and greatly aged Saddam was found by US soldiers in a hole in the ground covered with a rug and polystyrene sheeting in an orange grove near his hometown of Tikrit. A hut stood nearby, the last of the Iraqi dictator's many homes; this one boasted just the one room fitted out with two beds and a fridge containing a can of lemonade, a box of Belgian chocolates and a packet of hot dogs. No air-conditioning. No gold taps. 'I am the president of Iraq,' declared the bearded man in the hole, 'and I want to negotiate.' There was no negotiation. After the United States had dealt with their former strongman, he was handed over to his Shi'ite enemies, who taunted him to his death at the end of a rope and filmed his last horrible moments on their mobile phones.

While there can be no pity for Saddam Hussein, his story has been hugely important in shining a spotlight on the heartless double-dealings by the world's superpowers and their allies with the small and Third World countries that have fought their wars, economic and military, by proxy since 1945 and have done so at an accelerating rate over the past quarter of a century. The ironies and sheer complexity of these struggles have led to seemingly absurd situations. From 1979 and for the following ten years, the Americans fought the Soviet Union in the wilds of Afghanistan not with Marines and Harriers, but through the Mujahideen, a ragbag yet highly effective army of jihadist Muslims, financed and armed by the governments of Jimmy Carter and Ronald Reagan. Among the ranks of the Mujahideen were foreign adventurers including the wealthy Saudi Arabian Osama bin Laden. In hindsight, it seems absurd that Washington was so keen to spite the Soviets that it aided the man who devised the assault on the twin towers of the World Trade Center in New York some twenty years later and, if by default, led the US into a tangle of mistaken and even incomprehensible wars that would drag on until the present day. And it was these wars that saw the Harrier in action year after year in theatres far removed in every way from those it was designed to perform in during the Cold War itself.

Having bogged itself down in Vietnam, ostensibly fighting a war against the spread of communism, the US appeared to have learnt little or nothing when, along with its allies, it invaded Afghanistan in 2001 and Iraq in 2003. One of the great tragedies of Vietnam was that Ho Chi Minh, the hugely popular North Vietnamese leader, had longed for Washington to be his ally. Not only was George Washington his personal hero, but during the Second World War he had helped rescue US pilots and passed on intelligence about Japanese plans to the Americans. In 1945, he wrote personally to President Truman asking for US help in the liberation of Vietnam from French colonial rule now that the

Japanese had been defeated. Truman, who chose not to reply, took the side of the French; over the next few years, hundreds of thousands of Vietnamese starved as the rice they grew was shipped to France for a pittance. Ho Chi Minh, who had been a line manager with General Motors in Detroit in the 1920s, became a dedicated communist. American fears of the spread of communism were hardly dampened by Fidel Castro's military victory in Cuba in January 1959 and his subsequent conversion to communism, nor by Nikita Khrushchev's pledge of support, made in January 1961, to 'wars of national liberation'. The Americans went into Vietnam, full time, in 1965. Two years later, Dr Martin Luther King gave a speech in which he said:

> They must see Americans as strange liberators...
> even though they quoted the American declaration
> of independence in their own document of
> freedom, we refused to recognize them. Instead, we
> decided to support France in its reconquest of her
> former colony. Our government felt then that the
> Vietnamese people were not ready for independence,
> and we again fell to the deadly Western arrogance
> that has poisoned the international atmosphere for
> so long.

Ho Chi Minh died in 1969, but the United States lost its war in Vietnam. By the time Saigon fell to the North in 1975, however, some one-and-a-half million of the country's civilians had been killed. The United States had dropped 6,727,084 tons of bombs on Vietnam, compared with the 2,700,000 tons dropped by Allied bombers on Germany during the Second World War. American aircraft had also sprayed 3.5 million acres of farmland and rainforest with napalm and other chemical weapons: the effect of these will not finally wear off for many decades to come. Meanwhile, US dead amounted to some 58,000.

It was not as if the Americans had no idea of what they were doing. In 1968, James C. Thompson, who had recently resigned from the State Department over increasing US involvement in South-East Asia, wrote a prophetic article, 'How Could Vietnam Happen? An Autopsy', for *The Atlantic* magazine:

> There is a final result of Vietnam policy I would cite that holds potential danger for the future of US foreign policy: the rise of a new breed of American ideologues who see Vietnam as the ultimate test of their doctrine. I have in mind those men in Washington who have given a new life to the missionary impulse in American foreign relations: who believe that this nation, in this era, has received a threefold endowment that can transform the world. As they see it, that endowment is composed of first, our unsurpassed military might; second, our clear technological supremacy; and third, our allegedly invincible benevolence (our 'altruism', our affluence, our lack of territorial aspirations). Together, it is argued, this threefold endowment provides us with the opportunity and the

obligation to ease the nations of the earth toward
modernization and stability: toward a full-fledged
Pax Americana Technocratica. In reaching toward
this goal, Vietnam is viewed as the last and crucial
test. Once we have succeeded there, the road ahead
is clear. In a sense, these men are our counterpart
to the visionaries of Communism's radical left: they
are technocracy's own Maoists. They do not govern
Washington today. But their doctrine rides high.

It certainly did. Although the United States was defeated in
Vietnam, those same missionary ideologues were to mount
their high horses and ride off to do battle with anti-American
forces with increasing frequency and fervour in the decades
following the fall of Saigon. And they fell in along the way with
some very odd fellow missionaries indeed, none stranger than
Tony Blair, the right-wing British New Labour prime minister
who had the light of Jesus in his eyes and a love of George W.
Bush and what this oil man called his 'War on Terror' that defied
all understanding. Bush Jr was, of course, not just the draft-
dodging, war-mongering president of the United States who
took the United States and Britain into battle in Afghanistan in
2001 and Iraq two years later, but also the son of George H. W.
Bush Sr, the former US president and ally of Saddam Hussein
until America's strongman dared to invade Kuwait in 1990 and
to seize that country's hugely profitable oil wells. At least, Bush
Sr was a highly decorated US Navy pilot, who had signed up aged
eighteen and flown Grumman Avengers in the thick of action

against the Japanese from the deck of the 11,000-ton carrier USS *San Jacinto* in 1944–5.

This potentially toxic mix of zealous high-mindedness and realpolitik spilled over not when Saddam invaded Kuwait, but a decade later when Osama bin Laden and al-Qaeda attacked Manhattan using scheduled US airliners as guided missiles. From then on, US motives became a tangle of the politics of revenge, ideological zealotry, the show of arms, the wiles of the oil lobby and a variety of other factors. Taken together, they threatened to drag the country into the many Vietnams that Che Guevara, in a speech given at the United Nations in New York in 1964, believed would bring the United States to its knees.

I mention all this because such was the new world of war that the Harrier and those who flew, maintained and directed it found themselves in from 1990, when Saddam overstepped the mark. One of the great ironies of the situation is that the Iraqi dictator himself, despite being a Sunni Muslim, believed in the secularist state and was no friend whatsoever to fundamentalist Islamist jihadists. In fact, the reason the United States left him in power after Operation Desert Storm in 1991 was that Washington was concerned that, without its errant strongman, Iraq would be taken over by Shi'ite Muslims who would side with Iran and so create a climate in the region that was hostile to Western interests. When I travelled through Iraq in 2002, I spoke to Sunni and Shi'ite Muslims along with Sufis, Roman Catholics (Tariq Aziz, Saddam's imprisoned former foreign minister, is a Chaldean Catholic), Jews and Yazidis: while many despised Saddam, they were deeply fearful of US military intervention, which they –

unlike the oily British government mouthpieces I spoke to at the time – acknowledged was coming, and felt that without a strong, secular leader, Iraq would be plunged into bloody chaos and even civil war. As for democracy, most could only raise a knowing smile; as Dr Hamed Youssef Hamadi, Saddam's uniformed minister of culture, put it to me, his hand toying with the handle of a revolver, 'My dear, oil and democracy do not mix.'

Saddam's fatal error was in invading Kuwait. Iraq, which had laid claims on Kuwait, once a part of the Basra province of the Ottoman empire, since the early 1930s, had tried this once before, and failed. In 1960, just months before Kuwaiti independence, Harold Macmillan's Conservative government got wind of an invasion of what at the time was still a British protectorate by the Iraqi dictator General Qasim Abdul Karim. This was planned to coincide with the third anniversary of the 1958 Revolution during which the twenty-three-year-old, Harrow-educated King Faisal II and his family were murdered and the short-lived Hashemite kingdom became the Republic of Iraq; Qasim aimed to seize Kuwait the moment it won its independence. Britain, however, wished to protect its interests in the Persian Gulf, and, most of all, its supply of Kuwaiti oil. The concession for the exploitation of Kuwait's vast untapped oil reserves had been granted to the Kuwaiti Oil Company. This was 50 per cent owned by British Petroleum (BP) and 50 per cent by Gulf Oil of Pittsburgh, USA. The British government owned 51 per cent of BP. With so much at stake, Macmillan packed off Lord Home, his foreign secretary, to Washington to win US approval of his plans.

Once this was granted, Operation Vantage could begin. A fleet of a dozen Royal Navy warships converged on the Gulf the same week as the maiden flight of the second Hawker P.1127. HMS *Victorious*, later relieved by HMS *Centaur*, sailed with a squadron of dashing, twin-boom de Havilland Sea Vixens. These flew patrols over Kuwait while a force of 7,000 marines and infantry landed, along with Centurion tanks, armed personnel carriers, helicopters and artillery. RAF Hunters and Canberras were on alert from Aden, Bahrain and the British protectorate of Sharjah. It was an impressive display of force. Qasim backed down and Kuwait's independence was assured. The British maintained a plan for rescuing the state should Iraq try again until 1971.

In 1990, though, the coast had seemed clear. Saddam apparently believed either that the Americans had no fundamental objection to his annexing Kuwait or that he was powerful enough to fight them off. He was very wrong on both counts. It took seven months to plan and prepare, but when it was finally launched, Operation Desert Storm, a coalition of thirty-four nations led by the United States and sanctioned by the United Nations, proved to be a terrifying war machine. Opening with a massive aerial assault on 17 January 1991, the campaign saw very nearly a million UN soldiers – nearly three-quarters of them American – take on the Iraqi army. 'The great duel, the mother of all battles, has begun,' said Saddam in a state radio broadcast. It was all over within six weeks, during which time 482 coalition soldiers were killed, while the Iraqi dead numbered at least 25,000. Coalition aircraft under the USAF's Lieutenant General Chuck Horner had flown over 100,000 sorties, losing seventy-five aircraft, forty-four to Iraqi missiles and anti-aircraft fire and just one in air-to-air combat.

The UN forces were huge in number because the US, Britain and other guilty parties had helped build Saddam's army into the world's fourth largest. At the end of the war with Iran in 1988, it comprised 955,000 regular troops and a paramilitary Popular Army with 650,000 recruits, plus 4,500 tanks, 484 combat aircraft and 232 combat helicopters. Yet those tanks and most of those aircraft were standard Soviet-bloc hardware, suitably de-rated for export purposes and in many cases verging on obsolescence. In contrast, the US and its allies could call upon a veritable arsenal of hi-tech weaponry. They had Tomahawk cruise and AGM-130 air-to-ground missiles as well as Patriot interceptors, and their aircraft, armour and munitions benefited from the very latest digital electronics and guidance systems. All this, together with the sheer ferocity of the uncompromising assault led by General 'Stormin'' Norman Schwarzkopf, brought about colossal destruction of Iraqi infrastructure in and around Baghdad and the blitzing of Saddam's tanks and principal regiments along what became known as the 'Highway of Death' from Kuwait to Iraq. Ultimately, there was no possible hope of success for a regime that, although highly militarized, lacked the technology and command structure to resist an onslaught on this scale.

Saddam lost, yet he still got to mass-murder Kurds under the eyes of the Americans, drain the Qurna marshes, and set some 770 Kuwaiti oil wells on fire, causing the greatest amount of financial and ecological damage possible. In short, he was allowed to carry on. Various plots to topple him, including a failed US coup in 1996, came to nothing, but in October 1998 Bill Clinton's administration enacted the Iraq Liberation Act that called specifically for regime change and the overthrow of Saddam. The stage for the second act of the Gulf War had been set, although the justification for raising the curtain on it had yet to be found. And ironically, it was to be al-Qaeda, an organization Saddam despised, that would three years later provide at least part of that justification when it attacked the Twin Towers.

For the Harrier, this was a very different sort of war, one which was not going to involve popping up from forest clearings close to the East German border or even darting over Norwegian fjords. US Marine Corps AV-8Bs were involved extensively in the first Gulf War. Based on the USS *Nassau* and *Tarawa* as well as on land bases, they had gone into action on 17 January, initially against Iraqi artillery shelling Khafji, the border town between Kuwait and Saudi Arabia. Working in close collaboration with the US Army, AV-8Bs flew 3,380 sorties over 4,083 flight hours. Five were lost to Iraqi surface-to-air missiles, with two USMC pilots killed. General Schwarzkopf considered them to have been a great success, and from 1992 to 2003 AV-8Bs were kept busy policing the No Fly Zone over southern Iraq; this was not as peaceful a period as many people imagine and, although no Harriers were involved, Iraqi and US aircraft did clash.

Later, nine RAF Mk 2 Harriers – GR.7s – were sent to Turkey from RAF Laarbruch in early 1992 to police the No Fly Zone over northern Iraq and what was nominally, if not legally, Kurdistan.

The aircraft of all three front-line RAF Harrier squadrons – 1, 3 and IV – were equipped with reconnaissance pods that helped not only with the immediate problem in hand but also with evaluating how and exactly where a future war with Saddam might be fought. (Such a war seemed momentarily to inch closer in June 1993, when the Iraqis made an assassination attempt on George Bush Sr while the US president was on a trip to Kuwait.) The RAF Harriers performed well, although an engine surge that occurred when refuelling from a VC-10 tanker in November 1993 caused one pilot to eject over Dahluk. He was picked up by an American helicopter, while Kurdish villagers, who were duly rewarded with livestock and other presents, guarded the remains of his jet. The RAF was beginning to learn about the need to win hearts and minds as well as positions, 'kills' and battles. The No Fly Zone missions were handed over to RAF Tornados in January 1995.

But before both British and American Harriers became engaged in the 2003 invasion of Iraq, there were other combat missions to be flown. The first were during the Bosnian War of 1994–5. This vile affair was one result of the break-up of Yugoslavia, the kingdom and, latterly, communist federal republic that, in one guise or another, had held together the fractious countries, disputed territories and fathomless ethnic divides of the Balkans. From the end of the Second World War until his death in 1980, Yugoslavia was very much the fiefdom of Marshal Josip Broz, or Tito (a *nom-de-guerre* Broz adopted during the guerrilla war he led from 1941 against German and Italian invaders). A benevolent dictator – of sorts – Tito, who had fallen out with Stalin in 1948 and who suppressed nationalist sentiments inside Yugoslavia, created a non-aligned communist republic that became a favourite destination for British package holiday-makers in the 1970s and 1980s. What none of these sun-seekers could have known is that the country was soon to tear itself apart in the first war on the European mainland since 1945. Nor could they have known that this would be one of the most savage of all twentieth-century conflicts. Here, or so it seemed, was a well-ordered and even rather 'liberal' socialist state adorned with some of the most beautiful stretches of coastline to be found anywhere in the world, exquisite inland towns, venerable countryside and mountains that attracted swarms of enthusiastic skiers.

The Balkans nightmare began on 29 February 1992 when the Socialist Republic of Bosnia and Herzegovina declared its independence as the republics of Croatia and Slovenia had done the previous year. The problem was that Bosnia was a country whose population was divided between Bosniak Muslims, Catholic Croats and Orthodox Serbs. Bosnian Serbs now established their own republic with Radovan Karadžić, a part-time poet and psychologist, as president. Across the border in the Republic of Serbia, Slobodan Milošević saw this as his chance to create a Greater Serbia. Allying himself to Karadžić, and Serbian Croats, Milošević unleashed a war against Bosnia's Muslim population, pursued mostly by the Bosnian Serb army led by Ratko Mladić and by murderous Serbian paramilitary units including the Scorpions under Slobodan Medić and the White Eagles founded by Dragoslav Bokan and Mirko Jović. Their dirty and cowardly war was characterized from the start by the indiscriminate shelling of civilians, systematic mass rape of women including children, brutal massacres and a stated policy of 'ethnic cleansing'.

The United Nations attempted to create a No Fly Zone over Bosnia and safe areas within it, to protect its persecuted Muslim population. The Serbs ignored both. On 16 April 1994 an FRS.1 Sea Harrier flown by Lieutenant Nick Richardson, operating with 801 NAS from HMS *Ark Royal*, was shot down over Goražde, one of the nominally 'safe zones', by a shoulder-launched SA-7 surface-to-air missile. Richardson, who had been trying to bomb a pair of Bosnian Serb T-55 tanks, ejected and, scrambling to Bosnian Muslim lines, was rescued by the SAS; a French Super Puma helicopter took him back to the carrier. The *Ark Royal* was based in the Adriatic; she was relieved by her sister ship HMS *Invincible* with the Sea Harriers of 800 NAS. Together, the Sea Harrier squadrons flew 1,748 missions over the Balkans. A second aircraft was lost on 15 December 1994 when Lieutenant David Kistruck – in later life, General Manager Flight Operations, Virgin Atlantic – was forced to eject due to control failure while hovering alongside HMS *Invincible*.

NATO stepped up aerial attacks on Bosnian Serb positions the following July in the aftermath of the Srebrenica massacre. In a hugely deflating moment for both NATO and the United Nations, lightly armed Dutch troops guarding this 'safe zone' for Bosnian Muslims had proved unable to hold back Mladić's forces; although harried by aerial attacks, these were well supported by tanks and artillery. Air support was delayed at the crucial moment as the international bureaucracy of coalition warfare denied instant action when it was needed. Mladić entered the town, separating out men and boys from the ages of twelve to seventy-seven for 'interrogation for suspected war crimes'. Held in lorries and warehouses, more than 8,000 were murdered between 12 and 17 July. Less than a year before, the Greek Orthodox Church had declared Karadžić 'one of the most prominent sons of our Lord Jesus Christ working for peace' and decorated this protector of the 'western frontiers of Orthodoxy' with the Byzantine Knight's Order of the First Rank of Saint Dionysius of Xanthe. Mladić was his all too willing disciple. NATO launched Operation Deliberate Force in August. By the end of that month, twelve GR.7 Harriers of IV Squadron had flown from RAF Laarbruch in Germany to Gioia del Colle airbase in the heel of Italy to fly a total of 126 sorties against the Bosnian Serbs using free-fall and laser-guided bombs.

All the principal warring parties finally signed a peace treaty in Paris on 14 December 1995. Among those who eventually stood trial for genocide, crimes against humanity and breaches of the Geneva Conventions were Milošević, who died in 2006 before a sentence was handed down, Karadžić and Mladić. The courts at The Hague were still in session at the time of writing.

This, though, was neither the end of conflict in former Yugoslavia, nor the end of the Harrier's involvement in the Balkans. Trouble flared up again in 1998, this time in what had been the autonomous province of Kosovo in the south of Serbia. The Kosovan population is primarily Albanian, and, after Tito's death, demands arose for an independent republic. The Serbs saw this as an attempt by Albania to increase its territory. The result was a Serbian assault on Kosovo and more blatant savagery and 'ethnic cleansing'. NATO struck back on 24 March 1999 with Operation Allied Force, fought entirely from the air. In the name of Yugoslavia, Serbia declared war on NATO. Bill Clinton, the US president, and Tony Blair, the British prime minister, declared that this was 'ethical foreign policy' in action. This, perhaps, encouraged the Canadian Air Force to play such a key role in the operation: it was responsible for 10 per cent of all the bombs dropped in the defence of Kosovo. The Luftwaffe went into action for the first time since the Second World War. The Italians followed with their Mk 2 Harrier AV-8Bs, while the RAF flew GR.7s in ground-attack sorties and the Royal Navy patrolled with FA.2 Sea Harriers operating from HMS *Invincible*.

Finnish-Russian diplomacy led by Finland's president Martii Ahtisaari and the threat of an invasion by tens of thousands of US and British troops put an end to the Kosovo conflict in June 1999. Air strikes had been partly effective, but also controversial. President Clinton had exaggerated the numbers of civilians either killed or under threat in Kosovo at the time of Operation Allied Force, possibly as a justification for the extraordinary scale of the NATO assault on Milošević. Even without the benefit of hindsight, Operation Allied Force seems to have been something of a sledgehammer to crack a nut – a very tough nut, perhaps, and a very nasty enemy, too. New aircraft like the Northrop Grumman B-2 Spirit stealth bomber, equipped with satellite-guided 'smart bombs', were tested in action for the first time. The B-2s flew all the way to Serbia and back from their base at Whiteman, Missouri, yet for all the cleverness of their technology and weaponry, it was a B-2 that accidentally dropped a bomb on the Chinese embassy in Belgrade, killing three Chinese newspaper reporters.

Cruise missiles, meanwhile, were dropped from American B-52s, flying from RAF Fairford, or else launched from US warships and the Royal Navy submarine HMS *Splendid*. Tony Blair sent more RAF Harriers – altogether, sixteen GR.7s and seven FA.2s saw action in Serbia and Kosovo – charged with bombing ground targets in Kosovo. In Moscow, the Russian president Boris Yeltsin – possibly deep in his cups – warned of a Third World War unless NATO backed off. In the event, Russian troops were parachuted into Pristina, the Kosovan capital, as a peacekeeping force on 12 June, two days after Milošević signed a peace treaty and withdrew from Kosovo. By this time, NATO had mounted no fewer than 10,484 sorties, with the British contributing 1,018. And only then did NATO ground forces enter Kosovo. They did so as peacekeepers, a duty afforded them by a conflict fought entirely from the air.

Civilian deaths caused by NATO bombing may have amounted to 500; it remains difficult to uncover exact numbers. But without doubt, the aerial assault brought murderous Serbian aggression to a rapid halt and spared the lives of thousands of soldiers and civilians who might have been killed in a more prolonged land battle. The Serbians lacked convincing air power – their poorly maintained MiGs were no match for NATO jets – but their army was strong and well equipped with Russian tanks, artillery and missiles.

NATO countries, meanwhile, had little appetite for further loss of life among the enemy, civilian population or indeed their own numbers. In 1999, British airmen could expect to get home safely, and they had every reason to want to. A moving BBC news report in late June 1999 showed ten Harriers returning to RAF Wittering from the Balkans. The first pilot to step down was forty-one-year-old Squadron Leader Chris Huckstep, greeted by his wife Gill and their five young children.

Huckstep and his colleagues were, however, deeply concerned that their efforts – no matter how gutsy the pilots – had not been as effective as they would have liked them to be. Without troops on the ground, it was very hard to prevent the kind of violence against civilians in which the Serbs specialized. NATO aircraft were required to patrol above the range of shoulder-held missiles. Targets down below were tiny, all but abstract things.

Harriers were led to them by forward air controllers, one of whom, the USAF's Major Thomas Feldhausen, appeared in a *Frontline* documentary for American public television with Squadron Leader Huckstep and described how the system worked:

> I said, 'Okay, let's imagine you're in a car.' And I'm telling this on the radio. 'I want you to drive the car up until you get to the warehouse that's green on the left, and I want you to turn left there. I want you to go down the road until you see the fork.' And he's telling me all the time on the radio, 'Yeah, I see that. Yeah, I see that.'

Huckstep explained what might happen next:

> [I would be on the radio] saying, 'Found the target,
> happy with that. I can see the little tiny vehicles that
> we're talking about.' And then just as I round out to
> set up for the attack, the American calls. You know,
> 'Hold it!' or words to that effect. 'There's a civilian
> bus pulled up next to them.'

It was not just that Harrier pilots had to be sure what they were hitting when they went into the attack, but the fact that there were so many chains of command, so many checks and agreements to be made in this coalition war, all of which made their missions complex and highly demanding affairs. And, as Major Feldhausen remarked as he summed up the situation in Kosovo, 'Air power can do an awful lot of good, but it's never going to stop the ability of a guy on the ground of taking a can of gasoline and lighting a house on fire or lining a group of civilians up against a wall and shooting them.'

Deployed on board USS *Nassau*, and later USS *Kearsarge*, US Marines flew a dozen AV-8Bs over Kosovo from 14 April for the loss of one aircraft that crashed into the Adriatic while returning to the *Kearsarge* from a training mission. The American view of how the war should have been conducted was summed up for *Frontline* by Lieutenant General Michael C. Short, the Allied Air Force commander, and a highly decorated Vietnam veteran with 276 combat missions and 4,600 hours flying fighters under his gold-braided cap:

Let me shoot very straight with you. I believe before
the first bomb was dropped that the door should
have been closed with all those who wished to go to
war. And the United States should have said very
clearly, 'It appears NATO wants to go to war in the
air, and in the air only. If that is the case and that
is the sentiment of the nations here, we will lead
you to war. We, the United States, will provide the
leadership, the enabling force, the majority of the
striking power, the technology required. We will
take the alliance to war, and we will win this thing
for you. But the price to be paid is we call the tune.
We are not just one of nineteen.'

Short may well have had a point. As it was, Britain went alone
into Sierra Leone, with RAF Harriers of the newly formed
Joint Harrier Force, the following year. This beautiful West
African country, a British colony from 1808 until 1961, was
rich in diamonds, gold, titanium and bauxite, and yet the vast
majority of its six million people lived in dire poverty. To make
matters worse, the country was torn apart by a savage civil war
that spanned the 1990s. Corrupt governments were challenged
by the Revolutionary United Front (RUF), a guerrilla army of
malcontents formed by Foday Saybana Sankoh, a British-trained
former corporal with the Sierra Leone Army, with the backing of
Charles Taylor, leader of the National Patriotic Front of Liberia.

The civil war was a complex, ever-shifting affair involving
coups, changes of government and national leadership, and

atrocities that shocked a world that, by now, ought to have been unshockable. Sankoh's Army looted and raped with impunity, and chopped off the limbs of men, women, children and babies to get their own way, to spread terror and for fun. Fuelled by drugs, drink and savagery, the RUF killed at least 50,000 people, mutilated many more and displaced a third of the country's population. Boys and girls, fed on drugs and forced to kill their own parents, were abducted to serve as soldiers and prostitutes for RUF guerrillas.

UN peacekeeping forces sent late in the day came under attack, and 500 were kidnapped. In 2000, Britain's war-hungry prime minister Tony Blair made his one popular military intervention overseas: Operation Palliser. The idea had been to rescue British and other foreign nationals under threat in Sierra Leone. But when Brigadier David Richards arrived in Sierra Leone with 800 British paratroopers flown in from England via Dakar in Senegal, he was deeply shocked by the sights that greeted him.

Hospitals were crowded with those hacked by the machetes of the RUF; there were amputees on the streets of Freetown and crowds of desperate refugees. All were victims of Sankoh's own 'Operation No Living Thing'. Richards made a decision to arm government troops, to protect Freetown and the people of Sierra Leone, and to stop the president, the economist and barrister Ahmad Kabbah, from fleeing the country in a helicopter.

'It is the best thing I have ever done in the British Army,' Richards said later. 'I have no regrets, none at all. You can't look at a kid with his hand chopped off and just walk away. You have to sometimes make this choice, do what you think is right, even if people above you don't approve.' In London, however, Blair approved. Richards, now General Sir David Richards and currently Chief of the Defence Staff, was vindicated. The British pushed back the rebels and took on splinter groups like the murderous West Side Niggaz (known in the Western media as the West Side Boys), a loose group of brutalized young men, some of whom had tortured their own parents to death and were either drunk or as high as kites most of the time. They were influenced, they said, by American 'gangsta rap' culture.

Sea Harriers, at first, and then GR.7s – thirteen altogether – were flown from HMS *Illustrious* over rebel troops in May and June 2000, mostly to frighten them. This will sound hare-brained only to those who have not stood under a pair of low-flying, full-throttle Harriers: it is an aircraft that speaks with a voice of intense thunder. These sorties, though, also impressed upon rebels the power of the forces that might yet be stacked up against them, although it was difficult to see quite how effective the Harriers would have been in a prolonged guerrilla war with a light-footed enemy using dense jungle as cover.

From 1 April 2000 – an odd date to choose – the Royal Navy's Sea Harrier FA.2 squadrons and the RAF's Harrier GR.7 squadrons had been brought together as Joint Force Harrier (JFH) within RAF Strike Command. When the Sea Harriers were withdrawn in 2006 to save yet more money, 800 NAS was re-formed and equipped with GR.7s from 3 Squadron as it changed over to Eurofighter Typhoons. At the same time, the strength of Harrier squadrons was cut from twelve to nine aircraft. This allowed 801 NAS to convert from Sea Harriers to GR.9s.

Tony Blair, meanwhile, had won plaudits for the action taken in Sierra Leone, yet was to lose much of his credibility in Britain, if not in the United States, when he teamed up in gun-slinging fashion with President George W. Bush to invade Iraq in 2003, this time with the intention of instigating 'regime change', or ridding the country of Saddam Hussein. The invasion was based on absurd premises, among them the utterly mistaken supposition that Saddam possessed nuclear weapons he could deploy both quickly and credibly, and the erroneous belief that he had given succour to al-Qaeda. Worse still, no plans were made for the future of Iraq post-Saddam, and it seemed as if the British Cabinet had absolutely no clue about either the history of Iraq or the obvious fact that, nasty as he might be, Saddam was holding together ideological factions that would inevitably try and tear one another apart once the West's former strongman had been forcibly removed from office. In short, the wise counsel of both diplomats and foreign affairs specialists with first-hand knowledge of the area was either not asked for or simply ignored.

The force deployed against Saddam was astonishing, although not as massive as it had been in 1991. The Bush Jr regime had been limbering up for a showdown in the area with Operation Enduring Freedom, an attack on terrorist training bases and al-Qaeda strongholds in Afghanistan weeks after the breathtaking al-Qaeda assault on the World Trade Center in Manhattan on 11 September 2001. US Marines arrived off the coast of Pakistan the following month and flew attack missions from 3 November. In December, the USMC AV-8Bs were deployed from a base at

Kandahar, and from Bagram the following October. It was the start of a war that continues to this day.

The assault on Iraq began in 20 March 2003, when Baghdad was heavily bombed in a show of what the Americans called 'Shock and Awe'. Protests against the invasion held around the world on 15 February by some ten million in 800 cities had been dismissed by Washington and London; according to the *Guinness Book of Records*, it had been the largest protest in history. Well organized and largely well equipped, the invasion force – including a number of Polish and Australian troops – swept through Iraq in three weeks. Baghdad was seized, Saddam toppled and Bush announced, 'Mission accomplished.' Well, not quite. The last British and American combat troops finally left Iraq at the end of 2011 and the country in a mess. The British, in particular, had been humiliated; they might have helped win the war but they could not hold the peace, being eventually compelled to evacuate their forces from the southern city of Basra under cover of darkness. At least scores of thousands of civilians had been killed and the liberal democracy Bush and Blair believed would suddenly flourish in Iraq had unsurprisingly failed to take root.

In purely military terms, the invasion was quick and, for the British at least, as clinical an operation as possible. Operation Telic, commanded by Air Marshal Brian Burridge, saw 46,000 British soldiers scythe through Iraq by land and air. The RAF flew round-the-clock missions with impunity, even refuelling aircraft over Iraq. Twenty Harriers were based at Ahmed Al Jaber airbase in Kuwait, as were USMC AV-8Bs. The use of BAE Systems Thermal Imaging Airborne Laser Designator Pods allowed Harrier pilots to attack targets within what had become strict rules of engagement to ensure, as far as possible, that only legitimate military targets were attacked and hit. Pilots made use of GPS as well as hand-held binoculars: their attacks tended to be highly accurate. Tactical liaison between troops on the ground and Harrier pilots was close and reliable: about 30 per cent of all RAF Harrier operations were close air-support missions. Burridge spoke convincingly of the RAF and British troops moving 'nimbly' through Iraq, of trying 'not to break china' and of swift humanitarian aid. The Americans did not necessarily share the same view, although they did listen, sometimes, when Burridge explained how a particular air strike might look 'viewed from Paris, Berlin or wherever'. Warfare was coming under increasing scrutiny. It had done so since Vietnam, and even though George Bush Jr had got the United States excited about the fight against Iraq – one poll showed that, in January 2003, 44 per cent of Americans had been persuaded to believe 'some' or 'most' of the 9/11 hijackers were Iraqis – the president knew there had to be a limit to the number of US casualties, although he had little or nothing to say about the deaths, torture and mutilation of Iraqi civilians.

American Harriers flew in Iraq from 2003 to 2010. Over a thousand sorties were flown from sea during the 2003 war, the aircraft moving up to land bases when possible for closer and more urgent co-operation with the army. The aircraft were used successfully as tank-busters and as aerial artillery during the siege of Fallujah in 2004 – an operation that, while successful, witnessed the United States using white-phosphorus incendiary shells to flush insurgents from city-centre buildings.

By the summer of 2003, British Harriers had left Iraq. Fifteen months later, six GR.7s replaced USMC AV-8Bs at Kandahar, Afghanistan. Harriers would fly here for the following five years in a war that will have lasted for thirteen years by the time Britain and the United States pull out at the end of 2014. It was here that the Harrier mutated into its final form, the GR.9 and GR.9A. It does seem a little odd that the most impressive attack version of the Harrier should have been employed against such a low-tech enemy as the Taliban in a war that should never have dragged on for anything like so long.

The Taliban, a fundamentalist Islamic movement, established the Islamic Emirate of Afghanistan, with Kandahar as its capital, in 1996. It was recognized by just three other countries – Pakistan, Saudi Arabia and the United Arab Emirates. Its other great unofficial supporter was the United States. Washington liked the anti-Shia stance of the Taliban because this meant it was axiomatically anti-Iranian. The Taliban was also keen, or so it seemed, on plans for a trans-Afghanistan pipeline proposed by Unocal (Union Oil Company of California; now a part of Chevron). The Taliban's extreme behaviour could be laughed off when it appeared to be merely eccentric. According to Amy Waldman, then a reporter with the *New York Times*, one list of prohibitions made by the movement included satellite dishes, cinematography, musical equipment, pool tables, chess, masks, tapes, computers, lobsters, nail polish, fireworks, sewing catalogues, pictures and Christmas cards. According to an official US report, the Taliban had also banned clapping during sports events, kite-flying, drawings, stuffed animals and dolls. Men had to wear beards and hats while women were no longer to be educated or employed or allowed to play sport.

There was, though, nothing funny in these prohibitions; they were issued by unkind zealots who were soon enough doing terrible things to their fellow citizens. And the borders of Afghanistan and Pakistan were indeed safe havens for jihadist terrorists. Even so, the escalation of international war within this remote and largely poor country was a sorry episode. The very presence of British and US forces attracted fundamentalist fighters from various parts of the world, including those born and bred in Britain itself, while local farmers took down their guns from their racks and were loosely labelled 'Taliban', even though all they wanted was for the British and the Yanks to go home.

And given that military targets were often blurred with everyday civilian activities, it was very hard indeed to fight anything like a clean and just war against an enemy who could vanish as easily into a crowd in a marketplace as into mountain hideouts. As Colonel Richard Kemp, commander of British forces in Afghanistan from 2003 to 2006, remarked:

> The Taliban in southern Afghanistan are masters
> at shielding themselves behind the civilian
> population and then melting in among them for
> protection. Women and children are trained and
> equipped to fight, collect intelligence, and ferry
> arms and ammunition between battles. Female
> suicide bombers are increasingly common. The
> use of women to shield gunmen as they engage

NATO forces is now so normal it is deemed barely
worthy of comment. Schools and houses are
routinely booby-trapped. Snipers shelter in houses
deliberately filled with women and children.

The Joint Force Harrier (JFH) squadrons were on duty in
Afghanistan as part of Britain's Operation Herrick and NATO's
International Security Assistance Force (ISAF) for five years. They
returned home in June 2009 having flown more than 8,500 day
and night sorties and having spent over 22,000 hours airborne.
There were normally eight Harriers on duty – at first GR.7s
and then the more powerful, digitally wired GR.9s – and eleven
pilots supported by around a hundred engineers and fitters.
Each sortie lasted an average of eight hours with the Harriers
loaded to their aerial gunwales with every piece of weaponry
and hi-tech gadgetry they could carry. Each pilot, as Lieutenant
Commander James Blackmore, who flew many of those sorties
over Afghanistan and around its borders, has written, was 'pilot,
navigator, engineer, communicator, weapons officer and lawyer'.

The world of JFH pilots during those five years was as unlike
that of Battle of Britain Spitfire and Hurricane pilots, or indeed
jet pilots at any time during the Cold War, as can possibly be
imagined. There were no enemy aircraft to worry about or
intercept and little danger from weapons fired from the ground.
Instead, patrols and sorties were flown to support British and
coalition troops on the ground, to frighten and disturb Taliban
positions, using 'shows of force', and to maintain a presence
over warring territories. Contrary to the American experience of

the Harrier reported in the *Los Angeles Times* in 2003, the JFH Harriers performed extremely well. According to Lieutenant Commander Blackmore, 'Harriers never once lost a mission due to an unserviceable aircraft... the only times that the Harrier failed to get airborne in the five years of operations was if the weather curtailed flying.' And that wasn't often. When conventional jets were unable to take off because the airfields at Bagram, Kabul and Kandahar were snowed or iced in, the Harriers usually carried on with their relentless day-in, day-out close air-support missions.

When called by troops on the ground, Harriers were expected to be in the air within thirty minutes. The average time of a 'scramble' from Kandahar was sixteen minutes, with a record of eleven. This, as the pilots themselves say, was not bad considering the Harriers were a two-minute drive from their ops room. Take-off from Kandahar was not, however, a piece of cake. The elevation of the airfield is 3,330 feet, so the Harriers, unable to take off vertically when so heavily laden, needed to accelerate to about 200 mph before lifting into the thin air. As the speed limit for their tyres was a little under 210 mph, this left little margin, especially in hot weather. (The average high temperature in Kandahar in July is 40.2 °C, or 104.4 °F.) Levelling off at 100 feet, the aircraft would begin their climbing turns at 345 mph, soaring above this ancient settlement.

Kandahar may well take its name from Alexander the Great, who laid out a Greek-style city here in the fourth century BC; even then, the young Macedonian king was building on the foundations of one of the world's first cities. It seems such a shame that Afghanistan is known today mostly for ignorance, war, terrorism and the smashing of ancient monuments by religious bigots. It is a stunningly beautiful country, as those of us know who have had the privilege of travelling through it in interstices between its wars, and one with a thrilling past and a great culture. It is also, of course, a land of loosely aligned and warring tribes and factions who, in recent history, have taken on and defeated both the might of the British empire in the nineteenth century and that of the USSR in the twentieth. There is, in fact, nothing for the British, the Americans and coalition forces to win in Afghanistan in the twenty-first century. When foreign troops leave in 2014, the country will return to being what it has always been, a law unto itself. The one great hope, although a faint one, is that religious extremism there will abate and that people – especially women – will be able to lead educated, free and fulfilled lives.

As it was, the view of Afghanistan for Harrier pilots was usually at 16,000 feet, and either through binoculars or through their Digital Joint Reconnaissance Pods, which allowed them to zoom in to high-resolution images on the ground. This ability proved to be very important indeed and, doubtless, saved the lives of countless civilians and animals as well as soldiers. As Group Captain Harv Smyth told me recently:

> We could see things from the air that troops on
> the ground calling for us to strike couldn't. They'd
> be asking us to take out a target, but we might see
> schoolchildren or livestock appearing from around
> the corner of a building that might or might not be

sheltering a gunman. So, we'd make the decision
to hold fire. This might not always have been what
those talking to us on the ground felt they needed
at that exact moment, but we had to make those
instant judgments. We didn't want to kill a single
person too many. And the animals mattered, too.
Imagine if we had killed a local farmer's livestock;
this would destroy his livelihood and in all
probability turn him against us and into the arms
of the Taliban.

For Smyth, the commanding officer of IV Squadron in
Afghanistan, this kind of situation was also the reason why, for
all the talk of a future dominated by pilotless strike aircraft, it
will always be preferable to have someone looking down from a
cockpit, peering hard, thinking harder and making the kind of
judgment that might simply not be possible for a virtual pilot
sitting in front of a computer screen in a bunker thousands of
miles away. 'That virtual pilot inevitably sees the world through
a pair of "drinking straws",' Smyth added. 'He can't see the whole
picture, the children, the farmer, the cattle around the corner
and off the edge of the computer screen.' He continued:

We were scrambled one day from Kandahar on
Christmas Eve to take out a 'high value' Taliban
target driving along a road and being tracked by an
unmanned Predator drone. I picked up the target,
was given all necessary clearances, and then dropped

two laser-guided bombs that would have destroyed the moving car. But sixth sense – instinct – made me look out of the corner of my eye. The car was heading towards a compound where kids were playing. I was able to move the bombs away from the target. The 'bad guy' escaped, which might not have gone down too well with the virtual team in the bunker over in the States, but although you could say this was a tactical failure, it was a strategic success: we didn't kill a group of schoolchildren. With the latest laser technology, we could drop a bomb on a single person three or four miles away from 25,000 feet up; but sometimes you have to wait for a moment. Can I drop this bomb? Sure. Should I drop it? That's another question. We have a decision cycle, a mantra going in to attack: Find. Fix. Track. Target. Engage. Assess. The last is often the most important of all; a pilot might make a braver decision by not dropping a bomb.

It's not a computer game out there; it's real people and their lives.

Smyth, who had flown Harriers in action in Bosnia, Kosovo and Iraq, and on reconnaissance missions in Jordan in early 2003, was able to cite many examples of ways in which the small JFH fleet had been able to defuse dangerous situations on the ground without firing rockets or dropping bombs. This did cause clashes with American colleagues who, perhaps keen to imitate the creaking script of some Hollywood war movie, tended to believe in firing first and asking questions afterwards. Smyth recalled:

> US Army guys in a pair of Humvees found a giant weapons cache in a village. As they took a closer look, a big and angry mob of local people moved in on them. We were called in. 'Do something,' the Yanks told us, 'drop a bomb on the crowd.' I decided a low-level show of force might do the trick. We [Harriers always flew in pairs] came down to 100 feet and shot over the town's high street at 500 knots putting out flares. It was enough to scare the Jesus out of them. It worked. The Yanks were amazed and no one was hurt.

A combination of pilot judgment and hi-tech wizardry – notably the GR.9A's Joint Reconnaissance Pod and hi-fidelity Advanced Targeting Pod (SNIPER) – made the Harrier, in Smyth's words, 'the aircraft of choice' for ground troops seeking help from the air in Afghanistan. As he had said at the time:

> A lesser known piece of what we do is what has colloquially become known as non-traditional ISR [Intelligence, Surveillance and Reconnaissance]. We have for a long time studied how the Taliban do their business, and we know nine times out of ten where we think they will put IEDs [improvised

explosive devices]... Certainly in recent months our non-traditional ISR capability is coming more and more into play to counter IEDs; looking at vulnerable points, picking up areas of interest and trying to work out whether they were there two days ago.

The Tactical Imagery Wing guys can exploit these high-fidelity images [captured at high altitude by Harriers]; for example, determining the thickness of the compound's walls, which will then dictate how much explosive charge is needed to get through that wall first time, whether the windows have glass in them, if doors open out or in, and presence of livestock and dogs and potential escape routes. With this intelligence and information at his fingertips, the ground commander can develop an incredibly robust plan of how to execute the deliberate assault. It brings the fight to the here and now and allows us to keep one step ahead of the Taliban.

Meanwhile, women were now flying in action. One of Smyth's IV(AC) Squadron pilots was Flight Lieutenant, now Squadron Leader, Em Rickards, whom he described as 'exceptional'. Rickards wrote tellingly of her experience in the December 2006 edition of the RAF's *Spirit of the Air* magazine:

No day is ever the same in Afghanistan. Past are the pre-planned missions of Op Telic and Op Allied

Force with detailed routes, maps and target study.
Instead, the Harriers of 1(F), IV(AC) and 800(NAS)
Sqns typically launch into the brilliant blue skies
(and occasional dust storms!) above Kandahar, never
quite sure what mission awaits them.

This was indeed a new kind of aerial warfare, with highly
intelligent and well-informed pilots being asked to take on any
mission that might crop up, familiar or otherwise. Despite the
focus on sophisticated weaponry and guidance systems, Rickards
remembered to look out of the window:

For the pilots there is the added bonus of taking in
some of the breathtaking scenery of Afghanistan:
from thousands of acres of red desert, to thousands
of metres of soaring, jagged mountains that extend
north-east to the foothills of the Himalayas, and
vary from beige-brown to snow-clad through the
changing seasons. Indigenous living accommodation
consists of various sized compounds, housing beige-
coloured buildings, and surrounded by well-irrigated
and cultivated fields. In sharp contrast, on the edge
of this green area of civilization, arid landscape
begins again and stretches for hundreds of miles.
From several thousand feet it looks deceptively still
and peaceful on the ground, but clearly there is great
instability and insecurity.

During their five long years in Afghanistan – they were initially expected to serve six months – the Harriers flew mostly from land bases. But up to the end of their service with the British armed forces, the Harriers were based on carriers, too. One of the pilots to fly Harriers from the deck of HMS *Ark Royal* for the last time, on 24 November 2011, was Lieutenant Abi Marks. Speaking in 2010 to Gary Parsons of the website Key-Aero: the Homepage of Aviation, she had recalled her first deck take-off and landing:

> One of the most distinct memories is leaving the ramp on your first launch from the ship thinking, 'That's brilliant!' You don't carry a great deal of fuel for the first trip, as you're just going to do some circuits and then bring it back for the finale, the landing. I remember looking back at the ship from just 1,000 feet thinking, 'That's really small, I've got to get back on that!' and feeling a bit anxious. You're just concentrating on doing what you need to do to get it back on deck; you don't really have time to be nervous. It was when I got back down I was greeted by the boss, who said, 'Congratulations – welcome to naval aviation!' Finally I felt like a naval pilot.

Marks's senior officer, Lieutenant Commander Paul 'Tremors' Tremelling, explained further:

> It's one of the few human experiences that actually lives up to its billing. When you're doing a deck

landing, particularly your first one or in poor
weather, and you finally hit the deck, it's 'Wow,
that's not a way to pay the mortgage!' I wouldn't
trade this job for the world, but it does 'ring the
juice' out of you on some occasions. You shouldn't
have a cross wind if the chaps steering the boat
are doing their job properly – they should keep it
pointing into the wind – but it's the classic situation
when into wind is also into the fog bank. Then you
start to earn your pay.

Back in June 2009, however, the Afghan Harriers had returned
to RAF Cottesmore, handing over their role to Tornados. The
Americans, though, hung on to their AV-8Bs. A stark reminder
of the sudden dangers they faced made headlines worldwide in
September 2012 when Camp Bastion, the main British military
base in Afghanistan, and the largest British overseas military
camp built since the Second World War, was attacked by a Taliban
suicide squad dressed in American uniforms. Camp Bastion is
home to several US Marine aviation units. The squad destroyed
six AV-8Bs and damaged two more. Not since the Vietnam
War had so many US military aircraft been lost in a single day.
Lieutenant Colonel Christopher Raible, commanding officer of
the USMC Harrier unit, and Sergeant Bradley Atwell were killed
as they led a counter-attack against the enemy.

The bodies of seventeen attackers were found when the
shooting stopped. Afterwards, a Taliban spokesman said the
attack had been aimed at Prince Harry – Captain Harry Wales

– grandson of Queen Elizabeth II and an army helicopter pilot based at Camp Bastion. Later on, the spokesman added that the attack was also a riposte to a moronic video made in the United States, apparently by a Coptic Christian Egyptian, that had mocked the prophet Mohammed and resulted in violent protests in Egypt and elsewhere.

Meanwhile, US Harriers had been in action elsewhere in the Muslim world in previous months. Operation Odyssey Dawn was a UN mission aimed at maintaining a No Fly Zone over Libya during the uprising that led to the downfall and humiliating death of Colonel Muammar Gaddafi, the country's eccentric leader who had exported violence and supported a variety of unpleasant terrorist factions and regimes around the world. In February 2011, Gaddafi launched major attacks against his own people. The UN reacted quickly. Eight Italian Navy AV-8Bs from the *Giuseppe Garibaldi* joined USMC Harriers from USS *Kearsange* in attacks against Gaddafi's air capability between 19 and 31 March 2011. The League of Arab States recognized the anti-Gaddafi National Transitional Council as the legitimate government of Libya in August; the dictator was killed in October.

The intervention in Libya came too late for Britain's Harriers, however. The Conservative-Liberal Democrat coalition government's Strategic Defence and Security Review had been published on 19 October 2010 and among its many recommendations were that the MRA4 Nimrod Maritime Reconnaissance Programme should be scrapped and that the Harrier GR.9 should be withdrawn from service. There was a certain grim logic to the Nimrod decision – the project was running late and hugely over-budget – but common sense should have dictated that the Harriers would stay on until their replacement by F-35Bs from 2018. The decision to axe them was, though, ultimately made by politicians – and politicians, however well, or badly, they are advised by their civil servants and the military, tend to possess scant knowledge of warplanes and even less of the changing ways of warfare. Had the Harrier suddenly become a luxury the UK could no longer afford? Or was it now deemed surplus to operational requirements? Either way, it seemed perverse to get rid of an aircraft that was currently fighting an all too modern 'asymmetric' war in Afghanistan, and doing so very effectively.

Whatever the real whys and wherefores of the defence review, and we shall probably never be vouchsafed them, the Harrier has been placed in the role of aerial police officer for more than thirty years, and has performed this role remarkably well. It is an aircraft that air forces and navies will miss when it bows out for good. For the British, though, the Harrier's premature departure has been an especially hard blow, not least because there is a pervasive sense that the Harrier, along with the Hawk, will prove to be the last of this country's genuinely home-grown military aircraft. Of course, it was a Frenchman, Michel Wibault, who first conceived of how a V/STOL machine like the Harrier might be efficiently powered, just as it was the Americans who contributed financially and in other vital respects to what became the Mk 1 version of the aircraft and were instrumental in the development of the Mk 2. But the particular concept of the prototype aircraft, and the impetus to refine and develop it, were very British indeed. Without Hawker, without Camm, Hooper and Fozard in Kingston upon Thames, without Hooker and the engine wizards in Bristol, there would have been no P.1127, no Kestrel, Harrier or Sea Harrier, no AV-8A or AV-8B. This is an aircraft that still haunts us with its absence, reminding us that we are no longer a nation able to produce such superb machinery – except perhaps in the guise of Airfix kits, and even these are now manufactured in India – or to encourage our young people to become engineers, let alone pilots who actually fly.

Ralph Hooper's reaction to the coalition's decision was unequivocal and echoed that of his former boss, Sydney Camm. He told the *Daily Mail*, 'There is no one in the Cabinet with any kind of expertise in aviation. They are bloody politicians. God help us all!' He was, he added, 'both sad and angry. I was amazed when I found out. Everyone went home on Friday evening believing the government was going to run down the Tornados and keep the Harriers. They came to work on Monday and found out it had been turned around the other way.'

Meanwhile, in 2011 BAE Systems – which had long subsumed Hawker Aircraft – was to slip from second to third place in a league table of the world's biggest arms manufacturers compiled by the Stockholm International Peace Research Institute (SIPRI). Boeing took second place, with Lockheed Martin, the maker of the F-35, maintaining its lead. In some ways, and given that the overall sale of arms fell by 5 per cent – although SIPRI lacked figures for China – this might seem a good thing to those in Britain and elsewhere who abhor war and believe that far too much money is invested in instruments of death. Equally, it is interesting to note that arms companies including BAE have been shifting some of their focus on to defence systems designed to counter cyber-attacks, which can, of course, wreak havoc on modern digital economies. And yet, it is hard – very hard – not to think that the Harrier's half-century traces a technological and cultural revolution in a Britain that yearns to consume ever more and to make ever less, a nation that reaches puffily for the screen rather energetically for the sky.

And a year later, in 2012, Abi Marks, who had dreamed for so long of being a Navy fighter pilot, took redundancy.

CHAPTER 7

WING FEATHERS CLIPPED

The final new Harrier airframes were manufactured in 1995, as were the last Pegasus engines. The aircraft, however, continued to develop, with the last British upgrade of the type – the GR.9A – entering squadron service between 2003 and as late as 2009, the year before the government issued its compulsory redundancy notice on the Harrier. Further upgrades had been planned until the end of 2015, ensuring that the Joint Force Harriers would remain fighting fit until replaced by the Lockheed Martin F-35B. The Harrier has certainly had a long run, and Hawker's unusual little aircraft has proved to be highly successful. It still flies with the US Marine Corps, and with the Italian, Spanish and Indian navies, and these forces will only replace their Harriers when their chosen variants of the stealthy, supersonic Lockheed Martin F-35 are ready for action.

The British, though, have become a nation fixated with novelty. This chronic and galloping neophilia appears to have set in at much the same time as the government-endorsed consumer boom of the late 1950s, when Harold Macmillan, the Tory prime minister who despised old buildings, announced in a speech he gave to a Conservative party rally in Bedford in July 1957:

> Go around the country, go to the industrial towns,
> go to the farms and you will see a state of prosperity
> such as we have never had in my lifetime, nor indeed
> in the history of this country... Indeed, let us be
> frank about it, most of our people have never had it
> so good.

Shortly afterwards, in the early 1960s, highly competent and newly upgraded express passenger steam locomotives were ditched – damn the cost – with just a few miles under their steel belts and replaced with very expensive, underperforming and unreliable diesels. Common sense was bundled unceremoniously out of the station entrance as the railways were modernized by an odd new breed of men more concerned with image, consumerism, career status, the latest thing and what we know today, sadly, as 'brands'.

Now, five decades later, we have become stupefied by an ever-greater flow of ever-cheaper consumer gewgaws unloaded from container ships that have made the long journey from the Far East. Even as a dolefully deep recession hit Britain, Europe, the United States and much of the rest of the world from 2008 onwards, the lesson of countries like Germany and China, both of which remained keen on manufacturing and, as a result, less prone to the roller-coaster economic rides experienced by Britain and the United States, went unlearned. The idea of Britain reassessing its priorities and moving forward into broad sunlit uplands of futuristic design, engineering and manufacturing remained seemingly abhorrent to a nation still wracked by fervid consumerism.

Britain does still make some military machines – including Ralph Hooper and John Fozard's BAE Systems Hawk – and parts of several others including components of the Eurofighter Typhoon and the F-35B. Rolls-Royce continues to develop and manufacture civil and military aero-engines of the highest quality. And yet, unlike in Germany, which has a more or less integrated culture of design, research, innovation, engineering and manufacture, and finds relatively little need to outsource production to countries where wages are endemically low, what remains of British manufacturing industry works in a far more piecemeal fashion, with little intelligent or sustained support from either government or its system of education, one that continues to look down on industry, engineering, craft and the making of things.

Taken together, these concerns mean that Britain is both unwilling and unable to make military aircraft of its own – should it even want to – unlike the French, with the Dassault Rafale, and the Swedes, with the Saab Gripen. Given this situation and the fact that Britain cannot really afford to spend fortunes the country does not have to invest in a new nuclear deterrent, it might have been wiser to have kept a Harrier carrier and a fleet of Harriers in service while slowly adapting to the F-35B programme, thereby spreading future costs and maintaining an active force that could have been deployed at a moment's notice to global 'hot spots'.

As it was, the Hawker design office closed in 1985, but it had not been slack in coming up with new designs, one or more of which might well have superseded the Mk 1 Harrier and even negated development of the Mk 2. In fact, there had been several dozen proposals from the late 1960s, some more flights of the imagination than others, and at least one that progressed as far as mock-up stage. This, though, was the central purpose of any design office – to come up with a continual stream of new ideas and at the same time to work hard on the development, production and upgrading of aircraft about to go into production or already in service. Alongside V/STOL designs, the Hawker office produced drawings for simple fighters like the P.1201 of the mid-1970s; this featured a variable-incidence wing that, if the aircraft had been built, was to have encouraged a clean flow of air into the jet intake even when the P.1201 was pulling high g's. In practice, this proposal would have produced a highly effective dogfighter. The major effort, however, went into the design of supersonic V/STOL aircraft. The big question here was how to minimize the amount of the airframe exposed to the blast of a super-hot afterburning jet; aside from the basic issue of protecting the fuselage, there was also the specific need to reduce the heat profile of all military aircraft in the new era of heat-seeking missiles. One Hawker suggestion, the P.1212, featured a delta wing with a cut-back trailing edge and booms carrying fins, undercarriage and armament. Soon enough, this was developed into the P.1216, with its striking outboard tailplanes on booms. In a lecture he gave to the Hawker Association at Kingston in April 2003, Ralph Hooper recalled Margaret Thatcher's evident enthusiasm for the P.1216 on her prime-ministerial visit to the Hawker factory in December 1982. What she saw was a full-scale mock-up of an aircraft that has intrigued the school of 'what-might-have-been' aviation historians and model-makers ever since.

The putative P.1216 had been shot down by politics, yet this time not by government ministers unable to tell a Harrier from a Hunter, but by British Aerospace; the company was concerned that promotion of the aircraft might upset negotiations over who got to build which parts of the future Eurofighter or Typhoon. The P.1216 would certainly have been a handsome aircraft and, if it had made it into production, would have replaced GR.3 Harriers from the late 1980s. Its advantages would have included supersonic performance guaranteed by a plenum chamber-burning Rolls-Royce RB.422 turbojet. Lift, hover, forward and reverse thrust would have been gained through three rather than four nozzles, with one on each side of the fuselage's centre of gravity and one aft; all three, of course, would have been vectorable. While there was nothing fundamentally wrong with its design, the P.1216 would probably have proved a project too far for British Aerospace. And yet, the combination of supersonic performance and V/STOL capability would have meant a machine that might have taken on the roles both of fast tactical strike aircraft like the Jaguar and of the Harrier itself. Even though the P.1216 project was shelved, it did offer further proof of how far in advance of its international rivals Hawker was through the 1960s, 1970s and 1980s.

There were, however, to be a number of potential Harrier challengers. Some were to fail because their design was too complex or they were too expensive to develop, others because they simply didn't work. In the first category were the Heinkel-Messershmitt-Bölkow X-1 and X-2 VTOL jets of the mid-1960s. The first, which made its maiden flight on 20 September 1963, broke the sound barrier before crashing a year later. The second was cancelled in late 1965 because its six Rolls-Royce RB.145 turbojets were a luxury that neither German industry nor the German military could afford and certainly not in the rough and tumble of combat, where mechanical simplicity is often a virtue. The aim of the German military aircraft conglomerate had been to produce an aircraft that would supersede the F-104 Starfighter, offering V/STOL capability and a devastating turn of speed. Later, the American Rockwell company's futuristic-looking XFV-12 supersonic VTOL interceptor and strike aircraft was built in 1977 but cancelled four years on when, after a number of tests, it proved incapable of producing enough thrust for vertical flight.

The Russians came closest with the Yak-41, first flown on 9 March 1987. This was a supersonic development of the Yak-38 from a team led by Alexander Sergeyevich Yakovlev and designed primarily to protect the Soviet Navy's fleet at sea. Like the P.1216, it featured a top-mounted wing and twin booms. Where it differed was in its employment of not one engine like the Harrier, but three. The main engine, an R-79V-300 with 30,864 lbs of thrust for forward flight, was supported by a pair of RD-41 engines rated at 9,040 lbs each for vertical flight. Yakovlev's chief test pilot, Andrei Sinitsyn, achieved a first hovering flight on 29 December 1989, transitional flight on 13 March 1990 and a successful VTOL landing on the carrier *Admiral Gorshkov* on 26 June 1991. The dates are significant because between them the Berlin Wall came down, the Soviet Union exorcized Stalin and Lenin's ghosts, and the Warsaw Pact was dissolved. Not only would the *Admiral Gorshkov* no longer be on stand-by for a war against Western Europe and the United States, but both the Soviet state and an entire political system that had readied so many complex and potentially devastating machines for war were suddenly redundant.

To many commentators in the West, it seemed not only that the Cold War was over, but that history was also about to be rewritten. Given the liberalization of the global market and the triumph of Thatcherism and Reaganomics, it seemed that Western free enterprise was now the model for a global economy to follow. As nation followed nation into this apparently blissful world of free trade and rampant consumerism, there would be no other way forward.

For a brief time, the entire military apparatus designed and built up over the previous forty-five years to assure a nihilistic state of Mutual Assured Destruction if either NATO or the Warsaw Pact blinked first seemed not just unnecessary but even absurd. Now the most impressive aerial displays put on by the

RAF were not made with Cold War jets, nor even by the Harrier, but by the Red Arrows and their BAE Systems Hawks.

The Hawk was a simple and supremely agile jet trainer that had been designed at Kingston upon Thames by a team led by Ralph Hooper and John Fozard. It also soon proved itself an able light fighter and strike attack aircraft well suited to the needs of smaller nations. It could undertake point defence or deliver munitions in small and sometimes very nasty wars when the United Nations was looking elsewhere – wars about which no one in the rest of the world appeared to know, much less care, and in which complex military hardware and technology were neither affordable nor practical. For a while, and until NATO, the United States and Britain too became embroiled in small yet escalating conflicts in former Eastern Europe, Africa, the Middle East and Afghanistan, aircraft like the Hawk appeared to be a more rational, and profitable, way ahead for aircraft manufacturers than increasingly expensive and complex jets.

First flown on 21 August 1974, the Hawk has outsold the Harrier and remains in production in 2013. It began life in 1968 as a private venture by Hawker. The RAF had been asking for a replacement for its Folland Gnat jet trainers since 1964. When Hooper and Fozard set to work, the Hawk appeared very quickly indeed. The RAF ordered 175 aircraft in March 1972 and these were placed in service in late 1976. The Hawk could break the sound barrier in a shallow dive and, more importantly, could pull 9 g in a turn, well beyond the RAF's normal upper limit of 7.5 g. This meant that the little aircraft was a natural for the most ambitious air displays; it also meant that it was very strong. Fitted with underwing pylons, it could carry a pair of Sidewinder missiles along with a 30 mm Aden cannon in a pod under its belly, or a useful variety of ordnance. The US Navy was suitably impressed, and just as the Harrier became a great Anglo-American success story, so did Hooper and Fozard's latest aircraft. In the United States, the Hawk was manufactured by McDonnell Douglas as the T-45 Goshawk.

The Hawk's progress charted complex and very particular political and military developments around the world. In 1980, for example, the Finnish Air Force ordered fifty aircraft, assembled in Finland by Valmet Lentokonetehtaat (Valmet Aviation Industries). The Hawk was chosen because a Finno-Soviet treaty of 1948 allowed the Finnish Air Force just sixty front-line fighters. Hawks, however, counted as trainers; they also happened to suit operating conditions in Finland. Although the Harrier would have been a good choice, too, hiding in the country's great carpet of forests and taking off and landing on its lonely roads, the jump jet was a front-line fighter and so forbidden by the 1948 treaty. Although the treaty was rescinded in 1991 at the end of the Cold War, the Finns had become fond of the Hawk, ordering further aircraft and upgrading the entire fleet, which is now armed with Russian Molniya R-60/AA-8 air-to-air missiles and is expected to remain in service into the 2030s.

Being less expensive to buy and operate, and easier to fly and service than most conventional front-line fighters, the Hawk also proved very attractive to a number of distinctly unpleasant regimes. The Indonesian government of General Suharto bought Hawks in the 1980s and 1990s, but further sales were blocked, late in the day, by Tony Blair's New Labour government, which at the time preached an 'ethical foreign policy', due to the violation of human rights in East Timor. This tiny South-East Asian country had declared its independence from Portuguese rule in 1975. Almost immediately afterwards, Indonesia invaded and occupied East Timor, believing its newly independent neighbour had turned to communism. On the quiet, Washington and Whitehall supported the move. During the following fifteen years, some 18,600 inhabitants of East Timor were killed while, out of a population of about three-quarters of a million, a further 84,200 lost their lives through Indonesian actions that brought about illness and starvation. The UN finally sent in troops, with Indonesian agreement, in 1999; they stayed until 31 December 2012, although the sovereign state of Timor-Leste had been created ten years earlier. Today, far from being communist, the new republic is, along with the nearby Philippines, one of the world's most intensely Catholic nations. A dirty war had been fought, using British and American jets, rockets and machine guns against defenceless civilians, for no reason at all.

In January 1996, four protesters cut through a barbed-wire perimeter and broke into the BAE factory at Warton, Lancashire. Attacking a Hawk bound for Indonesia with hammers, the 'Ploughshare Four' – Lotta Kronlid, Andrea Needham, Joanna Wilson and Angie Zelter – caused £1.5 million worth of damage. Arrested, they were later acquitted when the jury at their subsequent trial at Liverpool Crown Court in July 1996 agreed that, under the auspices of the Genocide Act, they had used 'reasonable force to prevent a crime' – that is, the killing of further civilians. Sixteen Indonesian Hawks, however, were still on order three years later until the government ban took effect, and only after many more civilian deaths in East Timor.

Although the exact role of the Hawk in East Timor remains unclear, the relationship between Hawker, and later BAE, and questionable regimes in faraway countries of which we knew little, between war, human rights and the law, had clearly become far more opaque than it had been during the long certainties of the Cold War. Spare parts for Hawks sold, alongside second-hand Hunters, to Zimbabwe were banned after that country's involvement in the brutal Second Congo War of 1998–2003, a conflict involving several African countries and leading to the deaths of five million people. The brutish regime in Harare, under Robert Mugabe, turned to China instead, investing in the Hongdu K-8 Hawk look-alike. Sales of Hawks to Iraq, meanwhile, had been blocked in the 1980s at a time when Saddam Hussein was busily gassing Kurds in the north of the country. In 2010, seven years after Saddam's deposition, a new Iraqi government was lobbying to buy at least twenty new Hawks.

And yet, it was events, notably in Iraq, that saw sophisticated military aircraft and the Harrier in particular back in the front line – and in fact more active than they had been throughout the decades of the Cold War. Somehow it seemed odd, though, that the Harrier, initially placed into service to support NATO forces and to protect Western Europe against the mighty Soviet military machine, would end its days with the RAF and Royal Navy tackling small groups of local gunmen in the wilds of Afghanistan and fighting in a war that many had questioned since its beginning and that no one, except the most crimson redneck, really believed in by the second decade of the twenty-first century.

By then, there were those who evidently saw the Harrier as an artefact from a bygone age, a thing of dangerous and perhaps ineffable beauty. In 2010, visitors to Tate Britain were confronted by the sight of an FA.2 Sea Harrier hanging by its tail from the vaults of the Roman-style Duveen Galleries, its wings marked with feather-like brushstrokes and a slightly mangled Jaguar ground-attack jet sprawled across the marble floor. The installation was by the British artist Fiona Banner and entitled 'Harrier and Jaguar'. The Tate explained the work thus:

> Here, Banner places recently decommissioned
> fighter planes in the incongruous setting of
> the Duveen Galleries. For Banner these objects
> represent the 'opposite of language', used when
> communication fails. In bringing body and machine
> into close proximity she explores the tension
> between the intellectual perception of the fighter
> plane and physical experience of the object. The
> suspended Sea Harrier transforms machine into
> captive bird, the markings tattooing its surface
> evoking its namesake the Harrier Hawk. A Jaguar
> lies belly up on the floor, its posture suggestive of a
> submissive animal. Stripped and polished, its surface
> functions as a shifting mirror, exposing the audience
> to its own reactions.

'Harrier and Jaguar remain ambiguous objects implying both captured beast and fallen trophy,' wrote Banner herself, adding:

> I remember long sublime walks in the Welsh
> mountains with my father, when suddenly a
> fighter plane would rip through the sky, and
> shatter everything. It was so exciting, loud and
> overwhelming; it would literally take our breath
> away. The sound would arrive from nowhere, all
> you would see was a shadow and then the plane
> was gone. At the time Harrier jump jets were at the
> cutting edge of technology but to me they were like
> dinosaurs, prehistoric, from a time before words.

I, too, remember Harriers rifling through Welsh mountains, riding the contours, skimming across lakes and vanishing, thunderously, into the low vaults of rain-heavy Cambrian skies: mechanical dragons, perhaps, but never 'dinosaurs'. The metal husks of the aircraft were discovered, after the Tate show, in a scrap yard in the Harrow Road in north-west London; they had survived wars, but not Art.

James Dyson, the vacuum-cleaner magnate and champion of British engineering and manufacturing industry, bought a GR.7 Harrier to serve as a gate guardian in the car park of his headquarters in Malmesbury, Wiltshire. While Dyson's motive was a homage to British design and a powerful visual reminder of Hooper and Co.'s ingenuity, the Harrier he chose has a rather remarkable story attached to it. It was the aircraft that Wing

Commander Mark Leakey had crashed into the Mediterranean in November 1997. Leakey recalled:

> I was commander of a squadron, responding to Saddam's sabre-rattling. During a night low-altitude bombing detail on the ship's splash target using night-vision goggles and an infrared system, awful weather and twenty days without a break led me to over-correct on my approach. I could not stop the rate of descent, flew into the sea alongside the ship and briefly lost consciousness on impact. What I did not know at the time was that the aircraft had rolled on its back and I not only pulled the life jacket toggle, but also the seat-firing handle and had ejected down into the water. I should not have survived the impact [on crashing into the sea]; but having survived that, I should never have survived being ejected down into the sea.

He did, and it was not for the first time. In 1982, shortly after the end of the Falklands conflict, the engine of Leakey's GR.3 had given up the ghost. He ejected over the South Atlantic and was rescued by the crew of a Royal Navy helicopter. The Mediterranean crash, however, was to affect Leakey deeply. A medical check-up revealed that while he had survived the impact almost miraculously, he had a brain tumour; it would, most likely, kill him within ten years, but possibly within as little as nine months. Having lost his squadron, no longer flying and – mistakenly as it turned out – fearing a court martial,

Leakey turned to God. He recalled his upbringing in Burundi and Rwanda, his brother's early death from leukaemia, the violence he had witnessed in Africa at a young age, and his promise to himself to become a doctor to help luckless people in these poor, conflict-cuffed countries. He had put these things out of mind, though, after university when he joined the RAF as a fighter pilot, flying Harriers in Germany, Hawks in Wales and F-16s with the USAF from Tampa, Florida. Grounded, he thought about them again.

Two things happened next. First, Leakey was promoted, flying a desk initially with the MoD and, after a course at the Royal College of Defence Studies, moving on to become a principal staff officer with NATO and, after further promotion to Air Commodore, to an appointment as chief planner for British operations in Iraq, Afghanistan, Bosnia and Africa. Second, he became director of the Armed Forces Christian Union, a body founded originally as the Army Prayer Union in 1851 by Captain John Trotter when serving in India with the 2nd Life Guards. Leakey, who finally left the RAF after twenty-eight years, is also involved with Flame International, a group working for reconciliation in those parts of Africa most torn apart by conflict. By common consent, this former Harrier pilot has earned his wings a second time; his is truly a swords-into-ploughshares story, and the Harrier on display like some holy relic outside the Dyson headquarters is Leakey's unexpected and deeply affecting memorial.

Lieutenant Colonel Art Nalls, a God-fearing man, is cut from a slightly different cloth. 'As soon as I gun the engine,' he says, 'people put down their hot dogs and look upwards with their mouths open like a bunch of baby birds waiting to be fed.' That engine is a Pegasus and it powers the one and only Harrier flying in private hands. The FA.2 – XZ439 – is based at St Mary's County Regional Airport, Maryland. Lieutenant Colonel Nalls is a former US Marine Corps Harrier pilot who simply cannot let go of the aircraft he fell in love with years ago and, even though he has flown sixty-five different types of aircraft, still believes is the best of the best. Nalls left the Marines in 1990 after being diagnosed with an inner-ear condition. He was, though, determined to fly a Harrier again. How could he not?

Born in Fairfax, North Virginia, Art Nalls majored in aerospace engineering at the US Naval Academy at Annapolis, Maryland. Before being commissioned as a second lieutenant with the USMC in 1976, he won a place in the *Guinness Book of Records*. Nalls is not exactly a small man, yet his record was for making and riding the world's smallest rideable bicycle; it stood just five inches high. Nalls went on to fly North American T-2C Buckeye jet trainers from the deck of USS *Lexington*, then Harrier AV-8As from USS *Iwo Jima*. After successfully landing an AV-8A that flamed out at 17,000 feet near Richmond, Virginia (the first time this had been done in the United States – he was awarded an Air Medal) and with 900 hours on the Harrier and over 400 deck landings under his belt, in 1985 Nalls became a test pilot at Edwards Air Force Base, California, helping to put the AV-8B through its pre-service paces. He demonstrated the Mk 2 Harrier to the Spanish Navy on board the *Principe de Asturias* and to the Italians from the deck of the *Giuseppe Garibaldi*. Before his unexpected retirement in

1989, Nalls may well have clocked another world record, flying a total of six hours in Harriers without motive power. He had been testing the ability of their engines to relight after being switched off in flight rather than their qualities as gliders. Luckily for the intrepid Nalls, the Pegasus turbines fired up reliably and readily, although many pilots might have been disturbed to fly in such an accustomed silence for so many minutes before they could confirm as much.

Nalls moved on into the real-estate business, making enough money to think seriously of buying a Harrier, should one come up for sale, while improving parts of Washington DC that needed at least as much love and care as a second-hand jump jet.

Everett Aero, the specialist British ex-military aircraft supplier based at Sproughton, Suffolk, came up with the right machine at the right time. The Harrier on offer had begun life in 1979 as an FRS.1; it was later converted into an FA.2. After interviews with the British military and dealings with the relevant US authorities, and having loaded up with operating and maintenance manuals, Nalls handed over something like a million pounds – he will not say exactly how much he paid for the seven-ton aircraft, although the price was 'non-negotiable' – and shipped the FA.2 back to Maryland.

Since its return to the air after re-assembly on 10 November 2007, Nalls and Joe Anderson, a fellow former USMC Harrier pilot, have made over a hundred flights with their pet jet. It has a huge following. 'Watching the Harrier,' says Nalls, 'is like watching a magic show.' He talks fondly of the way his 'puppet without strings' dances, skates and plays in the air while hovering on a cloud of thrilling noise. While writing this book, I noted that Everett Aero had another FA.2 for sale in flying condition; a pair in flight would make a lot of people's day in Maryland. Even so, the costs of running a Harrier cannot be underestimated. In 2010, Nalls reckoned on burning up fifty gallons of fuel between hangar and runway each time he flew the aircraft. This equals a gallon every six seconds. Owning a Harrier is not for the cash-strapped, nor the faint-hearted. Twelve minutes into Nalls's second flight with XZ439, the hydraulic system failed. He had no brakes, no flaps and no landing gear. His one option, short of ejecting and losing the aircraft, was to land vertically. The US Naval Base at Pax River gave him permission to do so. It was Nalls's first hover in sixteen years. Before he attempted to do so, Nalls pushed the Harrier through a number of positive-g manoeuvres in an attempt to shake free the landing gear; the trick worked, and XZ439 came down to earth with a relatively soft bump and only minor damage.

Three years later, when the British Harrier fleet was abruptly grounded, it had seemed, for a moment at least, that the redundant aircraft might fly again, across the Pond and with the US Marine Corps. In fact, seventy-two GR.7 and GR.9 Harriers – forty of them serviceable and not originally scheduled for withdrawal until 2018 – were sold by the MoD to the US Marines in a deal completed in June 2011 and described by Admiral Sir John 'Sandy' Woodward, commander of the Falklands Task Force, as 'crass beyond belief'. The price was a give-away £112 million; the aircraft were not to be flown but instead to be broken up for spares to keep the USMC's AV-8Bs flying until the arrival of the F-35B, just one of which would cost most of the sum paid for all the second-hand Harriers.

The British Harriers were in fine fettle when they were packed off to the States. As Rear Admiral Mark F. Heinrich, chief of the US Navy's Supply Corps, put it, 'We're taking advantage of all the money the Brits have spent on them. It's like we're buying a car with maybe 15,000 miles on it. These are very good platforms.' As it was, the Harriers – sixteen of which might yet fly with the USMC – were shunted out to the Aerospace Maintenance and Regeneration Group, Tuscon, Arizona, where they were parked out in the open in what is effectively the world's largest aircraft cemetery. Back to its old 'Gotcha!' form, the *Sun* newspaper headlined a photograph of the Harriers with the words 'The Royal Flying Corpse'. At Tuscon, some 4,000 aircraft including B-52 Stratofortresses, F-14 Tomcats and A-10 Thunderbolts are grounded in 2,500 acres of desert where the sun blazes *High Plains Drifter*-style and summer temperatures rise to 40 °C, or 120 °F, and more. Jet aircraft do not fly here, but birds do and among them are falcons, eagles, ospreys, vultures, kites and, of course, harriers.

CHAPTER 8

WHAT FLIES AHEAD

At the end of 2012, and shortly after a visit to the F-35B Lightning II production line in Fort Worth, Texas for the *Daily Telegraph*, I received a package from Lockheed Martin, the makers of the Harrier's successor. Inside was a 1/48th scale model of the complex and stealthy V/STOL jet. I soon knew where it belonged. The following month an Australian army friend flew off to Afghanistan on a six-month assignment to pilot Westland Apache attack helicopters with British colleagues from Camp Bastion, and I gave the model to his bright-eyed eight-year-old son Blake. When he grows up, Blake wants to be a military pilot. If he does, he may well fly F-35Bs. And supposing he does and that he retires at fifty-five in 2059, he will still be able to fly F-35Bs then alongside whatever their replacements might be. It is quite a thought.

In 1979, Tommy Sopwith, the former chairman of Hawker Aircraft, told Sir Peter Allen, president of the Transport Trust, how 'we used to think of an aeroplane, then design it and build it in six weeks'. The great man was thinking of machines like the Pup and the Camel. It took twelve years to turn the first drawings of the P.1127 into the RAF's first GR.1 Harriers. The Harrier was then in service, and in action until the very end of its life with the RAF, for the following forty-one years. Lockheed Martin began work on the F-35 in 2001, although the project had been through an experimental stage over the course of the previous five years and the original idea behind this Joint Strike Fighter (JSF) dates from 1993. The first F-35B, the V/STOL version of the type, made its maiden flight in 2008, while production of the F-35 in all its variants is scheduled to end in 2037. As each aircraft is designed to fly in front-line service for a nominal thirty years, this means that F-35Bs will in theory be hovering above the decks of Britain's next generation of aircraft carriers until the late 2060s. Or when young Blake is due his bus pass.

Taken together, the active lives of these first- and second-generation jump jets will span more than a century. Tommy Sopwith lived to be 101 years old; in his century, he oversaw the production of around ninety different types in military service, some fifty with the Sopwith Aviation Company and a further forty or so with Hawker Aircraft Ltd. and its successors. As the twentieth century progressed and technology developed, the design and manufacture of military aircraft became increasingly complex and expensive. Aircraft were required to live much longer lives than they had in the days when Sopwith's team at Kingston could fly a new machine within little more than a month of sharpening a fresh set of pencils, rustling up a slide-rule and pinning a fresh sheet of paper on the drawing board. From planned start to finish, the F-35 programme will stretch across the same number of years it took to progress from the Wright brothers' *Flyer* to the Harrier's entry into RAF service and the first men on the Moon.

Considerable time and money have already been invested in the F-35, which is perhaps part of the reason why many critics, most of them confined to armchairs, have held it in their sights for a number of years: the slightest fault in development aircraft is inevitably jumped on by the media and bloggers as if they were willing the project, for whatever reason, to fail. Cost, though, remains the F-35's Achilles heel. Delays have caused serious friction between the Pentagon and Lockheed Martin. The total cost to the USA for development and procurement has been estimated at $323 billion, with a total life-cycle cost of $618 million per aircraft. Meanwhile, according to a 2012 US Government Accountability Report, F-35 costs have increased 93 per cent, in real terms, over the 2001 estimate.

The F-35A version of the aircraft first flew on 15 December 2006. The F-35B followed on 11 June 2008, with BAE Systems' test pilot Graham Tomlinson making the first full-stop in mid-air on 17 March 2010 and the first vertical landing the following day. The Navy's F-35C took to the air on 7 June 2010. The handover of the first F-35B to the British government, represented by the defence secretary, Philip Hammond, was made at a ceremony at Fort Worth on 19 July 2012, and on 16 November the US

Marines took delivery of F-35Bs at the Marine Corps Air Station, Yuma, Arizona.

Despite the negativity surrounding the programme, it is, of course, the F35-B version of this advanced warplane that will replace the Harrier, and so for this reason alone one needs to understand the aircraft. It is also a machine that, in one version or another, will be serving the air forces of a significant number of countries between 2015 and 2065. So might we even grow to be fond of it, as we have of the Harrier? And might it well prove the last piloted front-line aircraft produced by the US or Europe, as drones and other computer-guided aerial weapons make humans redundant?

I visited the Lockheed Martin factory on a blazing-hot December day, the lobby of its offices sporting a Christmas tree dressed in festive ribbons. Behind the management suites lay the mile-long aircraft assembly plant where B-24 Liberator bombers had been built in their thousands during the Second World War. This great industrial vista was relatively quiet since production of the F-35 was only just getting into its stride. Soon enough, though, Fort Worth will be rolling out 200 F-35s in peak years; the aim is to produce over 3,100 machines – a good deal more than the approximate total of 830 P.1127, Kestrel and Harrier airframes.

Outside the factory, an F-35B stood tethered and shimmering in the heat over a deep concrete 'hover pit'. It is a handsome machine, much larger than a Mk 2 Harrier, and is powered by one of the world's most powerful jet engines, the afterburning Pratt & Whitney 135 turbofan rated at 43,000 lbs of thrust. Empty, an F-35B weighs 32,300 lbs compared to the AV-8B's some 14,000 lbs. Its top speed is Mach 1.6 compared to the AV-8B's Mach 1.0. Much of this highly manoeuvrable stealth fighter's appeal stems from the fact that it can undertake a number of roles, allowing it to replace a host of existing military aircraft, from AV-8Bs and A-10 Warthogs to F/A-18 Hornets and Tornados. Indeed, such is the theoretical versatility of the F-35B that, when the Eurofighter Typhoon is withdrawn from RAF service in around 2030, it may well become the one and only front-line British military jet.

The test pilot at the Fort Worth 'hover pit' stepped out to meet me. He was Billy Flynn, a senior Lockheed Martin test pilot, with combat experience flying Royal Canadian Air Force CF-18s in Serbia and Bosnia. What Flynn was keenest to show me was not the aircraft as such but the high-tech helmet, made by the US-Israeli company Vision Systems International, he wears when flying the F-35. When he puts it on, he looks like a cyborg. 'Darth Vader never had a helmet like this,' he joked.

This carbon-fibre helmet packed with hi-tech gadgetry weighs just 4.2 lbs. It is laser-scanned to fit each F-35 pilot individually. 'This is an essential part of the F-35,' Flynn told me. 'It's what makes such a difference. Through it, I can see 360 degrees all around the airplane.' F-35 pilots can see the ground beneath their feet. 'It's a wild thing,' said Flynn. 'It's virtual reality! Strange? It needs refining, but it'll make a pilot and airplane an integral, all-seeing weapon.' Flynn said no F-35 pilot would want to trade it for anything else.

Just like their wartime forebears, present-day pilots who fly restored Spitfires will tell you that the aircraft feels rather like a suit or skin of metal clothes you have put on and that the sensation of being one with the machine becomes all too real once this lithe fighter is aloft. But what the F-35 offers is something quite different. The machine and its entire navigation, communications, reconnaissance and weapons systems see with the pilot: pilot and aircraft fly symbiotically. The F-35 will put an end to notes written on knee-charts, hand-held binoculars and any other form of traditional or analogue activity so familiar to Harrier pilots. In fact, all the test pilots and engineers I met involved in the F-35 project at Fort Worth and the US Naval Air Station Patuxent River, Maryland, where extensive flying tests are being carried out, spoke quite lyrically about the computer wizardry of this digital-era aircraft.

The pilots said it was the easiest combat aircraft they had ever flown. The computer-controlled systems, fly-by-wire and autopilot of the aircraft are such that the F-35 really does feel as if it can fly itself, leaving its pilots free to concentrate on the purpose of their missions. I can vouch for this, more or less, because I was allowed to have a go with the F-35 flight simulator at Fort Worth. Like Mk 2 Harriers, the F-35 offers the pilot a commanding view from a raised seat in a generous and well-laid-out cockpit. What is remarkable is how few conventional instruments and controls there are. But when the battery is turned on, the F-35's pilot systems light up on touch-pad screens, through head-up displays and, of course, through the ineffable workings of the cyborg helmet.

A touch of the starter button sets off an automatic engine, controls and safety check. The pilot needs to do nothing. This is a world away from the Harrier, let alone the aircraft I have flown with their analogue instruments, magneto checks, carb heat control and control surfaces connected by cables and wires to sticks and pedals. In just ninety seconds, the F-35 is ready to fly. The pilot's principal controls – a left-hand throttle and a right-hand multi-purpose control stick – are light, smooth and progressive. The virtual aircraft shoots up very quickly into what I take to be a 3D map of Afghanistan or somewhere like it, all mountains, deep valleys and vast desert plains. So far, so very normal for a fifth-generation supersonic military jet. But then come the real surprises. Not only will the F-35B land itself, but it will also hover at the touch of a button. Really. Once pressed, that button sets in train a process whereby the aircraft will stop in the air and hang there, a lid behind the cockpit opening to set a giant fan in motion as the rear nozzle rotates downwards. The pilot's hands are free. It is now the easiest thing to land vertically or to shoot off again in forward flight and into a very steep, very fast climb. In flight, the aircraft rolls and loops with the merest hint of firm pressure on stick and throttle. It really does seem all too easy, and yet the whole idea has been to make the F-35 a relaxed machine to fly.

As for launching weapons, this seems all too easy, too. The aircraft's complex radar and sensors find enemy aircraft flying far beyond the limits of the human eye. Because the F-35 sees in all directions, it can fire its weapons in all directions, too. A missile, mounted not on an external pylon but within a weapons bay, can be fired at a 'bad guy' with the F-35 pointing away from the target. It is very hard to miss as the latest technology ensures that missiles follow their targets automatically as well as with devastating precision. And, while a missile is finding its target, the pilot can be pressing on with other tasks. There is no need to look from the cockpit to see if the enemy has been taken out.

When I told the Lockheed Martin instructors – all of them former combat fighter pilots – that it seemed all too virtual for me, too much like a computer game, they laughed and told me that an entire new generation of 'HUD [Head-Up Display] Babes' had learnt to fly combat jets since the Harrier first went into service, but that they do make a point of reminding fighter jocks, they are flying real aircraft in real airspace.

It all seems so very logical and convincing – seductive, too – that one might have expected the various F-35s just to breeze into front-line service. The programme, however, remains a long way behind schedule. Design, development and testing have all thrown up teething problems that outsiders are determined to identify as fundamental flaws. Indeed, to say the F-35 is controversial is rather like saying Margaret Thatcher sometimes divided opinion. All modern military aircraft are astronomically expensive to develop, yet the cost overruns on the F-35 programme are unprecedented. Such figures are never easy to arrive at and can always be disputed, but the fly-away cost of a Dassault Rafale in 2012 was estimated to be $90.5 million (approximately £58.1 million), a Eurofighter Typhoon $104 million (£66.8 million) and an F-35B $237.7 million (£152.6 million). Should this stealthy new jump jet really cost so much, and is it worth so much, especially in an era where enduring economic recession and the availability of cheaper, rival technologies – drones, for example

– suggest that both politicians and the military need to cut costs substantially? And can Britain really afford to commission two large aircraft carriers and to fly F-35Bs from them?

Times have certainly changed considerably from 1993, when the F-35 emerged from the US Common Affordable Lightweight Fighter Project announced that year. In 1996, this duly morphed into the US Joint Strike Fighter Program, the purpose of which was to develop a stealth fighter to replace several front-line aircraft including the F-16 Fighting Falcon, a highly successful design from the mid-1970s still in production at Fort Worth, the F/A-18 Hornet and the AV-8B Harrier II.

'It's what we call a South West policy,' Steve O'Bryan, Lockheed Martin's fast-talking Vice-President, F-35 Business Development, told me when we met in the Oval Room of the company's offices at Fort Worth. A former F/A-18 US Navy pilot who flew on the first 'shock-and-awe' missions to Baghdad in 2003, O'Bryan explained how impressed he was by the efficiency, and profitability, of South West, the Texas-based airline that operates a single type of aircraft, the Boeing 737. Each of its 572 jets flies six trips a day. 'Like South West, everything's the same,' says O'Bryan, who predicts total sales of 3,100 F-35s, 'so everything's easier and cheaper, too.'

The US government alone plans to buy 2,443 F-35s in three variants. The F-35A is a strike fighter; it will take off and land conventionally and is intended to replace both the USAF's F-16 Fighting Falcons and A-10 Thunderbolt IIs. The F-35B is the V/STOL version for the Marines; it can operate from more or less anywhere. The F-35C is intended for the US Navy; it has folding wings for easier stowage on carriers, can be launched by catapult and is fitted with an arrestor hook for deck landings. The remaining 500 or 600 F-35s are to be bought, incrementally, by 'JSF partner nations': Australia, Canada, Denmark, Great Britain, Holland, Italy, Norway and Turkey. There may also be sales to Israel, Japan and Singapore.

Along with the United States, Britain is a 'Level 1 Partner', although it has paid just $2 billion, or 4 per cent of the current costs, while building a part of the aircraft and gaining 100 per cent of the benefits. As the US Marine Corps will receive their first F-35Bs before the RAF and the Royal Navy, both British services will also be able to see how the Americans get on with the new aircraft, and to learn from their experience. Quite how many F-35Bs Britain will finally order and place in service is a multi-billion-dollar question and one that will only be answered with any degree of certainty by the 2015 Strategic Defence and Security Review. Initially, Tony Blair and Gordon Brown's New Labour governments were to have ordered 138 F-35s, but this figure was revised downwards to forty-eight F-35Bs by David Cameron's coalition government. Even then, the politicians had been confused over which version of the aircraft they wanted; at first it was the F-35B, then the F-35A, and now it is the F-35B again.

This takes us back to politics. Two new Royal Navy aircraft carriers have been ordered – HMS *Queen Elizabeth II* and HMS *Prince of Wales* – but one may be sold on if finances prove too tight for comfort and this will mean a reduction in the number of UK orders from Fort Worth. However, as British jobs will be lost with each cancelled F-35B, future governments will need to think as hard about Britain's aerospace industry as they will about the nation's defence. As things stand, 15 per cent of each F-35 put into service around the world over the next twenty-five years will be made in Britain. So Rolls-Royce, BAE Systems, Martin-Baker and some 130 other companies spread the length and breadth of the country will still be able to participate in the design and manufacture of a leading-edge military aircraft. While some might entertain moral qualms about such undertakings and others anxieties about their spiralling costs, on balance this capability is probably one that any of the smaller, self-respecting post-industrial nations like Britain needs to retain – even if not necessarily to the extent of France and Sweden, two countries that still manufacture sophisticated and entirely home-grown combat aircraft.

'It's impossible for Britain to go it alone,' Air Chief Marshal Sir Brian Burridge told me. Burridge is the former commander-in-chief of British forces in Iraq in 2003, head of RAF Strike Command from 2003 to 2006 and, today, vice president of Strategic Marketing, Finmeccanica UK, where he is involved with the development of Italian-built F-35s. A highly experienced pilot with a first-class Cambridge degree in physics, he has climbed Mount Everest and is also a member of the council of the Defence Manufacturers Association. Burridge continued:

> The MoD has to think very hard in its 2015 review
> whether or not it wishes to develop the Typhoon, or
> to buy further F-35s, and nothing else. This would
> have quite profound consequences for European
> industry. Not to develop the Typhoon, which

still has potential sales in Oman, UAE, Saudi and
Malaysia, would mean that British expertise would
wither on the vine.

Burridge, like others concerned for British and European industry,
would like to see F-35s operating alongside upgraded Typhoons,
a pairing, perhaps, of twenty-first-century Mustang and Spitfire.
However, a number of factors – harsh economic conditions, the
changing face of warfare and the public's diminishing appetite
for military adventurism – mean that the very nature of the
fighter aircraft is rapidly mutating. 'We could go 100 per cent
unmanned after F-35,' Burridge said. 'It's a plausible position;
but there's a limit, politically and morally, for robotic warfare,
and [there are] a lot of questions concerning the ethics of extra-
territorial attacks and extra-judicial killings.'

As it was, shortly before Christmas 2012, Air Chief Marshal
Sir Stephen Dalton, the Chief of the Air Staff, announced the
formation of a new grouping known as Remotely Piloted Air
System (RPAS) pilots. Because they will have to gain basic flying
qualifications, this new generation of pilots will wear the same
'wings' and will stand – or perhaps sit, given the nature of their
job – to win much the same medals RAF pilots have cherished for
generations. The 'lethal precision of their weapons', Sir Stephen
told the Royal United Services Institute, means that RPAS pilots
will be seen increasingly as 'a cost-effective way to conduct
warfare'. They will not, though, be chasing the shouting wind in
the cockpits of Typhoons, nor flying F-35s through footless halls
of air; instead, they will be flying computer screens.

Meanwhile, at much the same time as Dalton's announcement, turkey vultures were winging low over the magnificent wooded estate of Pax River on the fringes of Chesapeake Bay as I drove in with Harv Smyth to observe F-35s on test. It was winter, breezy and close to freezing. At warmer times of the year, ospreys and bald eagles circle the 14,500-acre US naval air base, whose 22,000 personnel include twenty-two British pilots, engineers and commanders lodged with the F-35 test team. Among the latter I found the RAF's quietly spoken Squadron Leader Jim Schofield, who flew seventy hours in Harriers in combat in Iraq in 2003. He learned to fly, on a Piper Super Cub, before he could drive.

A pilot for the Shuttleworth Collection of vintage aircraft, Schofield is also a member of the Somerset-based Yakovlevs display team, flying sensationally aerobatic, piston-engined Yak-152s. Intriguingly, the Yak-141, that prototype vertical take-off and landing fighter jet intended for the Soviet Navy and first flown in 1987, was a significant influence on the F-35. This should not be surprising, since the Yakovlev Design Bureau had begun a partnership with Lockheed Martin in late 1991, immediately after the collapse of the Soviet Union and the end of the Cold War.

'I've flown ten front-line fighters,' Schofield said. 'The F-35 is by far and away the easiest. Flying it is a "no brainer", landing is very, very easy. I've flown the aircraft up to Mach 1.6 and pulled up to 7 g. The helmet gives me a God's-eye view. Astonishing. And, when you press that hover button, it's as if engineering and electronics have overcome the law of physics. Extraordinary.'

Peter 'Wizzer' Wilson, a BAE Systems test pilot who flew Sea Harriers with the Royal Navy from 1990 to 2000, told me:

> The new technology takes workload and risk away
> from the pilot. It's amazing how one press of a
> button will set in motion so much magic around you.
> The one time you get to hear something mechanical
> working hard is when the big [vertical lift-off]
> fan behind you spools up; it sounds like an angry
> mosquito! The [Rolls-Royce] fan is also very smooth
> in motion, which has really helped as we've practised
> precision deck landings at sea on USS *Wasp*; it's a
> quantum step in every way from the Harrier.

Flying the F-35 is neither as 'visceral' nor, to use Jim Schofield's term, as 'thrilling' as a Harrier, yet it is clearly more comfortable and far less demanding on the pilot than its Anglo-American predecessor. Meanwhile, the prototype F-35B – X-35B – is already a museum piece, housed in the Boeing Aviation Hangar of the Smithsonian Institution, Washington DC. It might seem an odd thought given the F-35 has yet to enter service, but however impressive such fifth-generation fighters might seem and however important they may prove to so many people's security, jobs and freedom, these machines are already beginning to seem a part of military aviation history. It is virtual pilots who are now reaching for the sky. From 2012, the RAF began flying General Atomics MQ-9 Reaper drone aircraft from Kandahar, Afghanistan with 'pilots' based back home at Waddington, Lincolnshire, a former home to Lancasters and Lincolns, Washingtons and Vulcans. To date, these ten robotic aircraft have been used, the RAF says, for surveillance missions, but they can be fitted with laser-guided bombs and missiles and will, doubtless, be used in combat. Aimed at saving the lives of servicemen and reducing costs, the Reapers, which cost $16.9 million (£10.85 million) apiece, are grim news indeed for advocates of manned military aircraft and those who make them.

As its enthusiastic and experienced pilots attest, the F-35 represents a quantum leap over the Mk 2 Harrier. But although the two aircraft employ rather different technical means to reach the same ends, it could be argued that, without the Harrier, there would have been no F-35B. The Harrier certainly blazed the way for V/STOL on the modern battlefield and at sea, and until the advent of the F-35B, it remained the world's only effective fighting aircraft with this capability. Whether the F-35B proves as successful remains to be seen. The Harrier has certainly set the bar very high.

THE WINDHOVER

Even with a crosswind, the 'plastic-wing' Harrier AV-8B twin-seat trainer feels certain in the hover. Kitted out with a Stability Augmentation System, it chevvies on an air-built thoroughfare in gently pattering rain with the confidence of a kestrel fluttering over the verges of country roads or, in this case, an American freeway. My skipper, sat up front, tells me she could still roll dangerously – and even fatally – if the aircraft side-slipped excessively. And the margins are tight. Sitting on a column of hot air thrusting down from the fast-spooling and noisy Pegasus turbine, it is impossible to forget that the Harrier's wings are, for these few minutes, all but redundant, and that an aircraft without wings is as every bit an oddity as a bird unable to fly.

The way the pilot checks wind direction and degrees of side-slip remains as special as it is simple and foolproof – that weathervane perched on the nose of the Harrier in front of the windscreen. It glows at night. And it takes pilot and passenger back to the earliest days of aviation – to windsocks at the sides of airfields – and to an era long before computers, head-up displays, fly-by-wire, digital technology and Stability Augmentation Systems. This seemingly crude device connects Harrier pilots to the elements in a direct and unambiguous fashion; when there is no wind flow over or under your wings, and you happen to be motionless fifty feet up in the air, knowing which way the wind is blowing is vital.

Throughout its life, the Harrier has relied on this little 'ten cent' weathervane that might have been fashioned in a medieval village forge or else bought from a local DIY store. Yes, it could have been replaced by a glowing digital gizmo, but then it would have become just one more piece of kit to weigh the Harrier down, to fiddle with, to maintain – and to go wrong. The weathervane works, its message understood as clearly and directly as the positions of the hands on an unmarked clock-face. There has been no need to improve it. And yet without it, this hover in American drizzle would have been much trickier than it was.

As the pilot guns the Harrier up and away from vertical to horizontal flight and into the sun, the aircraft is transformed into an aerial hot-rod, its acceleration sensational and climb rapid, its responses instant, fluent and thrilling. Its thrust is more than double that of a Hawker Hunter and a third greater than an English Electric Lightning's. It rolls, loops and, of course, 'viffs' with consummate ease. It is, without doubt, a fine and furious flying machine. With its high seats and bulbous canopy, it offers peerless panoramas of landscape and big skies. It can even seem normal – as normal as a fast military jet ever is – until it comes back to the hover, and attention switches to that life-saving weathervane again.

The basic quality of this simple device reminded me then, as it does now, of the sheer wonder of vertical flight in a winged aircraft that has never tried to ape a rocket or compromise its pilots' comfort and sanity. The very latest technological advances of the jet age were never quite enough, it seems, to ensure safe flying in the hover and at very low speed. Safely back on the ground, I read some informative and entertaining passages in Bill Gunston's book on the Harrier published some thirty years ago. The former RAF pilot – he flew de Havilland Venoms – and author was recalling the early days of the P.1127:

> As there were only small gyroscopic effects, [Sydney] Camm was hopeful that complex, triply-redundant three-axis auto-stabilisation would not be needed. Hugh Conway, former managing director of Shorts and well up in the SC.1 auto-stab problems [see Introduction], later became managing director of Bristol Siddeley Engines. He gave a long briefing to Camm on what had to be done. After he had gone, the Hawker boss said, 'We are only ignorant buggers here at Kingston, and don't understand all that science. We'll leave the P.1127 simple, and let its pilots fly it.'

Camm was only half-joking. The first flight of the P.1127 really was done as much on a wing and a prayer as it was by maths and science. Many of those involved in the project were unsure if the aircraft would take off vertically. Was the Pegasus turbine sufficiently powerful? How would the aircraft manage the transition to forward flight? How would she handle? Bill Bedford was concerned that his leg, weighed down in plaster of Paris, would be a burden. Bits of the aircraft, including its radio, were stripped away to reduce weight, while, according to Gunston, 'Hooker [technical director, Bristol Engines] suggested to Camm that "perhaps the first flight should be in the conventional [runway] mode, to check handling qualities". Camm snapped back, "All Hawker aircraft have perfect handling qualities; the first flight will be a VTO [vertical take off]."'

The test pilots made it all look easy, perhaps too easy in the case of John Farley, who, when demonstrating the aircraft, would fly down runways with the machine rotating around its yaw axis as if side-slip was a game to be toyed with. In practice, few, if any, Harrier pilots were able to match Farley's supreme mastery of the Kingston jump jet. As we have seen, 'shakers' were in due course fitted to the rudder pedals; the relevant pedal shook, encouraging the pilot to respond appropriately when the aircraft needed help to stay with the wind; Farley described the effect as like 'a rather nice relaxing calf massage'. The weathervane was added, too. These aids to safety were all the more welcome because in low-speed flight 'intake momentum drag', caused by air passing into the elephant-ear intakes on either side of the cockpit, inclined the Harrier to pitch or yaw, if not to roll: side-slip did that.

All this seems a world away from the hover-at-the-press-of-a-button capability of the new F-35B, but it is these idiosyncrasies and fundamental aspects of flight and the need to master them that have made Harrier pilots a breed apart. The Harrier itself still flies on, a truly legendary machine that, long ago, spread its wings from its Surrey nest to become the most radical and unlikely of great military aircraft. Perhaps some of the conflicts it has been engaged in have been questionable, yet the brilliance of its design cannot be denied and it seems a great pity that the Harrier will be remembered as the last British-born fighter jet – one of the last, in fact, of all British aircraft. Political hot air – Camm's fourth dimension – has seen to that.

ACKNOWLEDGMENTS

I am very grateful to all the individuals, pilots and aircrew who have assisted me in understanding the Harrier and experiencing it close-up. Special thanks must go to Ralph Hooper OBE, FREng, FRAeS, Group Captain Harv Smyth DFC, Commander Nigel 'Sharkey' Ward DSC, AFC, and Air Chief Marshal Sir Brian Burridge KCB, CBE, ADC, FCMI, FRAeS for helping me to place the Harrier in perspective in terms of design, combat – from the Falklands to Afghanistan – and politics.

Thanks must also go to Laurie A. Quincy of Lockheed Martin for facilitating my visit to see the F-35B in production at Fort Worth, Texas, and on test at Pax River, Maryland; to test pilots Billy Flynn, Peter 'Wizzer' Wilson and Squadron Leader Jim Schofield; and to Paul Davies of the *Daily Telegraph*, who sent me to report on the controversial new American jump jet.

My editor, Angus MacKinnon, who knows a thing or two about military aircraft as well as modelling them, commissioned this book and saw it through to take-off in print. Many thanks are due to him, to my unflappable desk editor Louise Cullen, to my copy-editor Ben Dupré, and, as always, to my high-flying agent Sarah Chalfant.

SELECT BIBLIOGRAPHY

Attrill, Mark,
Harrier: Inside and Out (Crowood Press, 2002)

Bicheno, Hugh,
Razor's Edge: The Unofficial History of the Falklands War (Weidenfeld & Nicolson, 2006)

Branson, Alan,
Pure Luck: The authorised biography of Sir Thomas Sopwith (Crécy Publishing, 2007)

Buttler, Tony,
British Secret Projects: Jet Fighters Since 1950 (Midland Publishing, 2000)

Calvert, Dennis J.,
Hawker Siddeley/BAe Harrier: Owners' Workshop Manual (Haynes, 2012)

Childress, David Hatcher,
Vimana: Aircraft of Ancient India and Atlantis (Adventure Unlimited Press, 1991)

Davies, Peter and Thornborough, Anthony M.,
The Harrier Story (Arms and Armour Press, 1996)

Dow, Andrew,
Pegasus: The Heart of the Harrier (Pen and Sword Aviation, 2009)

Evans, Andy,
BAe/McDonald Douglas Harrier (Crowood Press, 1998)

Farley, John,
A View from the Hover: My Life in Aviation (Seager Publishing, 2008)

Freedman, Lawrence,
The Official History of the Falklands Campaign. Vol. II: War and Diplomacy (Routledge, 2005)

Gordon, Yefim,
Yakovlev Yak-36, Yak-38 & Yak-41: The Soviet 'Jump Jets' (Ian Allan, 2008)

Gunston, Bill,
Modern Fighting Aircraft: Harrier (Lansdowne Press, 1984)

Hooker, Stanley,
Not Much of an Engineer: An Autobiography (Airlife Publishing Ltd, 1984)

Hunter, Jamie,
Sea Harrier: The Last British Fighter (Midland Publishing, 2005)

Jefford, C. G.,
The RAF Harrier Story (Royal Air Force Historical Society, 2006)

Jenkins, Dennis R.,
Boeing/BAe Harrier (Speciality Press, 1998)

Mack, Peter R.,
The Harrier Story (Sutton Publishing Ltd, 2007)

Markman, Steve and Holder, Bill,
Straight Up: A History of Vertical Flight (Schiffer Publishing, 2000)

Mason, Francis K.,
Harrier (Patrick Stephens Ltd, 1986)

Mason, Francis K.,
Hawker Aircraft since 1920, 3rd edition (Naval Institute Press, 1991)

Meyer, Ingolf,
Luftwaffe: Advanced Aircraft Projects to 1945. Vols. 1 and 2 (Midland Publishing, 2006 and 2007)

Meyer, Ingolf and Schick, Walter,
Luftwaffe: Secret Projects – Fighters, 1939–45 (Midland Publishing, 1997)

McLelland, Tim,
Harrier (Ian Allan, 2011)

Nordeen, Lon O.,
Harrier II, Validating V/STOL (Naval Institute Press, 2006)

Pook, Jerry,
RAF Harrier: Ground Attack, Falklands (Pen and Sword Books, 2007)

Robinson, Douglas H.,
The Zeppelin in Combat: A History of the German Naval Airship Division, 1912–18 (Foulis, 1962)

Robinson, Douglas H.,
Giants in the Sky: A History of the Rigid Airship (University of Washington Press, 1973)

Rolt, L. T. C.,
Aeronauts: History of Ballooning (Longman, Green & Co., 1966)

Swanborough, Gordon and Bowers, Peter M.,
United States Navy Aircraft since 1911 (Putnam Aeronautical, 1990)

Vann, Frank,
Harrier Jump Jet (Bdd Promotional Book Co., 1990)

Ward, Nigel 'Sharkey',
Sea Harrier over the Falklands: A Maverick at War (Cassell, 1992)

WEBSITES

www.harrier.org.uk
www.raf.mod.uk
www.seaharrier.co.uk

INDEX

Achgelis, Gerd: co-designer
of Focke-Wulf Fw 61, 24;
co-designer of Triebflügeljäger,
29

Afghanistan: 105, 240, 242, 245,
265, 277; Bagram, 233, 238;
borders of, 236; Camp Bastion,
246–7, 271; Kandahar, 232–3,
235, 238–9, 284; Operation
Enduring Freedom (2001–), 12,
14, 21, 33, 100, 150, 184, 207,
212, 215, 232, 239, 258, 262;
Operation Herrick (2002–), 237,
239; Soviet Invasion of (1979–
89), 187, 212, 239

Ahtisaari, Martii: President of
Finland, 225

Airborne Early Warning (AEW)
aircraft: 175

Aircraft Research Association: 77

al Qaeda: 232; 9/11 Attacks, 216,
220, 232; strongholds of, 232

Albania: 224

Alcock, Flight Lieutenant John: 114

Alenia Aeronautica: 206

Allen, Sir Peter: President of
Transport Trust, 68, 272

Allende, Salvador: regime of, 161

Ancient Greece: Athens, 20

Anders, Bill: background of, 121

Arbenz, Colonel Jacobo: regime
of, 161

Archytas: designer of *Pigeon*,
19–20

Ardiles, Lt. José: death of, 146

Argentina: 134, 140, 158, 166,
178, 205; Air Force (AAF),
163–5; Buenos Aires, 137, 159–
60, 164, 179, 182; Comodoro
Rivadavia, 163, 166; Córdoba,
141–2; government of, 181;
independence of (1816), 137;
Jewish population of, 141;
military junta of, 16–1, 131,
136, 140, 182; military of, 156–
7; navy of, 111, 139, 162–3; Río
Gallegos, 163

Argus: 26

d'Arlandes, Marquis: role in first
successful vertical-take off
(1783), 20

Armed Forces Christian Union:
formerly Army Prayer Union,
265–6; personnel of, 265

Armstrong, Neil: 26, 78

Armstrong Siddeley: merger with
Hawker Aircraft Company, 68;
subsidiaries of, 68; Viper, 78

Armstrong Whitworth: AW.681,
94

Auld, Lt. Commander Andy: RAF
squadrons led by, 176–7

Australia: 157, 205, 280; Cook's
Discovery of (1770), 180;
military of, 233, 271; Sydney, 44

A.V. Roe: 65, 69

Avro: 34–5; 504K, 105; facilities
of, 35; Lancaster, 285; Lincoln,
285; Vulcan, 69, 149, 167, 285

Avrocar: design of, 34–5; first free
flight (1959), 35

Aziz, Tariq: former Iraqi Foreign
Minister, 216

Ba'ath Party (Iraq): 209–11

Bachem, Erich: role in design of
Bachem Ba 349 Natter, 27

Bachem Ba 349 Natter (Viper): 29;
design of, 27–8; pilots of, 28

Bacon, Roger: 20

Bader, Douglas: 177

BAE Systems plc: 249–50, 281;
facilities of, 261; Hawk, 253,
258, 260–1; personnel of, 273,
284; Thermal Imaging Airborne
Laser Designator Pods, 233–4;
Warton incident (1996), 261

Bahrain: 218

Baker, Lt. Colonel Bud: 197

Baker, Valentine: 153

Balmer, Robin: 83

Banner, Fiona: 'Harrier and
Jaguar', 262–4

Barbie, Klaus: 141

Barker, Captain Nicholas: 156

Barkhorn, Colonel Gerhard: 104;
member of TES, 97–8

Barraza, Lt. Julio: 171

Barton, Flight Lt. Paul: 143–4

Batt, Lt. Commander 'Gordy':
1death of, 66

Bedford, Bill: 87, 143, 154;

background of, 81; Chief Test
Pilot for Hawker Siddeley, 78,
81

Begin, Menachem: 158–9

Belgium: military of, 67

Belize (Honduras): 132; Belize
City, 131; borders of, 130–1;
independence of (1981), 130;
UK military presence in, 130–1

Bell Aircraft: designs produced by,
43; facilities of, 43; personnel of,
43; X-14, 42–3; X-14A, 78

Benn, Air Commodore William
Wedgwood: family of, 110;
Secretary of State for Air, 110

Benn, Michael: death of (1944),
109; family of, 109–10

Benn, Tony: background of,
108–9; family of, 109–10;
Minister of Science and
Technology, 108–9

Berhoz of Khorasan, Prince: 21

Berlin Airlift (1948): casualty
figures of, 39

Blackburn Aircraft: acquired
by Hawker Siddeley, 53, 73;
Buccaneer, 69, 131; personnel
of, 73

Blackmore, Commander James:
237; Harrier squadrons led by,
13

Blair, Tony: administration of,
232, 260; defence policies of,
184, 280; foreign policy of, 215,
225–6, 230–3

Blériot, Louis: 65

Blot, Major Harry W.: 199

Boeing Company: 737 (Airliner),
279; 747 (Airliner), 94; B-29
Superfortress (Washington), 46,
285; B-52 Stratofortress, 149;
707, 159, 226, 269; Chinook,
171

Bokan, Dragoslav: co-founder of
White Eagles, 222

Bölkow: as part of EWR, 88

Borman, Frank: background of,
121

Bosnia and Herzegovina: 265,
275; ethnic Serbian population
of, 222–4; independence of